A Synopsis of American History

Volume I: Through Reconstruction

A Synopsis of American History

Volume I: Through Reconstruction

Eighth Edition

NEIL R. McMILLEN
with Charles C. Bolton

University of Southern Mississippi

Originally Under the Authorship of
Charles Sellers and Henry F. May

IVAN R. DEE, PUBLISHER

Chicago

A SYNOPSIS OF AMERICAN HISTORY. Copyright ©1997 by Ivan R. Dee, Inc. All rights reserved, including the right to reproduce this book or portions thereof in any form. For information, address the publisher at 1332 North Halsted Street, Chicago 60622. Manufactured in the United States of America and printed on acid-free paper.

The Library of Congress has cataloged the single-volume edition of this book as follows:
McMillen, Neil R., 1939–
    A synopsis of American history / Neil R. McMillen with Charles C.
Bolton. — 8th ed.
       p.   cm.
    Includes bibliographical references and index.
    ISBN 1-56663-160-2 (acid-free paper)
    1. United States--History.   I. Bolton, Charles C.   II. Title.
E178.1.M46   1997
973--dc21   97-1450

ISBNs for the two-volume edition:
Vol. 1, ISBN 1-56663-161-0
Vol. 2, ISBN 1-56663-162-9

CONTENTS

CONFLICTING HISTORICAL VIEWPOINTS

SPECIAL TABLES

MAPS

PREFACE

A *Synopsis of American History*, now in its eighth edition, provides students with a brief introduction to a complex subject. Our object in writing this comparatively slender volume is not to reduce the amount that students read but to liberate them from the traditional oversize textbook so that they may pursue their own historical inquiries in primary sources and specialized accounts. By design, then, the *Synopsis* is concise but chronologically inclusive.

This edition of a textbook first published nearly forty years ago emphasizes political history, which in our opinion affords the clearest organization of the nation's past. Yet we have defined *politics* broadly, and have endeavored to link it to the larger environment in which it functioned. Thus, while our focus is generally political, we also analyze the social, cultural, economic, intellectual, and diplomatic currents that give added dimension to American history.

In reducing a long and complicated story to a relatively few pages, we have found it neither possible nor desirable to avoid a point of view. While we have tried to be fair and judicious, we have not been reluctant to offer historical judgments. Appropriate reading in other books—the whole purpose of our synoptic approach—should enable students to accept or reject our interpretive statements. "For Further Reading" sections at the ends of chapters, though generally restricted to books that are readily available in college libraries, introduce students to the literature of each period. The sixteen essays called "Conflicting Historical Viewpoints" supplement the text and remind students of the subjectivity of the historian's craft; the Viewpoints highlight enduring scholarly controversies and suggest the development of scholarly thought through the years. Other pedagogical aids include nineteen time charts, which give a chronological summary of political and other important events. Three photo essays cover the Republic's early days, the Civil War and Reconstruction, and the Depression and New Deal era.

We wish to thank the many colleagues who, in one edition or another, read all or parts of this book and made many valuable suggestions. We tried to follow their suggestions insofar as they were consistent with the philosophy of the book.

In its first two editions, the *Synopsis* was the work of Charles Sellers and Henry May. Neil McMillen joined the enterprise in 1974 and, while he assumed responsibility for all revisions after that date, he shared co-authorship with Sellers and May in the third through the seventh editions. Although this book in many ways still bears their conceptual thumb prints, Sellers and May are no longer authors of record. Charles Bolton wrote the new material for the eighth edition.

N. R. M.

A Synopsis of American History

Volume I: Through Reconstruction

1

★ ★ ★ ★ ★ ★

Beginnings, 1607–1700

WHEN Christopher Columbus broke through the water barrier to the New World and became the first European to set foot on San Salvador, he opened a momentous chapter in the history of the Old World as well as the New. Already, a static and status-bound Europe was responding to new intellectual stirrings, growing trade, and competition among emerging nation-states in overseas exploration and commerce. The dramatic European discovery of the New World frontier accelerated these beginning currents of change into a 400-year revolution. The very knowledge of the existence of seemingly limitless space and resources in America set off a prolonged economic boom, quickened the spirit of enterprise, generated mounting pressures against the rigidities of the social order, and hastened Europe's entrance into the modern world of individualism, capitalism, and liberal democracy.

The development of America took place in the midst of this profoundly important transformation of the Atlantic world. The central characteristics of the emerging "modern" epoch, as the term is used here, were the increasing importance of individual autonomy and the growing faith that human beings could win secular salvation — wealth and "happiness" — through individual enterprise. By the nineteenth century, when modernity in this special sense reached its fullest development, this emphasis on the individual had given rise to the social philosophy known as *liberalism*. In its original meaning, liberalism was the conviction that the good of everyone would be served if all were left as free as possible to pursue their individual ends. In the economic sphere, liberal doctrines lent support to *laissez-faire* capitalism. In the political sphere, liberal doctrines encouraged a majoritarian democracy with some protection for the rights of minorities.

EUROPE DISCOVERS THE NEW WORLD

Although October 12, 1492 is the traditional date for the discovery of the Americas, Columbus was a relative latecomer to the New World. Many centuries before the Italian adventurer sailed west from Spain in search of trade routes to the Orient, Asian nomads entered the North American wilderness. The combined work of geologists, archeologists, and anthropologists suggests that this migration from the east was possible as early as the beginning of the Ice Age (perhaps 50,000 years ago). The mainstream of migration to the Americas, however, began some 11,000 years ago and continued for several centuries. Very likely these earliest discoverers traveled the "land bridge" across the Bering Strait; some may have entered the New World by crossing the Pacific Ocean to other points of entry. But however they came, the New World's first settlers were dispersed in a relatively brief time throughout the western hemisphere, from Alaska to Tierra del Fuego.

In our own millennium, the New World was rediscovered by eleventh-century Scandinavian sailors. Although the exploits of these colorful North-landers are also largely unknown, there is substantial evidence that Viking explorers sailed brightly painted, high-prowed ships from their settlements in Greenland to the North Atlantic coast of the Americas. About the year 1000, Leif Ericson led an expedition to "Vinland," a location possibly near Cape Cod but more likely in Newfoundland. During the next 10 to 20 years — four centuries before the French "discoverer" Jacques Cartier gave the region its name — other Viking parties probably scouted the vast reaches of the Gulf of St. Lawrence. These tentative Viking probings, however, had no lasting impact on North America. Whatever settlements the Norse established quickly disappeared. Theirs was an apparently isolated adventure without direct implication for future explorations in the great age of discovery.

Curiously it was Spain and not seafaring Portugal that was in the forefront of the bold exploration of the New World. Pioneers in the use of ships for trade and exploration, Portuguese mariners under the patronage of Henry the Navigator directed their swift, seaworthy caravels south along the coast of western Africa in search of gold and a passage to India. Some 25 years after Henry's death and 5 years before Columbus's first voyage to America, Bartholomeu Dias rounded the Cape of Good Hope. In 1498 Vasco da Gama reached India, and two years later India-bound Pedro Cabral was blown off course and happened upon the coast of Brazil. By that time, however, Spain had already seized the initiative in New World exploration. In fact Columbus, who had developed his considerable navigational skills in the service of the Portuguese, turned for the support of his first New World voyage to Ferdinand and Isabella of Spain only after being refused by the King of Portugal. Buoyed by the success of Columbus, the Spanish crown soon dispatched Vasco de Balboa, who discovered the Pacific (1513), and Ferdinand Magellan, whose expedition completed the first circumnavigation of the globe (1519–1522). By the early years of the sixteenth century, fully a century before the founding of the first permanent English colonies to the north, Spanish settlers occupied portions of Haiti, Cuba, Puerto Rico, Jamaica, and Panama. Soon thereafter (1519–1521), the resourceful Hernando Cortés, in the name of the Spanish crown, subdued the Aztec empire of

Montezuma to claim the vast treasure of Mexico. In the 1530s, Francisco Pizarro, following a nine-year seige, defeated the Incas to give Spain the even richer prize of Peru.

Initially, when the explorations of Juan Ponce de Leon, Francisco Coronado, and Hernando de Soto uncovered no gold or silver, the Spanish showed little interest in the region north of Mexico. Yet by the time the French and English began planting their North American colonies, the Spanish had already staked out Florida and present-day New Mexico and Arizona. A century later Spain added Texas, and in the eighteenth century extended its missions and fortresses (*presidios*) to California. Always secondary to Peru and Mexico in the Spanish scheme of things, these northern outposts served largely as buffers against hostile Indians and rival European powers. As the coming years would prove, these settlements were the most vulnerable New World possessions of an Old World nation rapidly declining in power and wealth.

The empire of New Spain in the south had its French and Dutch counterparts in the north with New France and New Netherland. Although the French and Dutch also sailed west in search of riches, they found it not in gold and silver but in fish and furs. Following the failed efforts of explorers Giovanni da Verrazano (1524), Jacques Cartier (1534), and Henry Hudson (1609), both nations abandoned their hope of a short cut to China and turned early in the seventeenth century to the less spectacular enterprise of colony building. In 1655 New Netherland managed to absorb a tiny Swedish outpost (New Sweden) along the Delaware River, but the colony soon became New York when the Dutch lost out to their commercial and colonial rivals, the English. The French proved more tenacious, but they too were to be driven from the continent in the eighteenth century.

The English also looked westward for a water route to the East. From the fifteenth-century voyages of John Cabot and John Rut to the eighteenth-century adventures of James Cook and Alexander Mackenzie, Britain searched for the elusive Northwest Passage. Failing here, the English became colonizers. Oddly, the area they eventually exploited was the last major segment of the New World frontier to attract Europeans. In the sixteenth century, while the Portuguese concentrated on Brazil, the Spanish on Central and South America, and the French on Canada, most of the intervening expanse of temperate and fertile country lay untouched while England slowly readied herself for overseas expansion.

English colonization in American differed in character and consequences from that of other European nations. England was closer to having a tradition of individual rights and social mobility, and the English exhibited earlier and more fully that spirit of individual enterprise that was to be a major force in the modernization of the European world. Henry VII and Henry VIII had destroyed the power of the feudal nobility, already weakened by the War of the Roses, and had established a strong centralized state. In so doing, the Tudor monarchs had encouraged the growth of the business middle classes, the merchants and entrepreneurs who were to be major agents of the modernizing process. Moreover, Henry VIII had welcomed the Protestant Reformation in England, and Protestant theology, with its spiritual individualism, reinforced the individualistic, enterprising spirit of English middle-class life. All of these influences culminated in a burst of national vigor and creativity in the late sixteenth century under the last of the Tudors, Elizabeth I. It was at this point that the English turned their eyes toward the New World.

A second crucial difference between England and the other major colonizing nations was that England entered into her colonizing ventures as a poor country. Though the Elizabethans dared to challenge the might of Catholic Spain, they were only on the threshold of holding major-power status, and the Queen's treasury had insufficient funds to support the New World ventures that seemed vital to England's grand strategic design. Private enterprise had to be enlisted, and the English responded to this national purpose with a mixture of patriotism, Protestant religious zeal, thirst for adventure, and greed.

Sir Humphrey Gilbert, one of the first individual colonizers, died in his effort to found a colony in Newfoundland in 1583. Gilbert's half-brother Sir Walter Raleigh then took up the task of establishing a colony in America. In 1585, he sent 108 male colonists, who landed on heavily wooded Roanoke Island in present-day North Carolina. They were unsuccessful in their search for gold and a route to the Pacific Ocean; instead, they encountered hostile Indians and experienced food shortages. Coming upon the colony during his explorations, Sir Francis Drake, the first Englishman to sail around the world, returned them to England the following year. Another group, composed of 117 men, women, and children, was sent out in 1587. Under circumstances that still remain a mystery, they had all disappeared from Roanoke when a supply ship arrived in 1591. These failures demonstrated that a colonizing venture was beyond the financial capacity of any one individual. The polished and daring Raleigh, a favorite of Queen Elizabeth, solved this problem by organizing a syndicate of London merchants, a profit-seeking "joint-stock company," to finance his second colonial venture in Virginia. The joint-stock device, forerunner of the modern corporation, dated back to the time of Henry VIII when English merchants had pooled their capital and shared the risks of trade with Russia by buying shares in the "stock" or capital of the self-governing Muscovy Company. Applied to America, this device not only made English colonization possible, but insured that it would be carried out under the direction of private entrepreneurs seeking private profits as well as national ends.

The private entrepreneurial aspect of English colonization and the individualistic character of English society interacted with the New World environment to produce important consequences. Everywhere in the New World, the absence of established institutions left people free to build new social orders, and abundant natural resources afforded a field for enterprise that led English Americans toward individualism and modernity.

The ready source of gold and silver that the Spanish found in their America reinforced the authoritarian social structure they had brought with them.

The fur trade played a like role in French America. The English colonizers at first also sought gold or a northwest passage that would open to them the Pacific and the riches of the fabled Orient. They, too, attempted to impose on their colonies a rigid form of social organization designed to promote corporate rather than individual ends. But the English New World, the temperate zone of North America, yielded no ready riches. Instead, it proved superbly fitted for the humbler pursuits of farming, fishing, and trade, tasks better adapted to individual than corporate enterprise.

Paradoxically, the English colonies flourished because they failed in their original corporate aims and thus left fields of enterprise open for individual English colonists. It was under these circumstances that English America surged into the forefront of the Atlantic world's drift toward modernity. This movement, with interesting variations, can be seen in the two colonial societies established in the first half of the seventeenth century, one on Chesapeake Bay and the other in New England.

THE CHESAPEAKE COLONIES: VIRGINIA AND MARYLAND

Following Queen Elizabeth's death in 1603, her successor, James I, made peace with Spain, thus freeing English human and economic resources for overseas ventures. Although this text focuses on the region destined to become the United States, England's seventeenth-century imperial reach was global; it stretched west from Ireland to Newfoundland and Nova Scotia, southward to Bermuda, and eastward to the subcontinent of India. It was to the west in the New World in 1606 that King James issued charters to two joint-stock companies to colonize the land that Raleigh had named Virginia in honor of the virgin Queen Elizabeth. The more important of the two Virginia companies, with headquarters at London, promptly sent out an expedition of 144 people aboard the *Sarah Constant,* the *Goodspeed,* and the *Discovery.* They reached Chesapeake Bay in April 1607 after an arduous voyage of four months. The 105 surviving English men and boys proceeded up a great river, which they named for King James, and founded Jamestown on a marshy peninsula — the first permanent English settlement in North America.

Hunger, hostile natives, and malaria took many lives in the early years before the settlers learned to cope with their alien and densely forested environment. All but 38 of the first arrivals died in the first year. Although the colony's numbers were replenished in 1609, out of some 500 inhabitants just 60 survived the "starving time," the fearsome winter of 1609–1610. Only the arrival of 300 reinforcements with a new governor, Lord De la Warr, persuaded the dispirited remnant not to abandon Jamestown and return to England.

Much of the settlement's early difficulties can be traced to the Englishmen's inexperience with farming and the unrealistic commerical aims of the enterprise itself. The colonists were eager to find instant riches in gold and silver, or a northwest passage to the Pacific. Many of them were gentlemen unaccustomed to physical labor and slow to do the mundane agricultural work necessary for survival. Placed under great pressure to produce profits for investors, initially the settlers planted few crops and failed to prepare for life in the wilderness. Those who lived through the first difficult winters did so because of the Indians of the Powhatan Confederation, from whom the English learned much New World lore, and with whom they exchanged knives and hatchets for corn.

Gradually, as both settlers and investors recognized that the area held no undiscovered short-cuts to the Orient and no quick profits from precious minerals, the policies of the Virginia Company shifted to develop trade. To make the colony more attractive to immigrants, the famous "headright" system was inaugurated in 1618. Under it, 50 acres were awarded to any individual who paid for the transportation of a settler who would agree to cultivate the land and pay an annual *quitrent* (or tax payable to a superior) of one shilling to the company. Although the system proved more beneficial to speculators who bought the land claims of settlers than to the settlers themselves, it did stimulate immigration. Toward the same end, the early "cruell lawes," which imposed a rigid military discipline on the colonists, were replaced by the "free lawes" of England. The settlers were also permitted to send delegates to the House of Burgesses, (Virginia Assembly); in 1619, as the first representative body in the New World, the Virginia Assembly organized itself on the model of the English House of Commons and claimed the right of local self-government.

The shift in company policy was a graceful adaptation to social fact: the fortunes of the colony were increasing only as people found opportunity to pursue their individual ends rather than the corporate ends of the company. John Rolfe, best known as the Virginian who helped gain peace with the Indians by marrying Pocahontas, daughter of the local chieftain, made a greater contribution to Virginia by developing, around 1613, a strain of Indian weed tobacco that achieved instant popularity in England. As the craze for tobacco in England created a flourishing market and high prices, Virginians poured all their energies into growing tobacco for individual profit, and company enterprises were left to languish.

The company made one final effort to recruit immigrants to staff its corporate enterprises, but the cost of promotion was too great, and the lure of tobacco quickly drew the new workers away. The company fell into factional bickering, and in 1622, after the death of Pocahontas's father, a new and more bellicose chieftain led the Indians in a massacre of the English farmers along the James River. About one-third of the settlers (347) were killed, and the devastation came up to the gates of Jamestown. The disaster, followed by bloody reprisals and a crop failure, so discredited the company that the King revoked its charter in 1624, and Virginia became a royal colony ruled by a governor appointed by the king. The headright system was continued, however, as was the House of Burgesses. Despite King James's reluctance to concede the principle of colonial self-rule, the crown interfered in Virginia's affairs less than the company had.

The high profits from tobacco brought quick recovery from the effects of the Indian massacre and made Virginia a land of opportunity for the disadvantaged and discontented. Gripped by such demographic and economic forces as rapid population growth, inflation, and the commercialization of agriculture with its need for fewer farmers, England teemed with farm and town workers available for colonial emigration. The poorest of English farm workers could emigrate as indentured servants of a Virginian who would pay their ocean passage. Labor was so dear and land so cheap in the New World that when the three to five years of servitude were completed, a servant could often buy a farm, plant tobacco, and perhaps acquire indentured servants of his own. The most enterprising and affluent of the early settlers accumulated both labor and land in abundance by importing indentured servants and acquiring headrights in the process. While these more successful planters filled the offices of colony and county government, Virginia society remained so fluid during most of the seventeenth century that the planters could not be said to constitute an aristocracy or ruling class.

For one category of immigrants, the Virginia environment produced not self-fulfillment but enslavement. In 1619, the year of the first representative assembly in British North America, a Dutch trading ship dropped anchor at Jamestown with the first cargo of Africans. The original English settlers had brought with them the traditional European prejudice against blacks, but there was no provision in English law for treating Negroes differently from other indentured servants. However, it was easier to take advantage of blacks. Torn forcibly from their African cultures and languages, they had few means of resisting oppression in the alien culture of Virginia. Conspicuously distinguishable from European servants, they could not run away and melt into the free population. Even as the conditions of servitude became less onerous for whites, masters gradually began holding black servants for life and claiming the labor of their children. By the middle of the seventeenth century, Virginia law was modified to define a separate status of permanent and absolute slavery for Africans. When the colony's evolving slave laws were first codified in 1705 and bondsmen were "adjudged to be real estate," blacks numbered perhaps 10,000 in a population totalling about 85,000. This was to be a land of opportunity for Europeans only. Indeed, it was through the exploitation of cheap black labor in the tobacco fields that some white Virginians began to amass great fortunes in the later seventeenth century.

While whites flourished in Virginia, a similar pattern of colonial life was being established under very different auspices farther up the shores of Chesapeake Bay. In 1632, King Charles I, successor of James I, granted to Cecilius Calvert, second Lord Baltimore, proprietorship (theoretically, personal ownership) of the feudal domain of Maryland lying between the Potomac River and the 40th parallel. The Calverts were a noble Catholic family who envisioned Maryland as a refuge for their fellow Catholics from Protestant England. The first settlement was established at Saint Mary's in 1634, when some 200 colonists, most of them Protestants, arrived aboard the *Ark* and the *Dove*. Soon both Protestants and Catholics were emigrating to Maryland to become tobacco growers like the Virginians. But unlike the early Virginians, they enjoyed peace with their Indian neighbors and experienced no starvation.

Due to a remarkable royal charter, Lord Baltimore had absolute political power and personal ownership of the land. In order to attract settlers and make the colony a success, the young Lord Proprietor shared both soil and power with them. Large grants of 3,000 to 6,000 acres were made to some colonists, mostly Catholics; they presided as manorial lords over large numbers of servants and tenants and came to constitute a kind of gentry. Most of the population were yeoman farmers, perhaps employing a few servants and leasing their lands from the proprietor on a basis nearly equivalent to ownership in return for a nominal tax or quitrent. The Calverts appointed a governor, but eventually allowed the inhabitants to elect an assembly that soon asserted its right to initiate legislation. The most notable piece of legislation was the Act of Toleration of 1649. This act promised less tolerance than is commonly believed; it applied only to orthodox trinitarian Christians and assured neither separation of church and state nor universal freedom of worship. Yet the act assured a measure of religious liberty to Protestants and Catholics. Within three decades of its founding, the colony had perhaps 13,000 inhabitants.

NEW ENGLAND: PLYMOUTH AND MASSACHUSETTS BAY

Meanwhile, far to the north of the Chesapeake colonies, a different kind of English colonization was taking place on the less hospitable coast of New England. The New England colonies were a direct outgrowth of a renewal of religious conflict in England. The more intense Protestants had never been satisfied with the moderate English Reformation as it was institutionalized in the Church of England. Calling themselves Puritans, they wanted to rid the English church of Roman Catholic practices and to "purify" it by eliminating the hierarchy of bishops and simplifying church ritual. The Puritans shared with Anglicans the predestinarian doctrines of the Swiss cleric John Calvin: a heightened sense of an inscrutable God's sovereignty and goodness and a recognition of depraved humanity's dependence on divine grace for salvation. The Puritans strove to live strictly in accordance with God's will and to create a community modeled on that of the earliest Christians.

Queen Elizabeth's astuteness had prevented the growing Puritan spirit from causing trouble during her reign, but her successors, the Stuart monarchs James I (1603–1625) and Charles I (1625–1649), invited conflict. James bluntly told the Puritans that they would either conform to the usages of the Church of England or be "harried out of the land." His son Charles married a French Catholic princess and supported efforts to compel religious conformity.

Early on, James harried one little band of particularly fervid left-wing Puritans out of England, and they took refuge in Holland. They were known as Separatists because they sought to separate from the Church of England and not merely to purify it. Although they were able to worship as they wished, after several years in Holland these Pilgrims, in order to preserve their identity, turned their eyes toward America. With support from a group of London merchants, they and additional recruits from England, totalling 101 men and women (87 of them either Separatists or members of Separatist families), set out for Virginia in the *Mayflower* in September 1620. Poor navigation brought them to the American coast at Cape Cod, north of the company's territory, and rather than brave further winter storms on the Atlantic, they established nearby the settlement of Plymouth. Half of this ill-prepared band died of illness and malnutrition during the first winter. The remaining Pilgrims were spared largely through the timely appearance of Squanto, a friendly Indian who spoke English, having spent some time in England after being kidnapped by a ship's captain. He taught them to fish and to grow corn. Thus, Plymouth Plantation endured, if it did not grow rapidly, as a "sweet communion" of simple and pious souls who eked out a living from poor New England soil and from trade in fish and furs. The first English community in New England, it was soon overshadowed and eventually absorbed (1691) by the larger, more prosperous Puritan colony of Massachusetts Bay. Its place in the American imagination, however, was assured by the eloquent history, *Of Plymouth Plantation*, left by its long-time governor, William Bradford, and by the first Thanksgiving, its celebration of the first harvest in the new colony. Not least of all, New England's first permanent settlement is remembered for the Mayflower Compact. This first American "constitution" was a self-governing agreement inspired by radical Puritan notions of church government; 41 adult males signed it on shipboard before the Pilgrims landed at Cape Cod. Under its terms, the colonists formed a "civill body politic" to govern themselves by majority will and promised "all due submission and obedience" to the "just and equall lawes" of the colony.

The main Puritan migration to New England was made possible when a group of well-to-do and influential leaders obtained from King Charles in 1629 a charter for the Massachusetts Bay Company authorizing settlement in the area north of the Plymouth colony. In a bold move, the leaders resolved to make this charter of a joint-stock company the constitutional basis for a holy commonwealth beyond the King's reach by moving charter and company officers across the Atlantic. All over England, Puritans subscribed funds and volunteered themselves, and in the summer of 1630, a fleet of 17 vessels carried nearly 1,000 people to establish a series of towns around Boston harbor. As conditions for Puritanism worsened in England, these original settlers were followed by thousands more. Within little more than a decade, New England had 20,000 people.

However foreign the Puritans' ideals may seem to later generations, their enterprise for a holy commonwealth was certainly one of humanity's nobler dreams. If one accepts the Puritans' premises that God is sovereign, that one's primary duty is to do His will, and that the major issue of life is whether one receives God's grace or salvation then it is hard to resist their conclusion that society should be constructed around a divine plan for human redemption.

The Puritans' theory of civil government was similar to their congregationalist theory of church government, and both were based on the idea of convenant. A true church was a group of the "visible elect" (those who appeared by their lives to be true recipients of God's grace) who had entered into a sacred agreement or covenant with God and each other to obey the divine will and establish a church to preach His word. It was then the business of the church members to choose as minister a man especially qualified by character and education to interpret divine will. (Women were, of course, generally denied education and were not eligible for the clergy.) This theory contained an element of democracy in that all members participated in the holy covenant, the choice of a minister, and the admission of new members; an element of aristocracy in that the minister once chosen should be accorded the authority due his special qualifications for interpreting God's will; and an element of monarchy in that God's will was sovereign.

The Puritans similarly believed that their holy commonwealth was founded on an implicit covenant with God and each other and that civil magistrates derived their authority from their special qualifications for interpreting God's will for the society. The Puritan commonwealth took its form from the corporate charter of the Massachusetts Bay Company. The stockholders or "freemen" of a joint-stock company met annually as a "Great and General Court" to decide major company policies and to elect the company's executive officers, a governor and a board of assistants or magistrates. When the Puritan leaders transferred the charter of the Massachusetts Bay Company from England to New England in 1630, only a handful of magistrates — the governor, John Winthrop, and a few freemen (stockholders) of the company who were also assistants — went along.

In their zeal to protect the religious objectives of the holy experiment, these few magistrates sought at first to make all rules, judge all cases, and govern alone. But within a year, a number of the leading settlers demanded a voice in government, and the magistrates decided that henceforth all adult male church members could be considered freemen and be allowed to attend the annual General Court to elect the governor and assistants. By 1632, three years after settlement, the General Court had forced the magistrates to concede it a share in the lawmaking power. As the population increased and the General Court became unwieldy, the practice was adopted of having the freemen in each town elect two deputies to represent them in the General Court. The evolution of the General Court as a representative legislative body was completed in 1640 when the elected deputies and the governor and magistrates began meeting separately, thus forming a bicameral legislature.

The Puritan commonwealth was theocratic in the sense that God's will was law, but not in the sense that ministers were given direct political power. The real power of the clergy arose from their authority as interpreters of God's will. With respect to civil matters, this function was ordinarily performed by the magistrates, but when they disagreed with the deputies, the magistrates could usually call the powerful authority of the clergy to their support. Nearly everyone believed that it was the duty of the state to support the church, to require church attendance by members and non-members alike, to enforce a strict morality, and to do anything else that would increase the chances of salvation for every member of the community.

The pattern of settlement reflected the religious aims of the holy commonwealth. Individuals were not permitted to buy land wherever they wished. The General Court, in a practice quite unlike that of Virginia or Maryland, insisted on compact settlement in contiguous towns. When warranted by population increases, the General Court would authorize a group of people to settle a new town adjacent to one already established. Thus, in orderly and controlled fashion, the original settlement at Salem was followed by ones at Charlestown and Boston and subsequently at Haverhill, Concord, and Sudbury, and then by others well beyond the Boston Bay area. Families were assigned house lots (the sizes of which were generally determined by social rank) in a compact village within the town's boundaries, and they worked the outlying agricultural lands they were allotted. The church was located in the village center, and villagers and the town and church officials were encouraged to guard, warn, and reprove each other against moral lapses. Freeman and nonfreeman alike were allowed to participate directly in the town meeting, which elected town officials and decided local policy.

Deeply believing that a trained intelligence was required to discern God's will, the Puritans were zealous advocates of education. The family was the basic unit of instruction. Although male dominance was an accepted principle and women were expected to regard their men with "a reverend subjection," the mother exercised considerable, at times decisive authority within the home. Day-to-day child-rearing, like most domestic matters, were her responsibility. Technically, at least, the father was responsible for educating his dependents; he saw to it that his children and servants mastered the rudiments of reading, writing, and arithmetic and that his sons learned a trade. Fathers were responsible, too, of course, for the religious and moral training and behavior of their families. In 1647, the General Court ordered every town of 50 houses to maintain an elementary school, and some of the larger towns supported public secondary schools as well.

Puritan theory required not only a decently educated general population but also a highly educated magistracy and clergy. More than 100 graduates of Oxford and Cambridge came to Massachusetts Bay in its first decade to fill this need. In 1636, the General Court established at Cambridge a college modeled on the English universities and named after John Harvard, a young English clergyman who bequeathed to it his library and half his estate. Bright boys from ordinary farm families attended Harvard, and about half of the graduates became ministers.

RHODE ISLAND, CONNECTICUT, NEW HAMPSHIRE

It was inevitable that the holy commonwealth's efforts to maintain social discipline and a uniform doctrine would lead to friction in a population filled with gifted, intense, and devout individuals. The most embarrassing troublemakers in the early days were Roger Williams and Anne Marbury Hutchinson, both of whom challenged the principle of religious uniformity. A brilliant young minister, Williams was a radical Puritan who arrived at the modern principle of separation of church and state on the not so modern ground that enforcement of religious uniformity impeded the soul in its search for religious truth. Such a view clearly threatened the commonwealth, and Williams's close friend Governor Winthrop warned him of his impending arrest in time for him to escape. Banished from the colony, he made his way south with some of his followers to Narragansett Bay in 1636. He established the town of Providence, and then the colony of Rhode Island, where he proclaimed the policy of complete religious freedom and inaugurated a democratic system of self-government. Receiving a charter from the English government in 1644, Rhode Island attracted dissenters from Massachusetts and Europe, flourished as a farming and trading community, and was a thorn in the sides of its orthodox Puritan neighbors.

Soon after Williams's exile, Anne Hutchinson, a gifted lay theologian and an uncommonly assertive Puritan woman, was also banished from Massachusetts to Rhode Island. She had been holding meetings in which she stressed the covenant of grace, which appealed to many Puritans. Because she believed that the continuing process of divine revelation could supplant orthodox scriptural interpretation, she was accused in the colony's General Court of disrespect for the clergy and the heresy of Antinomianism, which emphasized the primacy of inner faith and direct communion with God over outward religious observance and other good works. In today's more secular age, her doctrinal differences with the Puritan leadership seem small — matters of degree, not kind. Yet her outspoken criticism of established clerical authority — and her intrusion into affairs that the Puritan fathers thought were better left to men — assured her conviction as "a woman not fit for our society." After a brief imprisonment she along with her family and some followers fled to Rhode Island; she was killed in 1643 by Indians.

Another New England colony came into being when the strong-minded Reverend Thomas Hooker and members of his congregation in Cambridge became excited over the fertile Connecticut River Valley, 100 miles inland from the Massachusetts Bay settlements. Rivalry between Hooker and the other leaders probably figured in the fact that the magistrates departed from their rule of compact settlement and allowed the Cambridge people to go. Traveling overland in 1636, Hooker's followers founded Hartford and organized their own colony of Connecticut on the model of Massachusetts Bay. Other Puritan groups founded settlements at Saybrook and New Haven on the coast and maintained an independent status for a quarter of a century before merging with Hooker's valley settlements as the united colony of Connecticut.

Massachusetts Bay sought to maintain control over the sporadic settlements that grew up to its north. In 1679, the towns beyond the Merrimac River obtained a charter making them the separate royal colony of New Hampshire, but the Maine area beyond continued to be ruled from Boston.

ENGLISH STRIFE AND AMERICAN AUTONOMY

The Stuart monarchy of Charles I had little liking for the stiff-necked independence of Puritan New England, but Charles had his hands too full with Puritanism in old England to undertake any punitive measures across the broad Atlantic. English Puritans had become increasingly important leaders in Parliament's struggle against the arbitrary policies of the Stuarts. The long and bitter conflict culminated in civil war in the 1640s. Oliver Cromwell's Parliamentary army defeated the royalist forces, King Charles was beheaded in 1649, and Cromwell became the dominant figure in a Puritan Commonwealth.

Under these circumstances, the English colonies on the Chesapeake Bay and in New England had been left to develop as they pleased. The Virginians cared little who ruled in England so long as they were left alone to grow tobacco and pursue their individual fortunes. In Maryland, however, the Protestant majority took advantage of the English Civil War to overthrow the Calverts and the Catholic ruling class and to repeal the Act of Toleration.

The New Englanders became more independent than ever. The leaders of Massachusetts Bay regarded their holy commonwealth as a model for England and indeed for all humanity, "a Citty Upon a Hill, the eies of all people upon us." The early success of the Puritan cause in the English Civil War reinforced their faith that they were leading the way to a world organized under the will of God. With redoubled zeal to maintain a pure and undefiled commonwealth, they sought to eliminate religious error wherever it appeared. The Quakers caused the Puritans the greatest trouble. These adherents of the Religious Society of Friends represented a kind of radical Puritanism of lower-class origin that enjoined each person to follow the divine promptings of the "Inner Light" in his or her own soul. The antiauthoritarian Quakers felt impelled to bear witness to their faith in the most hostile places, and many of them came to Massachusetts Bay for this purpose. Although they were banished, they returned at the first opportunity. The authorities tried whipping, then cutting off ears, then the threat of hanging, but still the banished Quakers returned. Finally four were hanged.

But suddenly New England lost its sense of cosmic significance. The Puritan Commonwealth collapsed in England, and the Stuart monarchy returned to power in the Restoration of 1660. The new Stuart king, Charles II, restored Maryland to the Calverts and sought to strengthen his control over the other colonies, but the habit of independence had become so deeply ingrained that he encountered strong resistance. Though the New England magistrates and clergy ceased their persecutions and grudgingly began to tolerate Quakers, Anglicans, and other dissenters, they stubbornly sought other ways to maintain their autonomy and power in loyalty to the ideal of the holy commonwealth. But by now, this ideal was being weakened from within as well as from without.

PURITANISM IN A SECULARIZING
SOCIETY

The Chesapeake colonists had reacted to the New World environment and the lure of profits from tobacco culture by moving easily toward a society of merchants and staple-crop producers, based on individual enterprise and liberal institutions. In New England, an equally autonomous society had developed, but here institutionalized Puritanism was a brake against the pull of the New World environment toward modernity.

In emphasizing God's sovereignty and humanity's dependence, Puritanism (only somewhat more forcibly than Protestantism generally) was profoundly antagonistic to the modern spirit of optimism and confident individualism. Yet at the same time, Puritanism gave a powerful psychological impetus to individual striving. The Puritans were "moral athletes" who believed that "right living" was the best evidence (although no guarantee) that one enjoyed God's grace. Right living included working as hard and being as successful as possible in whatever worldly calling or business God had placed one. With these convictions, it was not surprising that Puritans were highly successful in their temporal pursuits, especially under the favoring circumstances offered by the New World environment.

Despite its scarcity of fertile soil, New England prospered from the beginning. Although fur trapping flourished only briefly and failed as game supplies dwindled, cod fisheries were developed early and remained a source of steady profit. Lucrative opportunities arose in trade with the English colonies in the East Indies and, to a lesser degree, with England and Spain. The Caribbean Islands produced only two crops — tobacco and sugar — for the European market, and New England colonists began to supply the islanders with food and other items they needed — fish, grain, staves, and livestock. These northern merchants also traded New World goods for manufactured products at Glasgow, Bristol, and London. Sometimes they exchanged rum for slaves on the coast of West Africa. Between the New World, the Caribbean Islands, and the Old World, a trading pattern, imprecisely called *triangular*, was established by the New Englanders. To facilitate their maritime endeavors, they built a flourishing merchant marine, which in turn stimulated a shipbuilding industry in New England.

By the middle of the seventeenth century, the Puritan colonies contained a growing class of successful and wealthy merchants and entrepreneurs, second-generation Americans with no memory of the persecutions once visited upon their forebears. Such people found it increasingly more difficult to maintain the fervid piety of the first settlers. Some could not put the search for salvation before worldly prosperity, and some did not feel helplessly dependent on the grace of an omnipotent God. There was no conscious parting from orthodoxy, no open rebellion against Puritan rule, but the religious fervor of the early commonwealth gradually ebbed. This became apparent when the children of the first generation of church members increasingly failed to give sufficient evidence of God's grace to be received into full membership themselves. Stubbornly retreating before the relentless tides of heterodoxy and secularism, the churches compromised; to retain influence, they opened their membership under a "half-way covenant" to those baptized children of church members who led exemplary lives and accepted the orthodox doctrines, but who were still unable to testify to a "saving faith," a convincing subjective experience of grace. Having blurred the distinction between the elect and the merely devoted, some churches soon went even further by permitting communion without public confession of faith.

Meanwhile, some of the more successful and less pious New Englanders began to argue that religious intolerance discouraged immigration and hampered growth and prosperity. These settlers also chafed under the orthodox leadership and disapproved of the continued defiance of royal authority. Thus when the British government finally lost patience with Massachusetts Bay, it found some allies among the Puritans. In 1684, Charles II annulled the Massachusetts charter, and the following year his brother and successor, James II, placed all the New England colonies, along with recently acquired New York and New Jersey, under the new and singular jurisdiction of the Dominion of New England. All legislative bodies were suspended, and the Dominion was arbitrarily ruled by a royally appointed governor, Sir Edmund Andros, and his council. But James's equally arbitrary rule at home was arousing opposition. When the King was overthrown in the "Glorious Revolution" of 1688, a series of popular demonstrations ousted the Dominion authorities in the American colonies.

In 1691, the Massachusetts Bay authorities had to accept from the new English monarchs, William and Mary, a charter that assured further secularization and seriously compromised the ideal of the holy commonwealth. The legislative power of the General Court was restored, but henceforth the governor was to be royally appointed, and property ownership replaced church membership as a qualification for voting. Under the new charter, the anticlerical elements gained increasing political influence and finally succeeded even in taking control of Harvard College.

The clergy sought to stem the ebbing of their spiritual and political authority by ever more fervent reminders of God's power and wrath and unwittingly contributed to the Salem witchcraft hysteria of the early 1690s. Before this frenzy subsided, 2 dogs and 19 innocent people died on the gallows, an old man was pressed to death by rocks, and some 150 others awaited (but would not suffer) a similar fate. Although belief in witches was almost universal throughout Christendom and although the Salem witch mania was modest and restrained compared to those of Scotland and Germany, the revulsion against the outrages in New England further undermined the prestige of the orthodox leadership. In all likelihood, the hysteria owed more to tensions resulting from a changing social, economic, and political order than to clerical excesses, but the tragic episode was another major setback for the Puritan hierarchy. By the turn of the century, the social and political leadership of the Puritan colonies was clearly passing into the hands of the enterprising commercial class that constituted the vanguard of modernity.

The Puritans have too often been viewed through the dark window of the witch trials. Until recently, much has been made of the somber, more repressive, and self-denying tendencies of these extraordinary people. Although their piety seems extreme to a more secular age, the Puritans were not necessarily the grim, self-righteous prigs of popular imagination. In a threatening and uncertain world, theirs was a purposeful community that proved immensely appealing to uprooted, discontented, and otherwise "unredeemed" Englishmen, that attracted an uncommon number of subtle minds, and that produced great intellectual vigor. Their modern critics have faulted their "hell-fire and damnation" religion, yet their ministers were well-educated men whose sermons were often models of lucidity. Nor were the Puritan faithful necessarily more stuffy or abstemious than other Anglo-Americans of the period; preferring moderation to total abstinence, they used tobacco and alcohol in moderation. Church records reveal that premarital sex could be forgiven the repentant Puritan, and that divorce was permitted for cruelty, adultery, and impotence. Marriage was often marked by tenderness and based on deep love between partners, who took pleasure in what one approving Puritan divine called the "Use of the Marriage Bed." In sum, these were appealing folk, sober and human, God-fearing and practical. They were not libertines, but they were probably no more puritanical than other seventeenth-century Englishmen on either side of the Atlantic.

FOR FURTHER READING

Samuel Eliot Morison's *The European Discovery of America* (1971) is a notable introduction to English explorations, and Wallace Notestein describes *The English People on the Eve of Colonization, 1603–1630* (1954). Gary Nash's *Red, White, and Black* (1992) explores the interactions between native Americans, Europeans, and Africans in colonial North America. The authoritative account of the early colonies is Charles M. Andrews's *The Colonial Period of American History* (4 vols., 1934–1938). The early history of the Chesapeake colonies is traced in James Horn's *Adapting to a New World* (1994), J. A. Leo Lamay's *The American Dream of Captain John Smith* (1991), and Wesley Frank Craven's *The Southern Colonies in the Seventeenth Century* (1949). Good recent explorations of colonial New England include Stephen Innes, *Creating the Commonwealth* (1995), and William Cronon, *Changes in the Land* (1983). Darrett B. Rutman, in *American Puritanism* (1970), provides a good introduction to early New England faith and practice; Perry Miller's classic two-volume study ably details *The New England Mind* (1939, 1953); and T. H. Breen's *The Character of the Good Ruler* (1970) examines Puritan political thought. Both Edmund S. Morgan's *Visible Saints* (1963) and Richard Gildrie's *Salem, Massachusetts* (1975) help explain the transformation of the Puritan commonwealth into a Yankee province. Important biographical and family studies include Edmund S. Morgan's brief study of Governor Winthrop, *The Puritan Dilemma* (1956); Morgan's *Roger Williams* (1967); Kenneth Silverman's *The Life and Times of Cotton Mather* (1984); and John Demos's analysis of Plymouth colony, *A Little Commonwealth* (1970). The best account of the social and economic context of the witch trials is Paul Boyer and Steven Nissenbaum, *Salem Possessed* (1974). John Demos, in *Entertaining Satan* (1982), places the Salem tragedy in broader perspective. In this period (as in all others) the student is advised to examine contemporary accounts, particularly Governor William Bradford, *Of Plymouth Plantation, 1620–1691* (1966) and John Winthrop, *Winthrop's Journal* (1908).

18

MAP 1: EUROPEAN SETTLEMENTS AND INDIAN TRIBES IN AMERICA, 1650

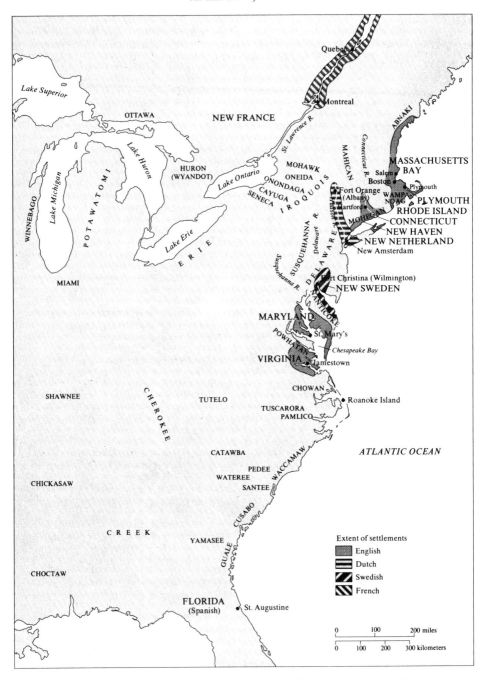

Source: Redrawn by permission of the Smithsonian Institution Press from B. A. E. Bulletin 145, *Indian Tribes of North America,* John Swanton, Smithsonian Institution, Washington, D.C., 1952.

2

★ ★ ★ ★ ★ ★

Britain's North American Empire, 1660–1763

BEFORE 1660, the English had little or no conception of a colonial empire. The isolated American settlements were rarely thought of, and the British government had been too distracted by political chaos to devise any systematic scheme of beneficial relations between colonies and mother country. The end of civil strife brought a new interest in America. Under the Stuart Restoration, the whole North American seaboard, from Maine south to Spanish Florida, was organized for settlement and exploitation, and an emerging theory of empire began to be embodied in a set of colonial policies.

THE PROPRIETARY COLONIES

The expansion of English settlement in North America was prompted partly by a desire to gain strategic advantages against other colonizing nations and partly by a desire to reward favored courtiers who had sided with the Stuarts during the Civil War. In 1663, Charles II granted a group of eight English noblemen the vast domain stretching south from Virginia to the borders of Spanish Florida and westward across the continent from sea to sea. This grant of Carolina was modeled on the proprietary grant of Maryland to the Calverts, and the eight Lords Proprietor were given title to the soil as well as political authority over the area. Carolina already contained a small population that had spilled over from Virginia into the area of Albemarle Sound. In 1670, an expedition from the British West Indies colony of Barbados established another settlement several hundred miles down the coast at Charles Town (Charleston); a contingent of French Huguenots (Protestants), Scots, and Germans augmented the English group.

Anxious to encourage immigration and make profits from rising land values, the proprietors promised religious toleration and adopted a liberal land system, including headrights. Settlers in the two sections (later to become the colonies of North and South Carolina) were allowed to elect an assembly and make laws in conjunction with a governor and council appointed by the proprietors. The northern settlements in the Albermarle district were blocked off by coastal sandbars from good ocean transportation, so this area came to be populated by small landowners whose isolation and independence made them difficult to govern. The southern settlements around Charles Town, on the other hand, quickly developed an export trade through profitable staple products — first deerskins and naval stores, and then rice and indigo. Brought to work the plantations, blacks outnumbered whites by the turn of the century, and a particularly brutal form of bondage based on the slave code of British Barbados became fully entrenched. Great plantations grew up on the tidal estuaries, and the planters came to constitute a tightly knit ruling class. They had their headquarters in Charleston, where they spent the malarial summer months in breeze-swept town houses.

While Carolina was emerging as a buffer against the Spanish to the South, the British were eliminating another competitor farther north: the Netherlands, the European nation most like England in the enterprising qualities of its people. Early in the sixteenth century, the Dutch merchant marine dominated the Far Eastern spice trade. Though their Far Eastern ventures absorbed so much of their slender resources and work force that they had little left for the New World, the Dutch were interested in finding a more direct water passage to the spice islands through North America. It was the search for such a northwest passage that led Henry Hudson in 1609 up the river that bears his name.

The Hudson River proved to be no northwest passage, but it did lead into the heart of the fur-rich Iroquois country, and by 1624, the Dutch had established trading posts that grew into the colony of New Netherland. New Amsterdam at the tip of Manhattan Island became a cosmopolitan trading center; a scattering of Dutch farmers spread out over Long Island, Staten Island, and across the Hudson from Manhattan; along the Hudson, vast manors were granted to wealthy patroons who exercised feudal authority over their tenants. Yet the preoccupation of the Dutch with the Far East, their authoritarian patroonship system, and the petty tyranny of its governors prevented New Netherland from flourishing like its English neighbors.

The English resented this Dutch intrusion into what they regarded as their domain. In 1664, Charles II granted the area between the Delaware and Connecticut rivers to his brother, the Duke of York (who ascended the throne in 1685 as James II). James promptly organized a fleet and sailed for New Amsterdam, which surrendered without a shot. He found his proprietary domain, which he renamed New York, to be larger than he desired, and he transferred some 5,000,000 acres between the Delaware and the Hudson rivers to two of his favorites as the proprietary grant of New Jersey. The New Jersey proprietors encouraged settlement by promising land and religious tolerance. Large numbers of Puritan New Englanders, Dutch New Yorkers, English Barbadians, and colonists from Scotland and England responded, making the region one of Anglo-America's most ethnically and religiously diverse colonies. In 1674 the grant was divided into eastern and western sections, and the original proprietors sold their rights to others. West Jersey eventually came into the hands of a Quaker group, which included William Penn.

Penn was responsible for filling one of the last gaps in the continuous band of English settlement along the Atlantic Coast of North America. The son of a British admiral, Penn had been a convert to Quakerism, a radical separatist fringe that carried Puritan doctrines of religious purification to the extreme of rejecting a clergy and the Sacraments. Reviled by Anglicans and Puritans alike, the passionate Children of the Light were often persecuted, and Penn himself spent time in prison for his religious convictions. While on missionary tours of continental Europe, he envisioned a political and religious refuge in America where not just Quakers but the persecuted and poor of all sects and countries could live in peace. The reigning Stuarts had owed Penn's father a large sum of money; in 1681, this debt and perhaps a desire to be rid of the Quakers led Charles II to grant William Penn the vast region between Maryland and New York — 29,000,000 acres, nearly the size of England. Penn later added to this tract by purchasing the former Swedish colony of Delaware. Penn arrived in the New World in 1682 and laid out Philadelphia between the Schuylkill and the Delaware rivers. Thus, the Quaker paradise was built not in New Jersey, but in what was called Pennsylvania.

Penn promptly began advertising his province, offering complete religious freedom, representative government, and the most generous land policy of any of the American colonies. The quick response from English Quakers, the Welsh, and persecuted German sects made Pennsylvania the most rapidly growing and populous area in British America. Penn himself spent several years there, and inaugurated a government that enforced the most humane code of laws in the world. Separate assemblies were provided for the Philadelphia area and the area of the "Three Lower Counties" of Delaware below Philadelphia; both had the same governor who was appointed by the proprietor. The preponderant Quakers continued for decades to govern the province in the generous spirit of Penn's "Holy Experiment," and Pennsylvania became for European liberals the pre-eminent symbol of a tolerant and prosperous New World society.

Thus, by 1682, Great Britain's North American empire had been almost completely rounded out. Georgia, the last remaining American colony of Great Britain, was not established until 1732. In that year, a group of English philanthropists persuaded the British government to appoint them trustees of the area south of the Savannah River, which was to be used as a refuge for imprisoned debtors and other deserving paupers. The leading trustee and first governor, James Oglethorpe, sailed with a contingent of settlers in 1733 and founded Savannah. The benevolent trustees tried to ensure a moral society of small farmers by limiting each settler to 50 acres and prohibiting the importation of rum and slaves. When this southern-most colony proved not to be the New World Eden that its promoters had advertised, these restrictions were relaxed to enable it to compete for settlers with its prosperous neighbor South Carolina. Yet Georgia remained for many decades a tiny outpost against Spanish Florida.

The failure of the Georgia restrictions was merely the final demonstration that corporate purposes, however high-minded, could not survive among the English in the New World. This lesson was forced upon the Virginia Company early, and the holy commonwealth of the Puritans resisted it only a little longer. The proprietary colonies founded after 1660 all promised religious toleration, representative government, and cheap land — policies designed to attract settlers by guaranteeing individual rights and opportunity. The characteristics of the English and the free environment of the New World led irresistibly toward a society permeated with the spirit of individual enterprise.

THE NAVIGATION ACTS AND THE COLONIAL ECONOMY

While the proprietary colonies were eschewing corporate purposes in the New World, officials in London were developing a series of policies designed to implement the larger corporate purposes suggested by an emerging concept of British empire. These policies were based on the theory of political economy known as *mercantilism*. Although the term was not coined by Adam Smith until 1776, mercantilism was widely practiced throughout Europe during the preceding century. This economic doctrine presupposed that nations were engaged in a continuous struggle for supremacy. Economic strength was valued for the military and strategic advantages it yielded, and was to be measured primarily by the accumulation of *bullion* (uncoined gold or silver). As nations lost gold and silver by buying things from other nations, the most self-sufficient nations were considered the strongest and healthiest.

Colonies held an important place in mercantilist thinking. England, like Spain, France, and the Netherlands, turned to empire in order to make itself economically less dependent on others. Colonies could also contribute to the prosperity of the mother country by providing a market for its manufactures. Finally, an extensive trade with colonies would support a large merchant marine, and in a period when merchant ships and seamen were easily converted to naval purposes, this increased the fighting strength of the mother country.

England with its scanty resources and abundant labor was ideally suited to gain from mercantilism. Although slow to develop consistent colonial policies, the British government under Oliver Cromwell attempted to exclude foreign shipping from its New World possessions. Following the Restoration, Charles II and Parliament sought additional control of colonial economic activity through a series of Acts of Trade and Navigation, enacted between 1660 and 1672 and augmented by subsequent legislation. The Navigation

Acts contained three major requirements. First, all trade between England and her colonies was to be carried in ships built, owned, and operated by the British or British colonials. Second, all European goods imported into the colonies — with a few exceptions — were to pass through England and were thus subject to British import duties. Finally, certain "enumerated articles" produced by the colonies (primarily tobacco at first but later nearly every export) were to be shipped first to England, even if destined for ultimate resale in other European countries. Ultimately, the colonies were forbidden to produce certain finished goods that competed with those made in the mother country.

The exclusion of Dutch merchants from the Chesapeake tobacco trade and the loss of the direct European market for North American tobacco contributed to a period of stringency in Virginia and Maryland in the late seventeenth century. The Navigation Acts clearly subordinated colonial trade to England's, but their effects were by no means uniformly negative for the Americans. Mercantilist policies were more easily legislated than implemented, and at least until the end of the French and Indian War (1763), the colonists were generally agreed that the advantages of the loosely administered British imperial policy outweighed its disadvantages. The British colonies were given a monopoly of the tobacco market in the mother country, and bounties were paid to colonial producers of indigo and naval stores. The exclusion of foreign-built and foreign-owned ships from the trade between England and the colonies was a great boon to the New England shipbuilding industry and merchant marine. Indeed, the Navigation Acts were the "cement of empire," a positive force that bound colony to mother country.

Certainly by the first half of the eighteenth century, the colonial economy was in a highly prosperous state. European demand for tobacco, sugar, rice, indigo, and naval stores rose even faster than the production in the southern and West Indian colonies could expand. As these colonies grew and concentrated ever more exclusively on the profitable staples, they provided an ever greater market for wheat, flour, ground vegetables, salt fish and meat, lumber, and livestock from the middle colonies and New England. Philadelphia and Baltimore became flour milling and exporting centers, and New York exported the furs brought into Albany by the far ranging Iroquois.

New England produced few or no staples for the mother country and at first did not seem to fit the mercantilist prescriptions for usefulness. But the New Englanders quickly made themselves indispensable to the operation of the imperial economic system. Carrying provisions from the mainland to the West Indies, they picked up cargoes of sugar and then proceeded to England where they loaded their vessels with manufactured goods for America. In another variation of this "triangular trade," they brought molasses from the West Indies to New England, manufactured it into rum, took the rum to West Africa and traded it for slaves, and then carried the slaves for sale to the West Indies or the southern colonies. Similarly they carried Chesapeake tobacco or Carolina rice to England, bringing back manufactured goods. Prospering greatly from this trade and from shipbuilding and fisheries, New England also became the heaviest consumer of British manufactured goods.

As the colonial economy matured, British officials found additional regulations necessary to maintain mercantilist aims. To prevent New England rum makers from importing their supplies from non-English sources, Parliament passed the Molasses Act in 1733, levying a prohibitive duty on foreign molasses or sugar imported into British possessions. But New England evaded the duty by systematic smuggling, and the rum trade continued to flourish. To prevent colonial producers from competing with British manufacturers, Parliament passed a series of acts between 1699 and 1750 forbidding colonists to export woolen cloth and beaver hats or to expand their production of finished iron products.

The most serious economic problem of the colonies — money supply — was greatly aggravated by British restrictions that grew out of the mercantilist preoccupation with bullion for the mother country's treasury. Because gold and silver coin was the only recognized money and because the colonists could neither import British coin nor mint their own, they had to rely on Spanish coin acquired in the West Indian trade. Even this was an unstable money supply for it was constantly drained away to offset colonial trade deficits with England. Thus, there was never an adequate money supply for an intercolonial exchange of goods and services.

Under these circumstances, the colonial governments finally resorted to issuing paper money. These issues were to be redeemed within a certain period and were accompanied by new taxes designed to yield a sufficient fund to pay for redemption. But if too much paper money were issued or if redemption were delayed, the paper money depreciated in value and creditors complained. Moreover, colonial paper money was worthless in England and caused trouble to English merchants who tried to collect from American debtors. The British government first sought to remedy the situation by instructing the colonial governors to veto all but the most soundly backed paper money issues. This failing, Parliament in 1751 forbade the New England colonies, where the worst abuses occurred, to issue any further paper for payment of debts.

ADMINISTERING THE EMPIRE

While British officials were groping toward a concept of empire, administrative agencies for colonial planning and control were haphazardly evolving in the British government. Soon after the Restoration, the king's principal advisory body, the noble Privy Council, designated a committee known as the Lords of Trade to consider colonial matters. But not until the Glorious Revolution of 1688 and the accession of William and Mary did colonial officials in London seriously consider the creation of a centralized empire of politically uniform and dependent colonies directly supervised by the imperial government. A supplementary Navigation Act in 1696 set up a system of admiralty courts in America to enforce commercial regulations and punish smugglers. This same legislation created in England a Board of Trade and Plantations (a group of bureaucratic experts on colonial matters) to advise the Privy Council through the Lords of Trade. While the Board of Trade had little direct power, it did attain considerable importance as the one agency of the British government that systematically considered all colonial matters. Gradually and over many years, the Board of Trade was able to implement some consistent policies of colonial control.

One basic aim of the Board was to convert all the corporate and proprietary colonies into royal colonies. This process, begun with Virginia in 1624 and New Hampshire in 1679, became a deliberate objective upon the accession of William and Mary. Massachusetts Bay, Plymouth, and Maine were organized into the province of Massachusetts under a royal governor in 1691. That same year the Calverts' Maryland proprietary was royalized, and in 1692, Penn's Pennsylvania and Delaware suffered the same fate. But the new policy was too weak to withstand the political influence of such powerful proprietors: Penn's domain was restored within two years, and the Calverts finally got theirs back after being converted to Protestantism in 1715. Despite these setbacks, the colonial reorganizers persevered, extracting East and West Jersey from their proprietors and uniting them as the royal province of New Jersey in 1702. The Carolina proprietors gave up South Carolina in 1719 and North Carolina ten years later, and in 1752 Georgia fell under royal control. Only the strong English respect for property and charter rights enabled Connecticut and Rhode Island to maintain their corporate status and Penn and the Calverts to regain their domains.

The British government had several means of control over a royal colony. Most important was appointment of the governor, who was sent out with a set of detailed instructions drafted by the Board of Trade and who had an absolute veto over the acts of the colonial assembly. Moreover all colonial legislation was sent to the Board of Trade for careful scrutiny, and anything objectionable could be disallowed by the Privy Council. The Privy Council was also a court of appeal from decisions of colonial courts.

Through these means, the Privy Council and the Board of Trade sought to restrain the provincial governments from acts harmful to either English merchants or the royal prerogative. But this restraint was not burdensome. Sir Robert Walpole, who became the king's chief minister in 1721, believed that it was in England's interest to let the colonies flourish without interference; his policy of "salutary neglect" continued until the 1760s.

Under these circumstances, the provinces became virtually self-governing. All had a similar form of government. Except in Rhode Island and Connecticut, which continued to elect all their officials, and in Massachusetts, where the assembly elected the council, the governor and council were appointed by the king or the proprietor for indefinite terms. The council and an elected lower house formed a bicameral assembly. The assembly could convene only when called by the governor, who could suspend its sessions or dissolve it at will. The governor's veto could not be overridden. But whatever the governor's legal authority, he had practical difficulties in resisting the assembly's will. Lax imperial administration, either through design or neglect, permitted colonial assemblies gradually to exercise powers and privileges that in practice, though not by law, shifted the center of colonial control from the executive to themselves. Although intended to be dependent assemblies, they became, in effect, little Houses of Commons and claimed broad Parliamentary authority over local affairs. They particularly insisted on the well established English principle that citizens could be taxed only by consent of their representatives. The governors were paid by the colonies, and an assembly's refusal to levy taxes or appropriate funds for the governor's salary was a powerful political weapon.

Disputes between governors and assemblies were legion. Often incompetent and invariably caught between the conflicting demands of the London officials and the local assemblies, the governors could satisfy neither group. The ablest among them achieved some success only through the astute distribution of favors and by horsetrading with leaders of the assembly. At times, a governor could fill the council with influential provincials who would side with him against the lower house. But except in the few areas of special concern to the Privy Council, the assemblies usually had their way.

As the decades wore on, Americans increasingly assumed that they had an inalienable right to self-government through their assemblies. The recurrent disputes with the governors taught them political sophistication and political skills that were to be invaluable when this right was challenged. Serious conflict with Crown and Parliament was to be avoided only so long as imperial authorities did not demand that colonial practices coincide with imperial policies.

THE ANGLO-FRENCH WARS

While the English colonies were growing strong and prosperous along the eastern seacoast of North America, the French were developing a different kind of empire to the north and inland. In 1608, one year after the founding of Virginia, Samuel de Champlain began a French settlement at Quebec on the St. Lawrence River. For years Champlain devoted himself to exploring the interior far up the St. Lawrence and into the Great Lakes country and to developing a flourishing fur trade with the Algonquin and Huron Indians of the region. The French fur traders were soon joined by a band of dauntless Jesuit missionaries who ranged far and wide over the wilderness of the north country preaching Christianity to the Indians. By the middle of the seventeenth century, there was a narrow zone of agricultural settlement along the St. Lawrence where humble French *habitants* worked peasant-style on the manorial grants of a rather down-at-the-heels class of feudal *seigneurs.*

Despite the fewer numbers of the French in America, their vigorous exploration and the good relations they had achieved with their Indian allies made them a formidable barrier to English westward expansion. Only the powerful Iroquois confederation in upper New York, hostile to the French-oriented Huron and Algonquin tribes, shielded Dutch New Netherland and the English colonies from contact with the French. But after the rise of Louis XIV in the 1660s, the French pushed their Canadian enterprise more vigorously and assisted their Indian allies in making war on the Iroquois. Meanwhile Louis sought to make France the dominant power in Europe as well as to expand its colonial empire in America and other parts of the world. England joined a series of alliances designed to block French ambitions, and the result was a series of four great wars (1689–1763) fought mainly in Europe but also between the French and English in America.

In the first three encounters — King William's War, 1689–1697; Queen Anne's War, 1702–1713; King George's War, 1744–1748 — the French and their Indian allies raided the New England and New York frontiers. Beginning with Queen Anne's War, the Spanish were allied with the French, so that there was skirmishing along the southern as well as northern British frontier. The only American territorial change that resulted from the first three wars was the transfer of Nova Scotia, Newfoundland, and the Hudson Bay country in the far north from France to England in 1713.

Meanwhile, during the intervals of peace, the French moved into the Mississippi Valley behind the English settlements. Around 1700, they set up posts in the Illinois country on the northern Mississippi and established themselves at Biloxi and Mobile on the Gulf Coast near the great river's mouth. New Orleans was founded as the capital of French Louisiana in 1718.

The final phase of the conflict between Britain and France in North America was the French and Indian War (known in Europe as the Seven Years' War). This conflict began when a group of Virginians sent agents across the Appalachians and into the upper Ohio Valley for the purpose of Indian trade and land speculation. The French responded by building a chain of small forts on the upper Ohio. Young George Washington, sent out in command of a force of Virginia militia in 1754, arrived barely too late to prevent construction of Fort Duquesne at the forks of the Ohio on the future site of Pittsburgh. He was driven off by the French, and the war began — though it was not officially declared for two more years.

All the major European powers were quickly drawn into the fighting. At first things went badly for the British in America and elsewhere. General Edward Braddock's army was routed within a few miles of Fort Duquesne, throwing the whole frontier open to several years of pounding by the French and Indians. The British seemed to have no overall strategy, and the colonies could not be persuaded to contribute very loyally or enthusiastically to the war effort. Delegates from eight of the colonies, meeting at the so-called Albany Congress in 1754, approved Benjamin Franklin's farsighted plan for intercolonial defense and unity, but this early plan for voluntary union failed to win the support of either the crown or the colonial assemblies. (Its implications, however, were not lost on a later generation of rebels who, during the imperial crisis that followed the war with France, would again entertain plans for a closer union.)

The situation changed dramatically in 1757 when the vigorous William Pitt assumed direction of the British war effort. Making the conquest of Canada his paramount aim, Pitt organized a series of offensives that culminated in the capture of Quebec by General James Wolfe in 1759. By the time the war ended in Europe, the British were victorious everywhere. In the Peace of Paris (1763), Britain gained French Canada and Spanish Florida, as well as acquisitions in India and elsewhere. The ownership of Louisiana was transferred from France to Spain.

No one had more reason to rejoice than the British Americans. Suddenly freed from the greatest threat to their security, they now looked west upon an unbounded arena of opportunity lying open to their enterprise. It did not yet occur to them that their new security and confidence might weaken their attachment to the mother country whose emergence as the world's most powerful nation they were now so loyally celebrating.

FOR FURTHER READING

The final volume of Charles M. Andrews's *The Colonial Period of American History* (4 vols., 1934–1938); Richard R. Johnson's *Adjustment to Empire* (1981); and Robert M. Bliss's *Revolution and Empire* (1990) are significant analyses of British policy and administration. Jack P. Greene has studied the struggles between colonial governors and assemblies in *The Quest for Power: The Lower House of Assembly in the Southern Royal Colonies, 1689–1776* (1965). Wesley Frank Craven describes *The Colonies in Transition, 1660–1713* (1968). The 13 volumes in the *History of the American Colonies* series, edited by Milton M. Klein and Jacob E. Cooke, are designed for both the serious student and the lay person. See, for example, Michael Kammen's *Colonial New York* (1975), and Joseph E. Illick's *Colonial Pennsylvania* (1976). *The Middle Colonies* (1938) are described by Thomas J. Wertenbaker. Mary Maples Dunn has written a good biography of *William Penn* (1967); Frederick B. Tolles deals with the changing role of Philadelphia's Quaker merchants in *Meeting House and Counting House* (1948); and Oliver A. Rink provides a useful survey of Dutch New York in *Holland on the Hudson* (1986). Francis Parkman's *France and England in America* (8 vols., 1851–1892) is still a useful account of the development of French Canada and the great struggle for empire in North America, but it should be read in conjunction with the more recent *France in America* (1990) by William John Eccles. The final phase of the French-English struggle in North America and the period after the French and Indian War are delineated authoritatively in Lawrence Gipson's *The British Empire Before the American Revolution* (15 vols., 1936–1970). Fred Anderson's *A People's Army* (1984) provides a vivid look at the American colonial contribution to the British war effort against France.

3

★ ★ ★ ★ ★ ★

A New Society,
1600s–1700s

Within the loose institutional framework of Britain's North American empire, a distinctly new kind of society had been taking shape. Inside this new society, the typical European was being subtly altered. "What then is the American, this new man?" the French immigrant Hector de Crèvecoeur was asking by the 1770s.

THE AMERICANS

De Crèvecoeur's American, in the first place, belonged to a numerous and rapidly multiplying people. The American population grew from about a quarter of a million in 1700 to two-and-a-half million by 1775, roughly one-third the population of England and Wales. The majority of these Americans were of English origin. But English immigration slowed in the latter part of the seventeenth century, and the continuing predominance of English stock owed much to the fecundity of Anglo-American parents.

The spectacular population increase of the eighteenth century was also based on a quickening of non-English immigration, much of it with little affinity for English culture and even less liking for British political control. From the founding of Pennsylvania in the 1680s, Penn's advertising attracted a steadily mounting flow of impoverished peasants from the war-ravaged states of the German Rhineland. By the 1770s there were around 200,000 industrious German farmers in the North American colonies. These so-called Pennsylvania Dutch (from the word *Deutsch*, meaning *German*) constituted a third of the population of that middle colony.

An even larger tide of immigration began flowing in the first decades of the eighteenth century from Ulster, the six counties of northern Ireland.

These Protestants of Scottish origin are called Scotch-Irish by their descendants, to distinguish them from the indigenous Roman Catholic population of the rest of Ireland; they had been transplanted to Ulster in the early seventeenth century as part of the campaign to subdue Ireland, the first overseas English colony. By the beginning of the eighteenth century, they were suffering from English restrictions on Irish trade and industry, increasing farm rents, and various civil disabilities against their staunch Presbyterianism. Under these circumstances, Scotch-Irish by the thousands, perhaps as many as a quarter million, crossed the Atlantic. Concentrated along the frontier as pioneer farmers and aggressive Indian fighters, they made up from one-twelfth to one-tenth of the entire population by the 1770s. Like Pennsylvania's Germans, the Scotch-Irish proved to be unwilling subjects of British rule.

Smaller groups from Europe included the Dutch and the French Huguenots. New Netherland had 8,000 Dutch residents at the time of its transfer to English control, and their descendants remained a substantial segment of New York's population. The Huguenots, or French Protestants, began leaving France when the revocation of the Edict of Nantes in 1685 ended religious toleration in that predominantly Catholic country. They did not come to America in large numbers, but their enterprising qualities made many of them successful and prominent. Probably the largest number came to South Carolina, where they were quickly assimilated to Anglicanism and emerged as a major element of the mercantile-planting elite.

Whether English or non-English, the European immigrants of the eighteenth century came mainly from the lower or middling orders of Old World society. Probably half or more of the settlers in the middle colonies crossed the Atlantic as indentured servants. Some were actually kidnapped and sold to America by dealers in human merchandise. Thousands more — orphans, pauper children, and prisoners — were sent abroad by public authorities. Not a few of them chose emigration as a welcome alternative to long imprisonment or execution for minor offenses. Some 40,000 English convicts were transported to North America in the six decades before the Revolution, and in Maryland, convicts made up the bulk of the servant class.

But whatever their legal status, most Europeans who embarked on the long voyage to America were the younger and more vigorous people from their home communities. Once free of indenture, even the lowliest among them was free to rise. Colonel John Lamb, a wealthy merchant and prominent political leader in New York in the 1770s, was the son of a man who had been taken from the gallows in England and transported to America, where he established himself as a solid citizen and laid the basis for his son's later success.

The African slaves, however, more than one in five of all Americans by 1775, came most unwillingly and had no chance to rise, whatever their vigor or ability. By the late seventeenth century, the very prosperity of the European immigrants was creating a growing demand for cheap and easily exploited labor. Yankee and European ship captains hastened to supply this demand, shuttling tightly packed cargoes of "black ivory" from the West

Coast of Africa and the West Indies for sale in British North America. Slavery became established in all the colonies, New York and Rhode Island as well as South Carolina and Georgia, but the readiest market for the black men and women who survived the horrors of slave ships was found in the southern states. There a privileged but growing class of planters depended on slaves to do the exhausting but routine plantation tasks of tobacco, rice, and indigo culture. By the eve of the Revolution, British North America held about 600,000 sons and daughters of once flourishing West African civilizations such as Ghana, Mali, and Songhai. In South Carolina blacks made up two-thirds of the population; in Virginia, nearly half; in New York, around one-seventh. Blacks contributed to the cultural and economic development of the emerging American society and in time developed a resilient and adaptive Afro-American subculture of their own. Unlike the other ethnic groups mentioned in this section, they were stigmatized by color, held down by the degradation of slavery, and shut off from the advantages enjoyed by others in the comparatively fluid New World order.

AMERICAN ENVIRONMENTS: NEW TOWNS AND THE OLD WEST

The acceleration of immigration and economic activity in the eighteenth century created a diversified society in the American colonies. Although the colonial population in 1775 was almost entirely rural, towns began to play an increasingly important role in colonial life. The early upsurge of commercial activity in New England was accompanied by a trend toward urbanization as Boston, Newport, and Salem became flourishing trading centers. Later, Philadelphia and New York emerged as major urban centers, and they eventually outstripped their predecessors. By the 1770s, Philadelphia's population of nearly 40,000 made it the largest American city or the second largest city in the British empire. New York was the second biggest city of British North America followed by Boston, Charleston, and Newport, the last having a population of around 7,000. The Chesapeake tobacco country, where oceangoing ships could sail directly up to the individual planter's wharf for trade, was the only area that did not develop a major urban center.

The colonial cities were scarcely more than overgrown villages compared to the older, larger, and more developed cities of Europe. Fewer than one out of twenty colonists living in 1700 and 1776 made their homes in cities. But the newspapers, pamphlets, and almanacs that formed the means of communication in the colonies were published in these cities, and in them flourished shoemakers, weavers, hatters, cabinet-makers, and artisans of countless other trades who satisfied most of the colonists' needs. The principal courts were found in cities, and in these urban centers lawyers emerged as an influential professional group. In short, the seaboard cities became dynamic sites of growth and change, sites of much of the evolving economic, intellectual, and political life of the colonies.

While towns were developing along the coast, the pressure of the population increase was forcing a line of settlement far inland. In this hinterland, or "Old West," a new society took shape by the middle of the eighteenth century. The distinguishing characteristic of this settlement was that it lay beyond the "fall line," the point where the rivers descended over rapids into the level coastal plain and became navigable. In the absence of good roads or other transportation facilities, the Old West lay too far inland to produce goods for market and thus became an area of pioneer subsistence farming, isolated from the coastal settlements and the Atlantic world. Nevertheless, to those who peopled it, the Old West seemed an agrarian paradise where the ease of acquiring farms of their own promised a degree of security, well-being, and independence that would have been unthinkable in the land-hungry Europe they had left behind.

New England's Old West included the northern and western hill towns and lay away from the coast and the deep inland extension of coastal society along the navigable Connecticut River. The old Puritan pattern of town planning broke down in New England as the provincial governments began disposing of blocks of new towns to land speculators who in turn sold farms to actual settlers.

South of New England, New York's Hudson River was a magnificent highway north into the interior. The Mohawk River, flowing east from the Great Lakes country into the Hudson at Albany, afforded the colonies their only easy avenue through the Appalachian mountains to the Ohio and Mississippi valleys. But fur-trading interests blocked settlement along the Mohawk until the early eighteenth century when the British government sponsored the resettlement of Germans above Albany.

The main current of German settlement flowed through Philadelphia and on inland to fill the broad and fertile lower valley of the Susquehanna. Beyond the Susquehanna, it washed up against the series of Appalachian ridges that run from the northeast through central Pennsylvania. Diverted down the valleys to the southwest, the Germans settled interior Maryland and crossed the Potomac into Virginia. Here some drifted southeast of the first great Appalachian range, the Blue Ridge, into the rolling Virginia Piedmont, but the main current moved on southwest up the Shenandoah Valley behind the Blue Ridge. By the 1750s, some Germans were pushing southeast from the upper Shenandoah across the Blue Ridge and down into the North Carolina Piedmont.

The German migration was followed and overlapped by the migration of the more aggressive Scotch-Irish. The Scotch-Irish filled in the gaps left by German settlements and then surged beyond them to the west and south. In Pennsylvania these hardy Indian fighters crossed ridge after ridge and filled valley after valley until by the 1770s they were on the waters of the Ohio occupying the area around Pittsburgh. Farther south, in the Carolinas, the Scotch-Irish pushed the Piedmont frontier up against the mountains; while in Virginia they pressed southwest through the mountain valleys toward the headwaters of the Tennessee River.

COLONIAL SOCIETY

The people of the Old West — the Yankee farmers of the New England hill towns, the Germans on the Mohawk, and the Germans and Scotch-Irish in the great curve southwest against the Appalachians from the Susquehanna to Georgia — soon complained of grievances against the older colonial settlements along the coast. The older areas continued to dominate the provincial governments by refusing to give the new settlements the representation to which their population entitled them. In Pennsylvania, the three oldest counties had only one-third of the province's population but elected two-thirds of the assemblymen. The frontier people complained that unrepresentative, Quaker-dominated assemblies were indifferent to such western problems as the need for an aggressive policy against the Indians. The most extreme case of indifference to frontier needs occurred in South Carolina where the new settlements were separated from the old coastal planting society by a wide belt of sandhills. Though the up-country people in the new settlements came to be a majority of the free population, the low-country people not only refused them any representatives whatever in the assembly, but also neglected to provide them with courts or local law-enforcement officers.

Not remarkably, the failure to give representation or consideration to the rapidly growing frontier settlements led to sporadic tensions and occasional outbreaks of violence. As early as 1676, Nathaniel Bacon led an armed rebellion in Virginia against the governor, Sir William Berkeley, who had ruled the province autocratically for 25 years in alliance with the wealthiest planters. Similar tensions among New Yorkers figured in Jacob Leisler's rebellion at the time of the Glorious Revolution. Great landlords periodically faced mob violence from their tenants in New York, New Jersey, and elsewhere. There was a bitter struggle between debtor and creditor interests in Massachusetts over an inflationary Land Bank scheme in the 1740s. In 1764, the Paxton Boys, an armed mob of frontier men, marched on Philadelphia in anger at the pacific Indian policy of the eastern-dominated Pennsylvania assembly. The most spectacular of these outbreaks occurred in North Carolina where the oppressive policies of the local ruling class finally goaded the people of the interior into systematic mobbing of the courts. The governor had to march an army against the insurgents, or the Regulators, as they called themselves, and in a ragged engagement at Alamance in 1771 dispersed them.

The tension between the old and new settlements was only a phase of a more general tension that accompanied the emergence of somewhat sharper class distinctions in the eighteenth century. The English who came to the New World in the seventeenth century had brought with them the traditional European notion that people should defer to their betters in a society of ranks and orders. Old World distinctions, however, made little sense in a fluid society of mobile individuals, and, consequently, class and property qualifications for voting were almost unknown in the early assemblies. Yet the very atmosphere of equal opportunity that eroded Old World notions made for new forms of inequality. In an environment of growing wealth and expanding opportunities, social and economic disparities widened as some inevitably became more successful than others. Eventually, a disproportionate share of wealth from trade and commercial farming fell into the hands of the most enterprising New England merchants and southern planters. As a result, the relatively simple society of roughly equal yeomen in the seventeenth century became a more highly stratified and differentiated society in the eighteenth.

This process of stratification was abetted by the British government, which actively encouraged the growth and political influence of a colonial elite. After the Glorious Revolution, London authorities replaced religious qualifications for voting with a property qualification in the new Massachusetts charter, and property qualifications became general in the colonies. Usually a voter had to be a "freeholder," the owner of 50 acres or a town lot. Royal governors generally sought to secure the support of the wealthiest colonials by bestowing important appointments and other favors on them. The provincial councils became the political strongholds of the very rich, while the assemblies were usually controlled by the merely well-to-do. Thus the eighteenth-century provincial governments were generally dominated by a local ruling class, the wealthiest members of which sometimes sided with the governors in disputes with the assemblies.

Too much can be made of socioeconomic conflict in eighteenth-century America. Unquestionably, this was a "deferential society." Marked by extremes in standards and styles of life, fundamentally elitist and class-conscious in character, American society was governed by men of privilege. Their starched ruffles and powdered wigs, their bearing, speech, and dress differed strikingly from those of ordinary folk, and their influence was usually derived from wealth and property. But prerevolutionary American society presented those outside the power structure with more opportunities for advancement than the older and more highly structured societies in Europe. Although hardly democratic by twentieth-century standards, this highly mobile New World society offered remarkably broad economic opportunities, relatively little poverty, and much class fluidity. Except for the anomaly of slavery and pervasive restrictions on the rights enjoyed by women, there was no real social stratification in the Old World sense. Even the property restriction on suffrage was hardly restrictive in a society of extensive land ownership. In some colonies, where the franchise was open to a vast majority of free male adults, there is evidence to suggest that suffrage was more widespread than the willingness to use it. To be sure, this remarkable breadth of franchise owed much to the availability of inexpensive land and very little to either constitutional theories or modern democratic notions. Even in a society that readily acquiesced to government by aristocrats, colonial rulers could not entirely ignore the needs and aspirations of the general population. Certainly, few historians would argue today that class tension was a principal, or even an important, cause of the Revolution. By the 1760s and 1770s, most scholars now agree, the Americans had already made significant progress toward a more representative social and political order for men. It would be some two centuries, however, before American women won even token admission to this circle of privilege.

COLONIAL WOMEN

With rare exceptions, women in colonial America were confined to the household sphere — child-rearing, home-making, and the moral instruction of servants and off-spring. The overwhelming majority of white women were married and lived on small farms, and in small and poorly lighted homes. Their days were crowded with the endless seasonal routine of colonial life: gardening and preserving food; spinning, weaving, knitting, and sewing clothes; making candles, soap, butter, and cheese; and laundering, cleaning, and cooking. Slave women typically worked in the fields, but on substantial southern plantations they also served as seamstresses, cooks, or midwives. Female indentured servants, who normally could not marry, devoted their hours to working for their masters. In towns a few women, usually widows, became shopkeepers or innkeepers; others worked as laundresses, nurses, or even skilled laborers; and some women operated "dame schools." Those women who found employment outside the home inevitably earned less than men.

Although colonial families were paternalistic, child-rearing was a shared responsibility. Children were required to be obedient to their parents. Wives were their husbands' "helpmeets" — not their slaves, but also not their equals. Husbands were the heads of their households, though marriages were often marked by affection and mutual respect.

Colonial women married at about the same age as American women do today: whites in their early twenties; blacks in their late teens. In an agricultural era when large families were an economic asset — and the means of birth control primitive — women commonly had 5 to 7 children, and not infrequently 10 or more. Throughout their years of fertility, the pattern for women was to be either nursing or pregnant, a fact that contributed both to their premature aging and to rapid population growth. The high mortality rate of children also fostered the desire to have large families.

Regional variations within colonial America make generalizations about life expectancy hazardous. In New England, with its healthful climate and pure drinking water, adults were remarkably long lived. A seventeenth-century New Englander who survived infancy could expect to live more than 60 years. In the malarial Chesapeake colonies, on the other hand, the death rate was frightful. Fully half the population died before the age of 20; the life expectancy was perhaps 45 years for men, less for women.

By law and by custom, a colonial woman's status was lower than a man's. Under the English common law of coverture, a wife's legal personality was submerged in her husband's. Under most circumstances, her income and her personal and real estate were not her own. She could not make a contract or a will; she had no legal control over her children; except in New England, she could not obtain a divorce. Women could not vote, rarely influenced economic decisions, and were legally subject in most colonies to physical punishment by their husbands. Perhaps their relative scarcity — not until the mid-eighteenth century did women constitute half of the population — gave them slightly more freedom than their English sisters. But even so, they were denied places in most professions, including the ministry, politics, and literature. Although Anne Dudley Bradstreet (1612–1672) distinguished herself as the first American poet, she was published anonymously. Some daughters of the colonial elite were taught social competencies in female seminaries, and a few were educated in European schools. More typically, young American women were encouraged to cultivate the practical arts, not their intellects. Except for domestic matters, education beyond the most basic rudiments was widely regarded as a male prerogative.

THE ENLIGHTENMENT

By the eighteenth century, the Atlantic world's advance into modernity had produced a new climate of thought known as the Enlightenment. The people of this optimistic age believed that a benevolent Creator had laid down certain "natural laws" regulating all phenomena for the purpose of producing human happiness. Human beings, it was believed, had been endowed by the Creator with powers of observation and reasoning that would enable them to understand and live by these natural laws and thus achieve happiness.

This faith of the Enlightenment received a strong impetus from Sir Isaac Newton's description of the physical world as a harmonious system of bodies regulated by simple natural laws (*Principia Mathematica*, 1687). Another English thinker, John Locke, persuasively applied the Newtonian kind of analysis to the moral and political spheres. In *An Essay Concerning Human Understanding* (1690), Locke analyzed the processes of observation and reasoning that enabled human beings to understand what kinds of behavior were conducive to happiness or, in other words, consistent with the Creator's natural laws for human behavior. Following Locke, thinkers of the Enlightenment exalted "reason" as the faculty that could lead humanity toward virtue, happiness, and perfection. Analyzing politics (*Two Treatises on Government*, 1689), Locke maintained that natural law ordained a government that rested on the consent of the governed and that respected the inherent "natural rights" of all.

Enlightenment thought was the theoretical expression of the emerging spirit of modernity. In British North America, society was too young and too busy with the processes of wresting a living from this new land to give much attention to metaphysical speculation. Indeed, how far any formal thought reaches into popular consciousness is problematic. Yet many thoughtful colonists gladly embraced Lockean ideas as explanations of what already seemed to them obvious. The better educated individuals often drifted from the tenets of orthodox Christianity toward the rationalism of *Deism*, the belief in an impersonal God, whose revelations came through natural law — not miracles.

The influence of Enlightenment thought can be seen in eighteenth-century American life. The esthetic principles of rational simplicity, order, and balance, for example, were exemplified in the colonial or Georgian architecture of the period. American writers imitated the simple elegance of the English authors Joseph Addison and Sir Richard Steele and sought to persuade their readers by rational argument.

The Enlightenment gave a great impetus to the maturing cultural and intellectual life of the colonies. Beginning with the Boston *News-Letter* (1704), newspapers sprang up everywhere; by 1765 there were 25, and every colony except Delaware and New Jersey had at least one. A hungry market developed for pamphlets on every conceivable topic. Artisans organized clubs for discussion and intellectual self-improvement. Booksellers flourished, many wealthier persons developed fine private libraries, and following the example of an enterprise launched by Benjamin Franklin in Philadelphia, subscription libraries were established in most towns.

By placing such a high value on intellect, the Enlightenment reinforced the religious impulse toward higher education. This combination of influences resulted in the creation of nine colleges by the 1770s. Harvard (1636) was joined by Virginia's William and Mary (1693), Connecticut's Yale (1701), and the Philadelphia Academy, which was originally founded as a secondary school by Benjamin Franklin and became in the 1750s the most modern and secular of the colonial colleges. Five other new colleges owed their founding most immediately to a great religious movement that seemed at first to oppose the spirit of the Enlightenment and modernity.

THE GREAT AWAKENING

The drift toward modernity had steadily eroded the seventeenth-century piety that the settlers had brought to all the early colonies and of which Puritanism was merely the most intense form. Religious observances were as strictly enforced in early Anglican Virginia as in New England, but the prosperity from tobacco soon converted Anglicanism into a bland and undemanding adornment of Virginia's genial country life. It was this kind of Anglicanism that became the established or official religion, supported by public taxation, in all the southern colonies and the three lower counties of New York. Anglican religious zeal was apparent only where the missionaries sent out by England's Society for the Propagation of the Gospel were at work and in New England where the Anglicans were an unpopular minority. Perhaps the most conspicuous example of the erosion of piety in the New World was the quick conversion of the Huguenots, those French counterparts of the Puritans, to the polite Anglicanism of the South Carolina planter class. Even the Pennsylvania Quakers, growing wealthy as a result of godly industry, frugality, and honesty, arrived at a point where the counting house seemed to overshadow the meeting house.

The decline of piety can be clearly traced among the theologically sophisticated and articulate Puritan Congregationalists of New England. By the end of the seventeenth century, the Reverend Cotton Mather, the last great defender of the orthodox order, was talking more about the necessity of right living in this world than about humanity's dependence on God for salvation in the next. The wealthy Boston merchants who founded the Brattle Street Church in 1699 did not require an account of conversion for full membership and chose a minister who preached a "free and catholic" version of Christianity emphasizing morality over piety. As the eighteenth century advanced, the most influential ministers in Boston, Charles Chauncy and Jonathan Mayhew, drifted into the "Arminian" heresy, which diminished human dependence on God by regarding human beings as capable of contributing to their own salvation by right living.

But a people conditioned to piety did not adjust easily to the clear, rather bland atmosphere of the dawning Enlightenment. The embers of the old intense faith still smoldered and, in the 1730s and 1740s, were fanned into a bright blaze of religious enthusiasm that burned up and down the length and breadth of the colonies. This American Great Awakening was only part of a general movement in the Protestant world including such parallel phenomena as an upsurge of Pietism in Germany and the Wesleyan revival in England. Beginning as an effort to reassert the earlier extreme piety against the rationalism and optimism of the Enlightenment, these awakenings appealed frankly to the emotions and ended by unconsciously accommodating Christianity to the modern spirit.

The American Great Awakening began in different places. As early as the 1720s, the Reverend Theodore J. Frelinghuysen touched off emotional revivals of religious feeling among the Germans in New Jersey's Raritan Valley. Nearby a group of ardent Presbyterian ministers began trying to stimulate intense religious feeling in place of the cold formalism of Calvinist orthodoxy. And at Northampton, Massachusetts in 1734, a gifted Congregationalist minister, Jonathan Edwards, stirred up a series of revivals by his powerful appeals to the religious emotions. All these streams merged into a general revival movement throughout the colonies when England's spellbinding evangelist, George Whitefield, swept through on his triumphant American tour of 1739–1740, leaving spiritual anguish and ecstatic conversion in his wake.

The Great Awakening was emotional, popular, and anti-intellectual. The revivalists were often poorly educated, and their fervent exhortations sometimes touched off extravagant reactions — barking, writhing, swooning — by their audiences. Revivalists maintained that a heart open to the divine spirit was more important than a highly trained intellect. The least temperate among them, the inflammatory James Davenport of New England, stirred up strife by accusing conservative, educated clergy to be the "dead husks" and "Old Lights" of spiritual emptiness. Sophisticated observers alleged that the "beastly brayings" of these "shouters" produced more hysteria than holiness. But in large towns and the countryside, and particularly in frontier areas and the South, more common folk responded with enthusiasm to the new evangelicalism. The more popular Protestant denominations — the Baptists, the "New Light" Presbyterians, and later the Methodists — grew enormously, and a religious pluralism swept the colonies. In appealing for an emotional response to God's grace and a commitment to an exemplary Christian life, the revival preachers often unconsciously suggested that salvation was available to all, not merely to the elect, and that the individual played an important part in the process. The Methodists came to espouse these Arminian (and modern) "heresies" quite consciously.

Paradoxically, despite its emphasis on sentiment over reason, the Awakening had as a major leader the most gifted colonial intellectual and perhaps the most creative of American theologians: Jonathan Edwards. This brilliant Congregationalist minister burned with a personal sense of God's majesty and power that would have been exceptional even among the first-generation Puritans. But he also had an understanding of the intellectual implications of Newtonian-Lockean thought that was equaled by few if any of his generation in Europe or America. In a series of impressive treatises, he turned the Enlightenment against itself, using the most advanced thought of his day to reconstruct the old Puritan vision of an omnipotent and inscrutable God. In a very real sense, this remarkable theologian was a transitional figure, a bridge between two ages, who sought to recast and modernize Puritanism in the light of eighteenth-century rationalism.

Few in his generation understood what Edwards was trying to do. His fellow revivalists gladly adopted his highly charged rhetoric and his advanced principles of human psychology, which recognized the importance and legitimacy of emotion. But most Americans had moved too far into modernity to share, even in seasons of religious exaltation, his vision of the beauty and fitness of God's awful sovereignty and the sinner's helpless dependence on the miracle of divine grace.

Finally, historians have also found political consequences in the fervid evangelicalism of Edwards's time. Spreading like a religious epidemic, the Great Awakening transcended political boundaries and thereby strengthened intercolonial ties. It has aptly been called the first truly American event. Perhaps it is too much to claim, although some scholars have, that without the Awakening there would have been no revolution, no independence. Yet this "great and extraordinary outpouring of the Spirit" touched more than the souls of enraptured colonists. By emphasizing the personal dimensions of salvation and undermining established religious institutions, the Awakening not only encouraged spiritual diversity and paved the way to the separation of church and state, but it also nourished the egalitarian colonial temper and the developing sense of American distinctiveness and thus hastened the break with Great Britain.

The Awakening prompted the establishment of three colonial colleges designed to train ministers for revivalist wings of the sponsoring denominations: the Presbyterians' College of New Jersey (Princeton, 1746), the Baptists' College of Rhode Island (Brown, 1764), and the Dutch Reformed Rutgers (1766). Two other colonial colleges were founded under nonrevivalist church auspices: Anglican King's College in New York (Columbia, 1754) and Congregationalist Dartmouth (1769), which began as an Indian school in New Hampshire. For all of its anti-intellectualism, this eighteenth-century resurgence of religious enthusiasm contributed mightily to the nation's educational development.

"THIS NEW MAN"

De Crèvecoeur's "new man," then, was a product of New World opportunity, whether the opportunity to acquire a farm of one's own in the Old West, to grow rich planting tobacco, to trade with the West Indies, or to achieve dignity and independence as an artisan in one of the growing colonial towns. According to de Crèvecoeur, Americans welcomed the optimistic tendencies of Enlightenment thought as something their New World experience revealed. In politics, they stoutly defended the English tradition of individual rights and aspired to control the representative institutions of provincial government in the interest of their group. In religion, they tended consciously toward Deism or Arminianism if educated; otherwise they reveled in the emotionalism of the Great Awakening while moving less consciously away from the orthodox piety of their ancestors.

"The American, this new man" took a fully developed form in the *Autobiography* of Benjamin Franklin. This son of a Boston candlemaker sat in Cotton Mather's congregation as a boy, assimilated Enlightenment thought while working on his brother's newspaper and while sowing wild oats in London, and returned to win wealth and prestige as a Philadelphia printer. Retiring from business while still in his early forties, he spent the rest of his life in scientific experiments that explained the nature of electricity, in developing a host of practical devices and projects for the benefit and improvement of his fellow citizens, and in public service culminating with attendance at the birth of a new nation.

Wise, humane, and practical, Franklin reflected the spirit of a people who preferred mobility to nobility, who, to quote Franklin, characteristically inquired of a stranger not *"What is he?* but *What can he do?"* Franklin was the quintessential American, simple, vigorous, independent, and uncorrupted by supposed Old World decadence. He embodied American self-awareness, that sense of an evolving new people, politically linked to the English, yet identifiably American, distinctive in character and culture.

The fascination with Franklin lies in the fact that he personified so many traits characteristic of his compatriots. De Crèvecoeur wrote that an American leaves "behind him all his ancient prejudices and manners, receives new ones from the new mode of life he has embraced, the new government he obeys, and the new rank he holds. . . . Here the rewards of his industry follow with equal steps the progress of his labor. . . . Here religion demands but little of him. . . . The American is a new man, who acts upon new principles; he must therefore entertain new ideas, and form new opinions. From involuntary idleness, servile dependence, penury, and useless labor, he has passed to toils of a different nature, rewarded by ample subsistence. — This is an American."

FOR FURTHER READING

J. Hector St. John de Crèvecoeur recorded his impressions of eighteenth-century American life in *Letters from an American Farmer* (1782). A readable overview of the period is Daniel J. Boorstin's interpretation of emerging New World attitudes and institutions, *The Americans: The Colonial Experience* (1958), but James A. Henretta and Gregory Nobles's *The Evolution of American Society, 1700–1815* (1987) is a more up-to-date survey of colonial society. European immigrants to America are described in Marcus Lee Hansen's *The Atlantic Migration, 1607–1860* (1940) and David Hackett Fischer's *Albion's Seed* (1989); Abbott Emerson Smith's *Colonists in Bondage* (1947) deals with indentured servants; and Herbert S. Klein's *The Middle Passage* (1978) describes the African slave trade. Winthrop D. Jordan's *White over Black* (1968) examines the development of white racial attitudes; Peter Wood's *Black Majority* (1974) examines black life in colonial South Carolina; and Gwendolyn Midlo Hall looks at *Africans in Colonial Louisiana* (1992). Carl Bridenbaugh's *Cities in the Wilderness, 1625–1742* (1938) is the standard study of early American urban life; he deals with the mechanic classes of the towns in *The Colonial Craftsman* (1950). Related works include such model social histories as Phillip Greven, *Four Generations: Population, Land, and Family in Colonial Andover, Massachusetts* (1977); Richard I. Melvoin, *New England Outpost: War and Society in Colonial Deerfield* (1989); Gary Nash, *The Urban Crucible: Social Change, Political Consciousness, and the Origins of the American Revolution* (1979); and Michael Zuckerman, *Peaceable Kingdoms: New England Towns in the Eighteenth Century* (1970). Daniel Blake Smith's *Inside the Great House* (1980) is an important analysis of eighteenth-century Chesapeake family life, and Allan Kulikoff's *Tobacco and Slaves* (1986) describes the development of colonial Chesapeake society. Studies of the southern colonies and backcountry include Carl Bridenbaugh's *Myths and Realities: Societies of the Colonial South* (1952), A. Roger Ekirch's *"Poor Carolina"* (1981), Richard R. Beeman's *The Evolution of the Southern Backcountry* (1984), and Daniel Usner's *Indians, Settlers and Slaves in a Frontier Exchange Economy* (1992). Wilcomb Washburn's *The Governor and the Rebel* (1957) is an interpretation of Bacon's rebellion; Richard M. Brown examines the *South Carolina Regulators* (1963). Laurel Thatcher Ulrich's *Good Wives* (1983) and Carol Berkin's *First Generations* (1996) explore the lives of colonial women. The intellectual and theological transformation of New England Congregationalism may be followed in Conrad Wright's *The Beginnings of Unitarianism in America* (1955). Jon Butler explores the importance of Protestantism in the development of American society in *Awash in a Sea of Faith* (1990), and Henry May examines the nature, development, and impact of *The Enlightenment in America* (1976). Norman Fiering looks at *Jonathan Edwards's Moral Thought and Its British Context* (1981). Carl Van Doren has written the best biography of *Benjamin Franklin* (1941), but Franklin's quality shines forth in his fascinating *Autobiography* (many editions).

4

★ ★ ★ ★ ★ ★

Toward Revolution, 1763–1775

AT THE CLOSE of the French and Indian War in 1763, the inhabitants of British North America considered themselves patriotic and loyal British subjects. Under British rule, the colonies had become flourishing and prosperous societies, affording to ordinary individuals well-being and opportunities without parallel in Europe and perhaps anywhere in previous human history. The British navigation laws had, by and large, fostered colonial prosperity; British fleets and armies had defended colonials against their Spanish, French, and Indian enemies; and a benevolent (or careless) home government had allowed them to develop representative institutions and to regulate their domestic affairs with only minor interference. Nourished on the British Whig tradition of limited monarchy stemming from the Glorious Revolution of 1688, the American colonists thought of their political rights and liberties as British rights and liberties.

Yet within 12 years, these same loyal British subjects were at war with the mother country. Although their relations with Britain until 1763 were relatively harmonious, the crisis of the next dozen years taught them that they had long since developed a deep attachment to the society they were creating in the colonies. Somewhat to their own surprise they learned that they valued the British connection only as far as, and as long as, it was compatible with their desire to preserve and perfect their free and semiautonomous American society. In one of history's most notorious instances of bad timing, British officials had chosen to tighten the lax administration of the Empire at the very moment when American colonials were beginning to feel their own separate identity. Colonial cries of imperial despotism and oppression were doubtless overdrawn, but the stiffening of British policy was at best untimely. The result was not only a deepening hostility to Great Britain, but a heightened sense of common purpose that would turn colonists into Americans.

TABLE 1.   EVENTS LEADING TO THE REVOLUTION, 1735–1776

Year	British Actions	American Actions
1735		John Peter Zenger tried for libel and acquitted.
1764	Revenue (Sugar) Act — duties for revenue. Currency Act.	James Otis, Jr., *The Rights of the British Colonies*
1765	Quartering Act. Stamp Act.	Crowd action. Sons of Liberty formed. Nonimportation agreements.
1766	Repeal of Stamp Act. Declaratory Act — asserting right of Parliament to legislate for colonies in all respects.	Nonimportation suspended.
1767	Townshend duties — revenue duties on various articles.	Crowd action. Nonimportation agreements. John Dickinson, *Letters of a Pennsylvania Farmer*
1770	Repeal of Townshend duties, except duty on tea.	Boston Massacre. Suspension of nonimportation.
1772		Committees of correspondence organized. *Gaspée* burned.
1773	Tea Act — giving East India Co. monopoly on colonial tea trade.	Crowd action. Boston Tea Party.
1774	Intolerable acts: 1. Closing port of Boston. 2. Restricting self-government in Massachusetts. 3. Allowing royal officers to be tried in England. 4. Allowing royal troops to requisition private buildings for quarters. Quebec Act — continuing nonrepresentative government in Quebec, tolerating Roman Catholicism in Quebec, and incorporating Ohio Valley in Quebec.	First Continental Congress: 1. Rejects Galloway's plan of union. 2. Adopts Continental Association, establishing committees of safety to enforce commercial nonintercourse with England. 3. Encourages Massachusetts to establish revolutionary government and prepare for military defense.
1775	Lexington-Concord — British troops skirmish with Massachusetts militiamen.	Committees of safety seize control. Second Continental Congress — appoints Washington to commmand continental army at Boston.
1776		Thomas Paine's *Common Sense* published.

THE NEW IMPERIAL POLICY

When Britain emerged victorious from the great Anglo-French wars, there were conditions that supported a new and more vigorous imperial policy. First, King George III, enthroned in 1760, was an ambitious and conscientious monarch who desired to play a larger role in governmental affairs than had his predecessors. Through manipulation of royal patronage and maneuvering of parliamentary elections he tried to re-establish the royal influence that earlier monarchs had exercised by right. Unfortunately, the king and his ministers proved to be less flexible and astute in dealing with the colonists than their easygoing predecessors had been. Yet probably any British ministry would have sought to strengthen the inefficiently managed imperial system at this time. During the war, the colonists had irritated the British by their reluctance to furnish troops, supplies, and money and in too many cases had actually prospered by trading with the enemy. Moreover, the empire had been greatly enlarged, and more efficient regulation seemed necessary everywhere if the colonial territories were to serve their purpose of benefiting the mother country.

The most pressing immediate problem was that of revenue to pay off the crushing debt incurred during the war and to support the increased costs of defending and administering the enlarged empire, costs that had multiplied fivefold since the war with France. Compared with English landowners, the colonists were virtually untaxed, and in London it seemed only fair that they should bear some of the heavy tax burden required for the defense of American territory.

The new and tighter imperial policy that grew out of these conditions was inaugurated by the ministry of George Grenville during 1763–1765, and it provoked colonial hostility. After Chief Pontiac's rebellion (an effort by the Ottawas and their allies to block English expansion into the trans-Appalachian region), the British had issued the Proclamation of 1763, which restricted colonial settlement on the new western frontier. The proclamation's intent was to minimize conflict with the Indians and to promote orderly disposition of crown lands. But the Americans, some of whom had settled beyond the Appalachians and were now ordered back, resented this British land grab and soon forced major revisions in the proclamation. The Currency Act (1764), which forbade the already hard-pressed colonies to issue paper money, and the Quartering Act (1765), which required them to provide shelter and supplies for British troops, also stirred American indignation. And the Revenue Act (better known as the Sugar Act) of 1764 met with colonial rage. This measure marked the first British attempt to levy import duties on colonial trade for the purpose of revenue rather than regulation.

Although the Sugar Act applied also to wine, coffee, silk, and linen, the duty on molasses seemed the most onerous. For years New England merchants had evaded an earlier levy under the Molasses Act of 1733 by smuggling molasses from the French West Indies for manufacturing rum. The new molasses duty was only half of the old, but it was rigorously enforced and crippled New England commerce. Shocked by the sudden vigor of imperial control after decades of salutary neglect, and squeezed by a postwar depression, the infuriated colonists protested that they could not rightfully be taxed except by their own elected representatives.

Either underestimating the strength of colonial opposition or not caring how strong it was, Grenville pushed through Parliament in 1765 the even more provocative Stamp Act. This measure required the colonists to purchase revenue stamps and affix them to all kinds of legal and commercial documents, newspapers, almanacs, playing cards, dice, and liquor licenses. This was taxation in a highly visible and odious form. Moreover, it most offended those who were most influential in shaping colonial opinion — merchants, lawyers, printers, and tavern keepers. An explosion of protest indicated not only how averse the colonists were to taxation of any kind, but also how attached they were to the representative tradition of British Whiggery and to the home rule that they had enjoyed with so little interference.

At question was the relationship of the colonial assemblies to Parliament. Claiming precedence over colonial lawmakers, Parliament denied that Americans were subject only to self-imposed taxes, and Grenville denied that Americans were being taxed without their own consent. As British subjects, he averred, they enjoyed "virtual," if not precisely direct, representation in Parliament. For the moment, few colonists were prepared to challenge Parliament's regulatory or legislative authority within the British Empire. But a growing number agreed that as British citizens, under the protection of the English Bill of Rights, they could be taxed only by their own assemblies — the only legislative bodies in which they were represented.

Colonial protest took many forms. Pamphleteers, including Massachusetts's James Otis, Jr. (*The Rights of the British Colonies asserted and proved*) and Maryland's Daniel Dulaney (*Considerations on the Propriety of Imposing Taxes*), argued in print the American case against the constitutionality of parliamentary taxation. From New Hampshire to South Carolina, resistance groups emerged. Often calling themselves the Sons of Liberty, these secret bands of artisans and small merchants burned effigies of Grenville, blocked the sale of stamps, besieged and sometimes destroyed the homes of crown officials, and intimidated agents of the British government in other ways. Colonial legislatures called for the repeal of the hated measures, and representatives from 12 colonies (all but Georgia) met in New York at the so-called Stamp Act Congress in October 1765. At this first intercolonial assembly since 1754, the representatives pledged loyalty to the king and "all due subordination" to Parliament, but denied Parliament's right to tax the colonists. The most effective protest against taxation without representation, however, was a nonimportation agreement sponsored by the colonial merchants that led to a boycott of British goods. This had such an effect on British manufacturers and exporting merchants that Parliament was persuaded in 1766 to repeal the Stamp Act. But Parliament did not surrender its claim to tax the colonists, for repeal was accompanied by a Declaratory Act asserting Parliament's right to legislate for the colonies in any and all respects.

That this was no idle claim was shown the very next year, 1767, when Charles Townshend, Chancellor of the Exchequer, pushed through Parliament the so-called Townshend Acts levying duties for revenue on a new class of previously untaxed articles. The new taxes were rendered more unpalatable by provisions for further strengthening the enforcement and collection machinery and by the stipulation that revenues from the act would be used to pay the salaries of royal officials in the colonies, thus robbing the colonial assemblies of their most potent weapon, the power to withhold salaries from uncooperative royal officers. The Americans, of course, protested. In his *Letters from a Farmer,* John Dickinson, a cultivated Philadelphian and a member of the Stamp Act Congress, rallied colonial support for a second boycott of British goods. Colonials protested, newspapers attacked British policy, and merchants employed the proven weapon of nonimportation agreements. And once again, in 1770, Parliament softened its stand, repealing all the duties except the one on tea.

Most colonists were willing to accept this action as settling the controversy, and the next few years brought a period of prosperity and relative peace between colonies and mother country. Except for New England merchants and, later, wealthy Virginia planters — two of the most powerful and articulate segments of the population — the trade regulations adopted after 1763 imposed no significant hardship on the colonial economy. Yet the British ministers were badly deceived if they supposed that imperial relations were as cordial as they had once been. During the seven years of controversy over parliamentary taxation, the Americans analyzed their relationship with the mother country and became increasingly conscious of their separate identity and the colonies' common interest. They had successfully defied what they viewed as the tyranny of the home government, and they were now more committed than they perhaps realized to republican principles of self-government.

THE RADICALS AND THE URBAN CROWD

Especially dangerous to continued harmony was a small but well organized and ably led group of American radicals. Since the 1760s, they had opposed any British effort to tax or regulate colonial affairs. Most of these radicals had led the more militant agitation against the Stamp Act and the Townshend duties; their hostility toward the British was often combined with a democratic resentment of elitist politics and aristocratic pretensions. In Virginia, for example, Patrick Henry's radical opposition to the Stamp Act simultaneously challenged control of the House of Burgesses by the most conservative wing of the planter oligarchy. In Charleston, though the radical group was led by the young aristocrat Christopher Gadsden, its rank and file was drawn largely from artisans, manual workers, and others from poor and middle segments of colonial society. In economically hard-pressed Boston the radical leader Samuel Adams, though backed by the wealthy merchant John Hancock, drew most support from socially immobile artisans and shopkeepers who welcomed an opportunity to strike at Bostonians with close royal ties. Anti-elitist sentiment was particularly apparent among the disfranchised and otherwise politically inarticulate classes: the propertyless working poor, apprentices, slaves, and women. These made up the crowds that contributed to the hellish fury of the 1765 Boston street demonstrations and that followed the impoverished shoemaker and war veteran, "Captain-General" Ebenezer MacIntosh, and burned Lt. Governor Thomas Hutchinson's elegant house. In such crowd actions, anti-British sentiment and class resentments melded, as the "unthinking multitude," including many not entitled to participate in organized politics, found purposeful and coordinated ways to influence events.

American men and women of every social level were politicized by changing imperial policy and joined in the protest against the Stamp Act and Townshend duties. The wealthier and more conservative among them, however, were dismayed by the excesses of the "lower ranks." These more conservative American Whigs (not a few of whom would become Loyalists) were satisfied when Parliament repealed all the offensive duties except the one on tea, while the radicals insisted on continuing to agitate against it.

The most dangerous radical leader was that superb organizer, agitator, and propagandist Samuel Adams, this self-styled "Populus" who had deep roots in the artisan class, despite having a Harvard degree. Through his control of the town meeting, Adams kept Boston in an uproar, though quiet returned to other areas. Adams exploited incidents like the Boston Massacre of 1770, in which an angry crowd goaded a small party of British soldiers into firing; they killed five persons, including the runaway slave Crispus Attucks. Adams's propaganda maintained the colonists' alarm over British "tyranny." In addition, Adams and his allies — notably such outspoken critics of wealth and power as William Molineux and Thomas Young — were creating a radical organization that joined Boston's merchant and laboring classes in an uneasy union.

Operating from his base in the Boston town meeting, Adams induced other Massachusetts towns to establish "committees of correspondence" to promote intercolonial resistance to imperial policy. The idea spread and, shortly, dissident Virginians urged the establishment of a provincial committee of correspondence in every colony. Naturally these committees came to be dominated by those with relatively radical attitudes. While the radicals were unable to dispel the complacency that prevailed in the comparatively prosperous years from 1770 to 1773, they created an organization that could seize the initiative whenever an opportunity arose.

THE SECOND CRISIS

Opportunity came when the British ministry of Lord North, in all innocence, undertook to aid the British East India Company by pushing through Parliament the Tea Act of 1773. The company was given the exclusive privilege of selling its tea directly to American consumers without paying the English export tax, thus increasing the company's profits, lowering the price of tea to Americans, eliminating widespread smuggling, and depriving American importing merchants of any share in the tea trade. But the cheap tea was still subject to tax under the Townshend duty.

The resentment of the conservative American merchants drove them again into alliance with the radicals, and the radicals made the most of this opportunity to renew violent agitation. Convinced that the British were using lower tea prices to seduce Americans into surrendering their liberties, again the radicals organized and resorted to mob action. In New York, Philadelphia, and other cities, the Sons of Liberty and committees of correspondence found a broad base of support. In the South, East India tea was locked in warehouses by Charleston patriots. In Boston in December 1773, colonists, ill-disguised as Mohawk Indians, boarded British vessels and dumped some 45 tons of East India tea in the harbor. Coming as it did only one year after angry Rhode Islanders had burned the British customs vessel *Gaspée*, the defiance of the Boston Tea Party shocked many Americans, but patriot leaders and the public in general agreed that to accept the Tea Act was to risk conceding Parliament's right to tax the colonies for revenue.

The British government, on the other hand, was now convinced that only punitive action could bring the rebellious colonists to heel. Promptly, Parliament passed a series of four "Coercive Acts" (known to Americans as the "Intolerable Acts"), closing the port of Boston until the Bostonians paid for the tea they had destroyed, drastically reducing the representative and self-governing features of the Massachusetts provincial government, allowing royal officials to be tried in England when accused of crimes in the colonies, and permitting the British army to requisition American buildings as quarters. However logical and necessary these measures appeared to a London government faced with colonial insubordination, they confirmed American suspicions of Britain's despotic designs. A fifth measure followed that, although not punitive in nature or actually one of the Coercive Acts, proved no more tolerable to the colonists. Through the Quebec Act of 1774, Parliament added to the Canadian province western territory claimed by several colonies, continued the autocratic rule in Quebec that had prevailed under the French, and afforded complete religious toleration to the province's Catholic population.

These measures threw the radical propaganda machine and committee organization into high gear. "The cause of Boston is the cause of all British America" was the message trumpeted everywhere during the spring and summer of 1774. Food, fuel, and money were collected for the relief of the beleaguered Bostonians, local nonimportation agreements sprang up on all sides, and a proposal for a continental congress to coordinate resistance won quick endorsement from the assemblies or from extralegal meetings of the assemblies in most of the colonies.

THE FIRST CONTINENTAL CONGRESS

In September 1774, an extralegal Congress of delegates from every colony except Georgia assembled in Philadelphia's Carpenters' Hall. Although sharing common anti-British sentiments and a commitment to the "cause of Boston," the 55 delegates were strangers to one another and not of one mind on the constitutional relationship of the colonies to England. The most radical among them embraced the doctrine of natural rights, denied parliamentary jurisdiction over the colonies, and argued that the colonists were subject only to the laws of their respective assemblies. Others did not assert the eighteenth-century doctrine of the rights of man, but their rights as English citizens instead; they recognized Parliament's power to regulate imperial trade, but denied its right to tax or otherwise interfere with internal colonial affairs. After some debate, the delegates unanimously adopted the defiant Suffolk Resolves, which condemned virtually all British trade regulations; they narrowly defeated a conciliatory plan for colonial government presented by Joseph Galloway of Pennsylvania, which was closely patterned after the Albany Plan of 1754. The first Continental Congress also created a "Continental Association," a detailed plan for nonimportation, nonconsumption, and nonexportation of goods between the colonies and Great Britain. To enforce the boycott, the delegates authorized every county or town to elect extralegal committees of safety. These committees were to circulate the Association among all citizens for endorsement and then to single out violators for boycott and for denunciation as "enemies to the rights of British America." Goods imported in violation of the Association could be seized, and the work of the local committees was to be coordinated in each colony by a provincial congress and a provincial committee of safety.

During the winter and spring of 1774–1775, the radicals began vigorously implementing this revolutionary scheme in every colony. A drastic decline in British imports quickly demonstrated the Association's effectiveness as an instrument of economic warfare; it was probably even more important as an instrument of political persuasion and coercion.

While nearly all Americans favored efforts to secure concessions from the British government, perhaps only a minority supported the aggressive tactics of the radicals. Many colonists were decidedly hostile to any action that threatened to break the British connection, and many more were simply confused or indifferent. But the Association and its committee system gave the organized and purposeful radicals a highly efficient means of committing the passive and often hostile majority to their program.

Though the committees were supposed to be elected, they were frequently in fact self-constituted bodies of the local radical leaders and in some cases were merely the old committees of correspondence continued under a new name. Where public denunciation failed to secure compliance with the Association, committees did not hesitate to employ threats and even physical violence. As the revolutionary crisis deepened, the committees increasingly assumed the powers of government, fixing prices, levying fines, and taking charge of local militia units.

Yet radical control was far from complete by the spring of 1775. The mercantile and officeholding aristocracy put up strong opposition in the northeastern port towns; up-country Carolina farmers were disposed to side with the royal governors against the provincial politicians who had oppressed them in the past and who were now leading the radical movement; and everywhere there were wide areas still so unexcited over British oppression that the radicals had made little headway. An additional impulse was needed and once again Samuel Adams's Massachusetts radicals supplied it.

WAR

British "despotism" was anything but a remote and idle threat to the Massachusetts radicals during the winter and spring of 1774–1775. As part of the British plan to crush the spirit of insubordination in Massachusetts, additional troops were sent to Boston, and their commander, General Thomas Gage, was designated military governor of the province. With the endorsement of the Continental Congress, the radicals took the momentous step of establishing a revolutionary provincial government under the old suspended charter and began training troops and collecting military supplies.

The inevitable clash came on the morning of April 19, 1775, when General Gage sent a detachment of British soldiers from Boston to seize the powder and arms that had been collected at nearby Concord and to arrest Samuel Adams and John Hancock. Warned by Paul Revere and William Dawes, the farmer "minutemen" (so-called because they were expected to "Stand at a minute's warning") challenged the British regulars at Lexington and Concord. Shots were exchanged, and by the time these surprised "redcoats" had run the 16-mile gauntlet of farmers' muskets on the road back to Boston, they had lost 273 dead, wounded, and missing. About a hundred patriots also were casualties in this bloody, first encounter of the Revolution.

Instantly the radicals sent special riders flying through the colonies with exaggerated accounts of the massacre of innocent Massachusetts farmers by British soldiers. Everywhere there was a burst of patriotic indignation, enabling the radical-dominated committees of safety to gain complete control. Royal governors were driven from their posts, troops were drilled, and royal forts and powder magazines were seized.

On May 10, a Second Continental Congress hastily assembled in Philadelphia. As a gesture to the timid, this radical-dominated body sent an "Olive Branch Petition" to the king as a final appeal for a peaceful settlement. When this petition was refused, the last vestiges of loyalty to the crown dissolved. Rapidly, a once-respected monarch was becoming, in Tom Paine's memorable words, a "royal brute." With all other acceptable avenues of resistance closed, Congress prepared for war. The thousands of armed New Englanders who had rushed to besiege Gage's redcoats by taking positions on the hills overlooking Boston were taken under the aegis of the Congress. And George Washington, who came to Philadelphia in the blue uniform of the Virginia militia, was named to command the emerging continental army. As resistance became rebellion, the 2.5 million British subjects in 13 New World colonies were awash in sentiments that would rapidly make them a single and independent people — Americans.

CONFLICTING HISTORICAL VIEWPOINTS: NO. 1

What Caused the American Revolution and How Revolutionary Was It?

Nineteenth-century historians rarely quarreled about the origin and nature of the Revolution. The war for American independence, they concluded, was a just and truly revolutionary struggle against the tyrannical and reactionary British imperial system. The colonial triumph ushered in a new era of human liberty, fraternity, and democracy. Indeed, to George Bancroft, author of the authoritative and justly celebrated History of the United States *(12 vols., 1834–1882), the Americans were God's chosen people and their revolution was part of the "grand design of Providence," a noble prelude to the "regeneration" of humankind.*

In the 1890s the patriotic distortions of this traditional view were challenged by two schools of historical interpretation: the imperialist and the progressive. Influenced by a turn-of-the-century spirit of Anglo-American accord, such imperialist historians as Charles McLean Andrews (The Colonial Background of the American Revolution, *1924) were more critical of colonial behavior than English policy. The quarrel with England, they argued, could be interpreted correctly only within the broad context of the British empire as a whole. Examining the imperial as well as the colonial point of view, they sympathetically concluded that the British Trade and Navigation Acts were not oppressive and that Parliament's efforts to tax the Americans were justifiable.*

While imperialistic scholars sought the origins of the Revolution in political and constitutional issues within the empire, the progressives focused on social and economic issues within the colonies themselves. Products of the reform mentality of the late nineteenth and early twentieth centuries, these liberal scholars addressed not only the question of home rule but the question of who should rule at home. As Carl Becker, the greatest of the progressive historians, expressed it in The History of Political Parties in the Province of New York *(1909), the American Revolution was actually two revolutions in one. The first, an external revolution, involved a conflict of economic interests between Great Britain and the American colonies. The second, an internal revolution, involved a class conflict between the haves and have-nots of colonial society. More recently, such distinguished historians as Lawrence Gipson* (The British Empire Before the American Revolution, *15 vols., 1936–1970) and Merrill Jensen* (The Founding of a Nation, *1968) still analyze the Revolution from the imperialist and progressive persuasions, and echoes of the progressive theme of colonial class tensions can be found in Gary B. Nash's* The Urban Crucible *(1979), a provocative analysis of the social and economic processes that shaped the Revolution.*

But in recent decades, new directions in historical thought have challenged earlier viewpoints. In the 1950s, for example, so-called consensus historians, apparently mirroring the conservatism of the Cold War pe-

riod, disputed progressive notions of class conflict. Arguing that American society was far more democratic, affluent, and fluid than the progressives had believed, such consensus histories as Robert E. Brown's Middle-Class Democracy and the Revolution in Massachusetts *(1955) and Daniel J. Boorstin's* The Genius of American Politics *(1953) concluded that the Revolution was essentially a conservative movement waged to protect traditional American rights and liberties from a changing and increasingly arbitrary British policy.*

*Edmund S. Morgan (*The Birth of the Republic, *1956), Bernard Bailyn (*The Ideological Origins of the American Revolution, *1967), and other scholars who stress the causal importance of ideas have also discounted internal social and economic cleavage theories. Colonial patriots, Bailyn wrote, although not unmindful of their pocketbooks, were genuinely alarmed by the changing course of imperial policy and deeply affected by the anti-authoritarian tradition of English thought. Possessed of "real fears, real anxieties, [and] a sense of real danger," they viewed their opposition to parliamentary taxation as a struggle of liberty against the corrupting force of power. Thus the new intellectual history has returned to the nineteenth-century conclusion that constitutional rights and lofty values lie at the heart of the American Revolution. Although embracing neither Bancroft's patriotic and religious excesses nor his undue criticism of British policy, it finds the old master correct when he argued that the colonists revolted in the name of liberty and republican ideals.*

Radical or New Left scholars, such as those who contributed essays to Alfred E. Young's The American Revolution *(1976) or Edward Countryman, author of* A People in Revolution *(1981), have added yet another dimension to the debate. Not without justification, they indict their fellow historians for overemphasizing the attitudes and behavior of social and economic elites to the neglect of the great mass of human society. In the radical view, the Revolution can be correctly interpreted only from "the bottom up," the vantage point of colonial nonelites. Regardless of the perspective, however, there is little likelihood of unanimity of historical opinion.*

FOR FURTHER READING

Edmund S. Morgan's *The Birth of the Republic* (1977) is an excellent introduction to the period from 1763 to 1789, and John C. Miller's *Origins of the American Revolution* (1943) offers a narrative overview of the events leading to conflict. John R. Alden has assessed the role of *The South in the Revolution, 1763–1789* (1957); Rachel Klein's *Unification of a Slave State* (1988) explains the coming of the Revolution in South Carolina. Arthur M. Schlesinger, Sr., *The Colonial Merchants and the American Revolution* (1918) is dated but still commands attention, while John W. Tyler's *Smugglers and Patriots* (1986) updates Schlesinger's account. Pauline Maier's

From Resistance to Revolution (1972) provides a synthesis of the role of colonial radicals in the development of hostilities; Rhys Isaac's *The Transformation of Virginia, 1740–1790* (1982) demonstrates how religious conflict helped shape revolutionary political culture; and Marc Egnal's *A Mighty Empire* (1988) examines the range of opinion on British imperial policy among the American colonial elite. Bernhard Knollenberg traces *The Origins of the American Revolution* (1961); Edmund S. and Helen M. Morgan brilliantly analyze *The Stamp Act Crisis* (1953); Hiller B. Zobel surveys *The Boston Massacre* (1970); Benjamin W. Labaree details *The Boston Tea Party* (1964); Peter D. G. Thomas examines *The Townshend Duties Crisis* (1987); and Robert A. Gross surveys *The Minutemen and Their World* (1976). Both John C. Miller's *Sam Adams* (1936) and Bernard Bailyn's *The Ordeal of Thomas Hutchinson* (1974) are readable biographies, and Pauline Maier's *The Old Revolutionaries* (1980) is a collective portrait of five first-generation patriot leaders.

5

★ ★ ★ ★ ★ ★

Independence Achieved, 1775–1783

THE FIRST YEAR OF WAR

The military struggle began slowly, and during the first year no really decisive engagements occurred. In June 1775, shortly before Washington arrived to take command of the poorly organized American forces on the hills surrounding Boston, General Gage managed to drive his besiegers from one of their strongest positions, Breed's Hill. But the misnamed Battle of Bunker Hill cost the British some 40 percent of their force, and these frightful losses demonstrated that the Americans, though outnumbered, could not easily be dislodged. During the months that followed Washington methodically converted his untrained militia into a disciplined army and tightened the ring around the British.

With Gage's army encircled in Boston, the ebullient Americans undertook, during the winter of 1775–1776, a two-pronged offensive against Canada. The forces led by Richard Montgomery and Benedict Arnold surmounted great hardships and won some early successes, but in the end the reluctance of the Canadian population to join the rebellion forced a retreat.

In the first year of the war, perhaps the most important struggle was among the colonists themselves. Because neither the British nor the American leaders were prepared to compromise, few people doubted that the issue could be resolved by means short of full-scale war. But only two-fifths of the colonial population actively supported the Revolution. Perhaps one-fifth of all whites — from every social class and ethnic group — remained loyal to the British. Some 55,000 American Tories actively joined the British cause. Another 80,000 went into exile in Canada, the Bahamas, or England. Other neutral or potentially subversive elements included pacifists, apolitical western frontiersmen, indentured servants, slaves, and Indians.

MAP 2: THE AMERICAN REVOLUTION

For the most part, the revolutionists managed to neutralize British efforts to exploit these indifferent or resentful peoples. But several thousand slaves cast their lot with the British in the hope of freedom; a greater number capitalized on wartime confusion by running away. However, the much-feared wholesale enlistment in the black army of John Murray, Lord Dunmore, last royal governor of Virginia, did not occur. Prodded by British actions, General Washington lifted an initial ban on black enlistment and initiated active recruiting. Some 5,000 blacks (slave and free, mostly from the northern colonies) joined the Continental army, serving in both integrated and all-black units. Similarly, though most Native American tribes had legitimate grievances against the colonists, Indians (with some exceptions) generally chose to remain neutral, rather than to ally with the British.

Faced with these actual and potential internal divisions, Congress and the colonies imposed severe penalties on those suspected of loyalty to the crown: censorship, ostracism, disfranchisement, loss of public office, confiscation of property, and detention. Those women believed to be aiding the British cause were treated as harshly as their male counterparts and received "disrespectful Indignities." Though excesses and wrongful persecutions did occur, the American Revolution produced none of the wholesale imprisonments or executions of dissidents that have tarnished some other revolutions. Given the dangers posed by so many subversives, real and imagined, the penalties imposed on the Loyalists do not seem disproportionate.

In March 1776, General Gage finally abandoned the increasingly difficult task of holding Boston and sailed away with his army and hundreds of Loyalists to the British stronghold at Halifax, Nova Scotia. His departure did not mark a decisive American victory, but rather the end of a year of stalemate in which each side had consolidated its position and prepared for the real struggle yet to come. During that fortunate year of respite a new American nation animated by fresh and exciting ideals had been coming to birth.

"CONCEIVED IN LIBERTY"

Few Americans admitted that they sought independence from England until months after the Revolutionary War had begun. Yet the pressure of events increasingly forced them into independent acts and steadily prepared them for an open break.

The question of independence was connected in an indirect, but important way with the acceleration of democratic tendencies inherent in the revolutionary movement. While home rule was the primary issue in the Revolution, a political upsurge of the lower orders of the social hierarchy raised the important secondary issue of "*who* should rule at home?" The Liberty Boys who rioted against the Stamp Act or the Townshend duties were making a bid for political status. Perhaps more important, the revolutionary agitation opened an avenue by which ambitious persons of the "middling sort"

(Samuel Adams, Patrick Henry, and their counterparts in other colonies) could rise to influence. The revolutionary movement offered such "new men" an opportunity to gain power by espousing radical measures and appealing indirectly to the inchoate democratic aspirations of those heretofore without influence in government.

The success of these "new men" was due in considerable measure to a favorable climate of ideas. The revolutionary era was one of those periods in history when ideas had great consequences. All Americans, including the most conservative and aristocratic, believed that the Glorious Revolution of 1688 and its great Bill of Rights had guaranteed to every British citizen certain rights — especially rights of liberty and property — upon which no government could rightfully infringe. In the British tradition of dissent dating to the Civil War (1642–1649) and the Commonwealth (1649–1653), Americans believed that government — power and authority — was naturally aggressive and tended to go beyond legitimate boundaries at the expense of liberty. In the spirit of that tradition, Americans distrusted government and were eager to restrict it lest force and compulsion dominate liberty and virtue. Their opposition to the new imperial policy was based on the claim of Britain's Whig party that this was an arbitrary exercise of power, a violation of this heritage of English rights. "Liberty and Property" became the slogan of the Revolution; a fear of the transgressions of authority became the controlling concept of an emerging American republicanism.

The ideas of British Whigs carried democratic implications that could be applied to government within as well as outside of the colonies. When the colonial leaders argued for the Whig principle of "no taxation without representation" in imperial relations, inadequately represented Americans required no great imagination to apply the same argument to domestic affairs or even to expand it into the more general principle that government should be representative of the governed, meaning *all* the governed.

These democratic implications of seventeenth-century British libertarianism were refined and reinforced by the larger stream of Enlightenment thought. Confident that the Creator desired human happiness, the people of the eighteenth century were drifting toward the notion that all people were equal in their "natural rights" and that the only just end of government was to maintain a state of society in which all could enjoy their rights to the fullest possible extent. Since liberty was the most precious of these rights, government should be restricted to the smallest possible compass that would enable it to keep individuals from invading each other's liberty, and since all persons were potentially rational, government should rest on the consent of the governed. The second of John Locke's *Two Treatises on Government* (1689) was a most trenchant justification of revolution on the basis of the natural-rights argument.

During the later stages of the revolutionary crisis, the colonial leaders broadened the basis for their claim to autonomy from their rights as British citizens, according to the Whig tradition, to their rights as human beings, according to the natural-rights tradition. Directly or indirectly, Americans were thinking in Lockean terms as they decided for revolution, drafted their

Declaration of Independence, and established a republican system of government.

Americans did not rebel against England, as conservative Tories often charged, to overthrow the established social order and advance the leveling spirit of democracy at home. Compared to subsequent European revolutions, the American Revolution was essentially conservative, begun for limited political and constitutional purposes and accomplished without major internal upheaval. Unlike the toppling of anciens régimes in France (1789) and Russia (1917), the overthrow of royal tyranny in America was followed by no shattering changes in class, economic, or property arrangements. Yet large segments of the population rallied to the movement for colonial autonomy because they were aroused by the logic of rebellion. Moreover, while creating broad support for their movement, revolutionary leaders sought out new groups that had previously played little part in public life. Consequently, the new provincial congresses organized at the war's start encompassed a more diversified membership than the previous colonial assemblies and councils.

This rise of the lower orders affected how the colonial ruling group reacted to the Revolution. Many gentry were alarmed into being Loyalists by their fear of having a government "independent of rich men." A larger number (conservative Whigs) continued to furnish leadership to the revolutionary movement but resisted independence. They hoped to win colonial autonomy while restoring the British connection as a means of preserving the dominance of the aristocrats within the colonies. A third segment of the gentry (radical Whigs) was so deeply infected with the revolutionary ideology that they worked closely with the new men who spoke for the lower orders, espousing independence and paving the way for a new distribution of political power.

It was this last group, especially Richard Henry Lee of Virginia and Samuel and John Adams of Massachusetts, who controlled the Continental Congress in the early war years. On the question of independence, they were aided by the drift of events. The British government showed little disposition to conciliate the Americans and every disposition to wage vigorous war against them. The importance of aid from Britain's ancient enemy France became increasingly apparent, and it was hoped that independence might pave the way for a French alliance. Finally, Americans of all classes were gradually beginning to sense the exciting possibility of building a new and independent society based on natural rights and the implicitly democratic principles of revolutionary rhetoric. How rapidly this feeling had spread was demonstrated by the tremendous public response to Thomas Paine's anonymous pamphlet *Common Sense*, a spirited defense of the American cause, published in January 1776. Advocating both independence and democracy, Paine's slashing document sold several hundred-thousand copies.

A new American, who emigrated from England only in 1774, Paine did not create the sentiment for independence; he merely crystallized an often unspoken but rapidly growing attitude. Once catapulted into the arena of open debate, the idea of independence rapidly overcame conservative opposition. On July 2, the Continental Congress resolved that "these United States are, and of right ought to be, free and independent states"; two days later the Declaration of Independence was adopted.

Drafted by Thomas Jefferson, with the help of Benjamin Franklin and John Adams, this remarkable document was for the most part a long and exaggerated catalog of British violations of American rights. Designed in large part as propaganda for world consumption, the Declaration offered no subtle interpretations of events. It was the hapless George III — not Parliament, the source of most colonial grievances — who was made the villain of the piece. What made the Declaration a momentous factor in history, however, was its opening section, which distilled in a few sentences of enduring prose the essence of the Lockean, natural-rights theory of government: "We hold these truths to be self-evident, that all men are created equal, that they are endowed by their Creator with certain inalienable Rights, that among these are Life, Liberty, and the pursuit of Happiness. That to secure these rights, Governments are instituted among Men, deriving their just powers from the consent of the governed. That whenever any Form of Government becomes destructive of these ends, it is the Right of the People to alter or abolish it." Much of subsequent American history was to be a working out of the implications of the principles so ringingly enunciated here.

THE NEW STATE CONSTITUTIONS

As the colonies became states, they adopted explicitly republican charters — documents that not only expunged what the Americans thought to be British tyranny, but assured protection against future infringements on liberty. The object of the present controversy, Jefferson said in the spring of 1776, was the reordering of the American polity, the shaping of a virtuous society of independent men living in harmony and equality under republican institutions. By the time the Declaration of Independence was adopted, four colonies had already applied its idealistic principles in drafting their state constitutions. Directed by the Continental Congress to create new governments "under the authority of the people," the other states followed suit, except for Rhode Island and Connecticut, which continued to operate under their unusually liberal colonial charters. The writing of constitutions was unprecedented (Britain's consisted of laws and custom and was not written) and significant — unmistakable evidence that Americans wanted the limits of governmental power and citizens' rights clearly delineated. With British authority destroyed, Americans were free to perform the act that lay at the root of all legitimate government according to Lockean theory: they entered into a "social contract." The new state constitutions were conceived of as voluntary compacts among all the people, creating governments of limited and explicitly defined powers. In several states, the people elected special conventions to draft the fundamental compacts; in several others, the constitutions were submitted for popular ratification; but in a majority of cases, the existing provincial congresses themselves drafted and promulgated the new constitutions.

However adopted, the new constitutions uniformly reflected the distrust of governmental power — especially "ever restless, ambitious, and ever grasping" executive or gubernatorial power — that arose from the Enlightenment's liberalism and from the colonists' experience with British authority. To prevent the encroachment of power upon liberty, most states followed Virginia's constitution, including a bill of rights specifying in detail the rights of citizenship (freedom of speech, freedom of the press, trial by jury, and the like) that no government could rightly abridge. All the constitutions sought to minimize the danger of arbitrary power by building "checks and balances" and a "separation of powers" into the very structure of government. The executive, legislative, and judicial functions were exercised by separate bodies, and except in the unicameral states of Pennsylvania, Georgia, and Vermont (which became a state in 1777), the legislatures were divided into two houses that were expected to act as checks on each other. The senates, by common consent, were designed to represent society's wisest and best, and were to serve as checks on excesses of the popular will, as reflected in the lower houses of representatives.

The checks and balances principle, however, was tempered by memories of the long struggles between the colonial assemblies and the royal governors. The new constitutions made the legislatures dominant and the governors relatively impotent. Governors in most cases were elected annually by the legislatures, were denied veto powers, and were subject to impeachment. Moreover, the awesome power of appointment, the most dangerous threat to free government, was given to most state legislatures, rather than to governors.

Along with restrictions on the governmental power, the new constitutions also tended toward more representative government, toward *actual* as opposed to *virtual* representation. These impulses toward closer supervision of legislators were reflected in annual elections, residential requirements for lawmakers as well as for voters, and (in five states) proportional electoral districts that gave representation to back country settlements. Although the state constitutions did not grant *universal* white male suffrage (Massachusetts raised its property qualifications for voting), and no state granted female suffrage, these charters generally extended the privilege of voting, either by reducing the colonial freehold (property) requirement or by opening the polls to most taxpayers. As a result, men of moderate means, petty entrepreneurs, and farmers gradually joined the well-to-do gentry in the conduct of public affairs.

The Revolution thus weakened the social hierarchy, opening new opportunities, both economic and political, for enterprising men outside of the aristocratic and wealthy elite. Yet incongruities in the ideal of human rights remained. It may have been true, as a French traveler observed in 1788, "that the Americans more than any other people are convinced that all men are born free and equal." But that doctrine applied only to white males. For blacks, the revolutionary ideology of republicanism did contribute to the gradual abolition of slavery in northern states, where the institution was least profitable. The nation's free black population grew dramatically, and even in the South more liberal manumission statutes were adopted. However, race distinctions were all but universally applied, and slavery (a truly "peculiar institution" in any republic) survived the Revolution by many decades.

The condition of women improved marginally, and only in such areas as educational opportunity and less stringent divorce laws. Along with these, perhaps there was a greater freedom to select marriage partners and slightly more reciprocity within matrimony. The origins of American feminism can be traced to the remarkable Abigail Adams's oft-quoted plea of 1776 — "Remember the Ladies" — and to the wartime emergency that temporarily enlarged the woman's sphere. Yet during the War for Independence and for many decades thereafter, General Washington's view of the female patriot's proper role — "passive, admiring, and quietly suffering" — was widely, if not universally, shared. The revolutionary generation seemed oblivious to the sexual implications of republican thought.

THE ARTICLES OF CONFEDERATION

As the Continental Congress still had no regular constitutional authority, it began working on a plan for a confederation that would provide sufficient powers to conduct the war and to unite the states once victory was achieved. After protracted debate, the Articles of Confederation were finally approved by Congress in 1777, though a dispute over the western lands claimed by some of the states delayed final ratification until 1781.

The Articles of Confederation established not a government, but a confederation of sovereign states. Because the Revolution was being fought to abolish central control and because liberty was deemed safe only when government was kept close to where the governed could watch it, the Confederation was given only the powers to: (1) conduct foreign affairs by negotiating treaties and making war and peace; (2) control Indian affairs; (3) set standards of coinage, weights, and measures; (4) settle disputes among the states; and (5) conduct a postal service. Although an improvement over the voluntary arrangement under the Continental Congress, the Confederation was a less than perfect instrument of national unity. It could not raise money or troops except by requisitions on the states. It had no power to make laws binding individual citizens and no means of enforcing its will on either citizens or states. Each state was to have a single vote in the Confederation Congress, the votes of nine states were required to approve all important measures, and the Articles could be amended only with the approval of Congress and the legislature of every state. The Articles did not provide a separate judicial branch or an executive division to carry out policies Congress might adopt. Yet the Articles did represent a move toward national unity;

for the first time, there was a permanent agency that could speak for the citizens of the 13 American states.

THE CAMPAIGNS OF 1776–1777

The Declaration of Independence had just been adopted and the constitution-making process was well under way in the states and the Congress when the British launched the American war in earnest. In July 1776, the greatest military force Britain had ever sent abroad sailed into New York harbor; hundreds of ships carried 32,000 soldiers under the command of Sir William Howe. Anticipating the British strategy, Washington had moved his army to the vicinity, but his greatly outnumbered forces were easily pushed off Long Island, out of Manhattan, steadily through New Jersey, and across the Delaware River into Pennsylvania.

The 43-year-old Washington was a leader of imposing presence and command, but he had little combat experience and was probably no military genius. Indeed he lost more battles than he won. Yet his courage and tenacity kept his army intact and the American cause alive. When he assumed command, his troops were largely without uniforms and without a semblance of unified command. Pay was low; both enlistments and rations were short. The men were eager to return to family and farms. The officers were often elected and poorly qualified for leadership. War materials, always in short supply in this undeveloped country, had to be captured or imported from Europe. Yet by good fortune and force of will, this sober, aristocratic Virginian prevailed. With the assistance of such foreign advisers as the Count Casimir Pulaski, the Baron von Steuben, and the Marquis de Lafayette, he built a force of some 8,000–10,000 regulars. (There were an additional 7,000 short-term militiamen.) Wisely avoiding decisive engagements, he waited until the British ceased offensive operations for the winter, and on Christmas night, 1776, he daringly ferried his troops back across the icy Delaware and fell upon unsuspecting British forces at Trenton and nearby Princeton, New Jersey. With these small but brilliant victories to buoy American hopes, he went into winter quarters at Morristown.

The following summer of 1777 was the time of greatest military peril for the infant American nation. From Canada, General John Burgoyne launched a British offensive by way of Lake Champlain toward Albany and the lower Hudson Valley. Sir William Howe had the opportunity to move up the Hudson from New York City to join Burgoyne and cut the colonies in two. Instead, the indecisive Howe succumbed to the temptation of occupying the rebel capital at Philadelphia, brushing aside what resistance Washington's outnumbered army was able to offer at the Battle of Brandywine.

Freed from the threat of Howe to their rear, the American commanders in the Hudson Valley, Horatio Gates and Benedict Arnold, were able to put up a stubborn resistance against Burgoyne's advance from the north. Far from his base of supply and harassed on every side by farmer militia, the British commander was finally forced to surrender his entire army at Saratoga in October 1777. The importance of this victory and the narrowness of the American escape from a crushing military catastrophe cannot be exaggerated. Thanks to a combination of British lethargy and American determination, it now appeared for the first time that the patriot bid for independence might succeed.

THE FRENCH ALLIANCE AND THE
SOUTHERN CAMPAIGNS

Even the victory at Saratoga could not make up for the feebleness of the American war effort. Driven from Philadelphia to York, Pennsylvania, Congress struggled ineffectually during the winter of 1777–1778 with the problems of supply and funds, as inflation rose sharply and paper money issued to finance the war became increasingly worthless. Meanwhile, cold and hunger in the winter camp at Valley Forge decimated Washington's ragtag army. Often local American farmers and merchants traded their goods for British coin and supplied enemy forces encamped in the relative comfort of nearby Philadelphia. But the patriot cause saw its share of profiteering, official corruption, provincial rivalries, disaffection, and desertion, though subsequent generations remembered only the gallantry and sacrifice of the revolutionaries.

Across the Atlantic, the Saratoga victory was bearing fruit. From the beginning of the conflict, Americans had hoped that France would avenge her recent defeat by Britain by giving them aid. As soon as independence was declared, Congress sent the engaging and inimitable Franklin (who affected a fur cap and homespun airs for the occasion) to seek an alliance in Paris. The French government proved willing to furnish supplies and funds secretly, but before siding with them openly, it wanted assurance that the Americans had a real chance of winning. Saratoga furnished this assurance, and in February 1778, the treaty of alliance was signed. As a result, France's ally Spain was also pulled into the war with Britain, and soon afterwards the Netherlands were drawn into the conflict because of their insistence on continuing trade with the French and the Americans. Spain and the Netherlands furnished much needed loans for the American war effort, but France became the main source of both the money and the munitions that enabled the Americans to keep fighting. In addition, the French sent an army and a powerful naval force, without which victory would have been impossible.

Military activity was at a stalemate for a year following Saratoga as the British prepared for another offensive, this time aimed at the southern colonies. Landing at Savannah, Georgia, in December 1778, the British army under the aggressive Lord Cornwallis easily took Charleston and occupied most of South Carolina. When the Americans finally marched against him in August 1780, they were soundly defeated at Camden, and Cornwallis was able to push his invasion northward. By this time, however, the American forces in the South were under the able command of Nathanael Greene. At King's Mountain and at Cowpens, severe defeats were inflicted on contingents of Cornwallis's army, and in March 1781, the British army sustained heavy losses in a hard fought but inconclusive battle at Guilford Court House, North Carolina. Cornwallis, despairing of subduing the vast and hostile southern interior, withdrew his seriously weakened army to Yorktown on the peninsula between the York and James rivers in tidewater Virginia, where his forces waited to be evacuated by the British fleet.

But it was not the British fleet that appeared. By a miracle of good fortune and good timing, Washington and the French commanders were able to march the combined Franco-American army down from the north just as the French fleet appeared off the Virginia coast. Thus caught between a hostile army and a hostile navy, Cornwallis had no alternative but to surrender his 7,000 British and Hessian troops on October 17, 1781. As he did so, legend has it, a British military band played "The World Turned Upside Down."

THE TREATY OF PEACE

Cornwallis's surrender finally convinced the British government that the effort to subdue the Americans was too difficult and too expensive to continue. Despite considerable advantages in population (11 million to 2.5 million), economic resources, diplomatic alliances, and military experience, Britain suffered from disadvantages in pursuing the war. Its problems included maintaining communications with, and providing supplies to fighting forces who were 3,000 miles away; it took some two to three months to send messages or to convey arms and men to the colonies. Able to raise only one-third of its troops in Great Britain, the crown relied heavily on German mercenaries and American Tories, in roughly equal numbers. These British troops, though often skilled in formalized European-style warfare, were ill-prepared to fight in a remote and savage wilderness without major industrial or population centers and without adequate roads. (As in later wars of colonial liberation, the imperial power found it easier to control the towns than the countryside.) Although the British navy — the world's largest — controlled the seas until 1781, and the well-trained Redcoats usually defeated American armies when they could catch them, these advantages brought little ultimate success. The country was too vast, the population too deeply committed to resistance, the indigenous guerrilla forces too elusive, and the costs too great to be borne indefinitely. In the end, a once-confident and often blundering Britain was outlasted by militarily weaker, but more resourceful and determined colonial forces.

Following the debacle at Yorktown, Lord North resigned his ministry, and a new ministry came to power prepared to negotiate with the Americans. Although John Adams, Benjamin Franklin, and John Jay were already in Europe for such purposes, a peace settlement was delayed for some time by the crosscurrents of international politics. The Franco-American alliance committed each party to continue fighting as long as the other was fighting, and the Franco-Spanish alliance committed France to continuing the war until Spain won Gibraltar from England. This seemed to mean that the

Americans could not make peace with England until Spain regained Gibraltar. But when the American commissioners uncovered evidence that the French were arranging that the Spanish and British control the northern and southern portions of the American land between the Allegheny Mountains and the Mississippi, the Americans felt absolved of their obligation to negotiate in concert with the French.

Seeing an opportunity to detach the Americans from French influence, the British accepted an American proposal for separate Anglo-American negotiations. By thus playing off one power against the other, the American commissioners won an exceedingly favorable treaty. Besides recognizing the independence of the United States, the British also acquiesced in giving up a generous extent of territory, stretching from the Atlantic to the Mississippi and from the Canadian border on the north to the Florida border on the south. These terms were agreed upon by late 1782, but peace did not come officially until Spain and France ended hostilities in early 1783. In this general settlement, Florida was transferred from Britain to Spain to compensate for Spain's failure to win Gibraltar.

FOR FURTHER READING

Gordon S. Wood's *The Radicalism of the American Revolution* (1992), Edward Countryman's *The American Revolution* (1985), and Robert Middlekauff's *The Glorious Cause* (1982) are the best overviews of the American Revolution, but John R. Alden's older *A History of the American Revolution* (1954) is still useful. A good general military history of the war is Marshall Smelser's *The Winning of Independence* (1972). Don Higginbotham, *The War of American Independence* (1971), and John Shy, *A People Numerous and Armed* (1976), analyze the unconventional character of the armed conflict; and R. Arthur Bowler examines *Logistics and the Failure of the British Army in America* (1975). Also excellent for military and naval history are two biographies: Don Higginbotham, *George Washington and the American Military Tradition* (1985), and Samuel Eliot Morison, *John Paul Jones: A Sailor's Biography* (1959). Diplomatic histories of the period include William C. Stinchcombe's *The American Revolution and the French Alliance* (1969), Lawrence S. Kaplan's *Colonies into Nation* (1972), and Reginald Horsman's *The Diplomacy of the New Republic* (1985). James Henderson's *Party Politics in the Continental Congress* (1975) closely examines congressional politics during a crucial period. For the political thought that influenced the development of new political institutions during the revolutionary years, see Morton White's *The Philosophy of the American Revolution* (1978) and Carl L. Becker's *The Declaration of Independence* (1922). Studies of loyalists in the American Revolution include: Robert S. Lambert's *South Carolina Loyalists in the American Revolution* (1987), Philip Ranlet's *The New York Loyalists* (1986), and Robert M. Calhoons's *Loyalists in Revolutionary America, 1760–1781* (1973). Peter S. Onuf in *The Origins of the Federal Republic* (1983) describes the conflicts surrounding the formation of the new state governments; Jackson T. Main analyzes *The Upper House in Revolutionary America* (1967); and Merrill Jensen offers a controversial analysis of the drafting of *The Articles of Confederation* (1940). Important contributions to an understanding of the republican ideology of the Revolution include Bernard Bailyn's *The Ideological Origins of the American Revolution* (1967), J. G. A. Pocock's *The Machiavellian Moment* (1975), and Gordon S. Wood's *The Creation of the American Republic* (1969). The social effects of the war are explored in J. Franklin Jameson's pioneer study *The American Revolution Considered as a Social Movement* (1926) and in James K. Martin's *In the Course of Human Events* (1979). The black experience during the Revolution is covered in Sylvia R. Frey, *Water from the Rock* (1991), and Benjamin Quarles, *The Negro in the American Revolution* (1961). David Brion Davis's *The Problem of Slavery in the Age of Revolution* (1975) is a landmark study that explores the context for an emerging abolitionism. Mary Beth Norton in *Liberty's Daughters* (1980) and Linda K. Kerber in *Women of the Republic* (1980) offer differing perspectives on the impact of the developing republican ideology on women's rights.

6

★ ★ ★ ★ ★ ★

A Nation Emerges,
1780–1788

THE NEW NATION brought into being by the Revolution covered a thinly populated but vast expanse of territory six times the area of England and Wales combined. Ninety-five percent of its 3 million people lived in the countryside. Most of them were near the seacoast, but even here they were so dispersed that there were only six cities with more than 8,000 inhabitants. Philadelphia, with fewer than 40,000, was largest, followed by New York, Boston, Charleston, Baltimore, and Salem. (By contrast, contemporary London had 750,000 people, and Paris, 500,000.) Transportation facilities from one part of this far-flung republican empire to another were rudimentary, and communication was so infrequent that the letters carried by the postal service amounted to only one per capita per year.

Nevertheless, the shared experience of the Revolution had given Americans a sense of national pride and optimism about the future of their experiment in liberty. But because not all Americans agreed about what that future should be, the decade of the 1780s was one of conflict. It was also, as time would prove, the richest and most intense period of American political and constitutional thought.

THE AGRARIAN-MINDED AND THE
COMMERCIAL-MINDED

One fundamental division was between what might be called the *agrarian-minded* and the *commercial-minded* portions of the population. The great majority of the people were small farmers. Measured against the Europe that they or their peasant forebears had left behind — the Europe of arbitrary government, heavy taxes, military conscription, state churches, and rigid social distinctions — America seemed a virtual paradise. In America, the dream of land ownership — the key to security, independence, and dignity — could be realized by the great majority.

To these small landowners, secure on their acres, far from cities, often illiterate or semiliterate, the American utopia w.s already at hand. Provincial and typically adhering to the more orthodox brands of Protestantism, they regarded the farmer's way of life as morally superior to all others. They were deeply suspicious of cities, of change, and of those ambitious and probably evil urban people who grew rich by commercial manipulations. This agrarian mystique was also shared in good part by many southern planters and by many of the great landlord families in New York's Hudson Valley.

Less numerous but equally influential were the people who saw America's future in terms of general economic growth and national strength. This commercial-mindedness was centered in the cities and especially among the merchant and professional classes, the best educated and most cosmopolitan parts of the population. Included also were a good many farmers and planters who lived close enough to transportation and cities to produce commercial crops for foreign and domestic markets.

The division between the commercial-minded and the agrarian-minded merged into the other major political division of the 1780s: there was a tendency for the agrarian-minded to be democratic-minded and for the commercial-minded to resist democratic tendencies. However, the two alignments did not coincide completely. Thomas Paine, for example, was among the most effective advocates of both democracy and commercial expansion, while much of the leadership for the agrarian forces was provided by elitist gentry from the great landholding families.

With some important exceptions, then, the political struggles of the 1780s involved two rough groupings. On one side were those who favored leadership by the gentry, vigorous and more centralized government, and policies designed to foster national strength and economic growth through encouragement to entrepreneurs. On the other side were persons resentful of any pretensions to superiority, deeply suspicious of all government, and mistrustful of even their own elected representatives. They consequently wanted government kept as decentralized as possible, as inactive and inexpensive as possible, and subject to the check of frequent and democratic elections.

CONFLICT WITHIN THE STATES

The state governments were the principal arenas of conflict between the two groups. The conflict was in part a straight struggle for control, as in Pennsylvania where displaced conservatives warred unrelentingly against the ultrademocratic constitution of 1776 and the power it gave to western farmers and the lower orders of Philadelphia.

Religion was frequently another divisive issue. In New England (outside Rhode Island where religious freedom had always prevailed), the Congregationalists were persuaded to surrender only part of the exclusive privileges they had enjoyed by law before the Revolution. But in New York and the southern states, the members of the formerly established Anglican church were reduced to an equal footing with those other denominations. In Virginia, the Anglicans of the wealthy and conservative tidewater area managed to stave off this movement until 1786 when James Madison's coalition of liberal gentry, back-country Baptists, Methodists, and Presbyterians pushed through the legislature Jefferson's Statute for Religious Freedom.

The greatest cause of alarm to conservatives was the democratic legislatures' apparent disregard for property rights. In some states, property-minded persons fought against wholesale confiscations of the property of Loyalists, and they were even more alarmed by the movement for debtor laws and state-issued paper money.

Paper money had been used during the colonial period with both good and bad results, but the collapse of the Continental currency during the Revolution had utterly discredited the whole idea with merchants and creditors. Yet the return to a specie (gold and silver) currency at the end of the Revolution, the collapse of the brief boom that followed, and the ensuing depression of 1785–1786 produced a severe deflation. People who had borrowed money during inflationary times found that they had to repay their debts in money that was worth much more than the money originally borrowed and at a time when money of any kind was hard to obtain.

Under the pressure of desperate debtors, seven state legislatures authorized issues of paper money, while in several other states, creditors and merchants barely averted such demands. The paper issues were relatively beneficial where taxes were levied to support them, but in other instances, the old story of rapid depreciation was repeated. Some states tried to compel creditors to accept the paper money in payment of debts, and creditors were said to flee the state of Rhode Island to avoid payment in depreciated paper.

The conflict became most violent in Massachusetts, where debtors and small farmers of the interior simply could not find enough of the scarce specie to pay their debts and heavy state taxes. As the courts began imprisoning large numbers of defaulting debtors or foreclosing on their farms, armed mobs started breaking up sessions of the courts. By the winter of 1786–1787, the interior was swarming with a virtual insurrectionary militia of several thousand debt-ridden farmers whose principal leader was a Revolutionary veteran named Daniel Shays. Finally, a state army of 4,000 marched into the area and quelled the disorders after a series of minor skirmishes. Meanwhile, accounts of "Shays's Rebellion" had further alarmed property-minded conservatives in all the states, convincing many of the need for revising the Articles.

PROBLEMS OF THE CONFEDERATION

In the early 1780s, conservatives were already seeking to guard against the localism and democratic irresponsibility of the states by strengthening the Confederation government. Under the leadership of the "financier of the Revolution," Robert Morris, a Philadelphia merchant who had grown wealthy from war contracts, they had persuaded Congress to appoint full-time executives to superintend departments of finance, war, foreign affairs, and marine. Morris himself became superintendent of finance and exercised great influence in all areas. His primary concerns were economic stability and the attachment of monied interests to the central government. Toward those ends, Continental paper money was abandoned, and Morris sought to finance the government by borrowing, partly from American citizens. In the process, he encouraged the creation of a powerful class of public creditors (bond buyers) who had a vested interest in a government that would be strong enough to pay its debts.

But the Confederation government could neither pay its debts nor effectively carry on its ordinary operations as long as it had to depend for income on voluntary contributions by the recalcitrant states. Morris's whole program hinged on getting the states to approve the "Impost of 1781," a proposed amendment of the Articles of Confederation that would give Congress the power to levy limited import duties to pay the Confederation debt. But Rhode Island refused to ratify, and all further efforts to give Congress any taxing power failed to get the required unanimous approval of the states. Meanwhile, the coming of peace dissipated the atmosphere of emergency, and the drive to add vigor to the Confederation government stalled.

Through the mid-1780s, national-minded persons could only grumble helplessly at the impotence of the Confederation in many areas. Lacking any means of enforcing its policies either on the states or directly on their citizens, the Confederation was unable to deal effectively with unseemly quarrels among various states over boundaries, western lands, and state-levied tariffs and trade restrictions.

The Confederation's weakness was most evident in foreign relations. Partly because the United States could not enforce uniform commercial regulations in its own territory or threaten uniform retaliatory regulations against other countries, it was unable to secure favorable commercial treaties with the leading European powers. More serious, Spain and Great Britain threatened the territorial integrity of the new nation in the Southwest and Northwest respectively.

Spain had lost Florida to Great Britain at the end of the Seven Years' War in 1763 but had gained formerly French Louisiana (the entire western watershed of the Mississippi and the "island" of New Orleans east of the river). Then, in 1783, Spain regained Florida, making her the dominant power on the southwestern borders of the United States. Moreover, Spain would not be bound by the 31° northern boundary of Florida specified by the Anglo-American treaty, but occupied territory north of that line and claimed the greater part of the Southwest. These claims she actively buttressed in the 1780s by gaining control over the southwestern Indians and restricting the Mississippi River trade through New Orleans. When the Confederation proved powerless to protect new settlements in the Tennessee-Kentucky area against the Indians or to secure them a right to trade down the Mississippi, many settlements sought the protection of Spain, and for a time there was a serious danger that the western settlers would cooperate in making the entire Southwest a Spanish territory.

Great Britain understandably treated her former subjects with great contempt, closing her West Indian possessions to American trade, restricting American trade with England, and refusing to enter negotiations for a commercial treaty or even to send a minister to the new nation. Most threatening of all, she continued to occupy military posts along the northern frontier within territory she had ceded to the United States, and from these posts she retained dominion over the Indians of the northern Ohio Valley and encouraged them to resist the advance of American settlement.

The British found justification for these actions in the failure of the American states to live up to their obligations under the Treaty of Paris. Congress technically complied with the treaty by urging the states to restore confiscated property to Loyalists, but it could not force the states to do so. Nor could it prevent the states from violating the treaty by impeding the collection of debts that Americans owed to British merchants. The Confederation authorities could counter British complaints on these points only by demanding payment for several thousand slaves that the British armies had carried away from the southern states.

THE CONFEDERATION AND THE WEST

For all its weaknesses, the Confederation had one magnificent achievement to its credit: the creation of a great national domain west of the Appalachian Mountains and the formulation of a system for land sales and territorial government by which this West and later Wests would become a spectacularly expanding "empire for liberty."

Even before the Revolution, pioneers had crossed the mountains to form pockets of settlement in a few areas. New Englanders had moved up and across the Connecticut River to populate the green hills of Vermont. Resisting the claims of New York and New Hampshire to the area during the Revolution, Ethan Allen and his "Green Mountain Boys" created an independent republic that was not admitted as one of the United States until 1791.

Farther south, other pioneers had established themselves on the upper waters of the Ohio River in the Wheeling-Pittsburgh area, and still others had pushed southwestward through the valleys of the Virginia mountains to found the Watauga settlement on the headwaters of the Tennessee River in what was to become the northeastern corner of Tennessee. During and immediately after the Revolution, these outposts became staging areas for further advances of settlement into the country north of the Ohio, through Cumberland Gap into the Bluegrass region of what would later be central Kentucky, and over the Cumberland Plateau into the Nashville basin of what would later be middle Tennessee.

Seven states laid claim to various parts of the trans-Appalachian empire. Virginia, making the most of the vague boundaries specified by its colonial charter, claimed Kentucky and all the territory north of the Ohio River. New York had a shadowy claim to the Ohio Valley resting on Indian treaties, while

Massachusetts and Connecticut argued that their boundaries extended indefinitely westward, cutting across the Virginia claim. Farther south the two Carolinas and Georgia asserted that their boundaries extended all the way to the Mississippi.

Even before the war was over, under heavy pressure from landless states, Congress had urged that these western claims be ceded to the Confederation to create a great common domain. Virginia led the way in 1781 by offering its lands north of the Ohio, and by the end of the 1780s all except one of the landed states had followed suit. Georgia finally ceded its western lands in 1802, while, in 1792, Virginia passed the sovereignty over its remaining western territory directly to the new state of Kentucky that was created from it.

Congress lost no time in providing for land sales and a governmental system in the new public domain. The Ordinance of 1785 established a "rectangular" system of survey. Land was to be divided into squares one mile from north to south and one mile from east to west. "Townships" six miles square were to be laid off, each of which would contain 36 one-mile-square (640-acre) "sections." As the line of settlement advanced, these sections were to be auctioned off to the highest bidders, with a minimum price of two dollars an acre.

A year earlier, in the Ordinance of 1784 (drafted by Thomas Jefferson), Congress had declared that territorial governments in the public domain should evolve as quickly as possible into new states fully equal to the original states. The process by which this was to happen was altered by the so-called Northwest Ordinance of 1787, adopted to meet the wishes of the Ohio Company, a group of New England land speculators who were promoting a settlement in the Muskingum Valley of what was to become southeastern Ohio. The Ordinance of 1787 established a Northwest Territory in the area north of the Ohio and east of the Mississippi rivers; this area was to be administered first by a governor appointed by Congress. When the population of the territory reached 5,000, the people were to elect a representative assembly and a nonvoting delegate to Congress. Eventually the Old Northwest was to be divided into not less than three and not more than five states, and when the population of any of these proposed states reached 60,000, it could be admitted to the union on an equal footing with the original states. During the territorial stage, civil liberties and religious freedom were guaranteed, a system of free public education was called for, and slavery was excluded. Thus Congress laid down the pattern of territorial evolution by which the United States was to become a continental nation of equal states.

THE MOVEMENT FOR A
STRONGER GOVERNMENT

Many Americans — particularly subsistence farmers — were generally satisfied with the Confederation. Indeed, it often functioned reasonably well. But, amid a growing awareness that the Articles could not meet important national needs, others grew more impatient with its weakness and more determined to secure a strong national government in its place. The unpaid public creditors constituted a standing lobby for change. Merchants wanted a uniform commercial policy that could force concessions from the great trading nations. The artisan class and infant industrial sector wanted a uniform tariff policy that would protect them from the competition of British manufactures. The elite of many states dreaded the possibility of irresponsible popular control of state politics. Creditors and wealthy persons cried out for protection against debtor legislation, paper money, and the assaults of the unpropertied on property. Frontier people demanded more vigorous defense against the Indians and their British and Spanish abettors. And the more cosmopolitan and national-minded patriots wanted their country to assume a position of greater strength and dignity among the nations of the world. Quite obviously the reasons for the discontent were nearly as numerous as the people who advocated a stronger government. The pressures for revising the Articles could be traced as much to dissatisfaction with state government as to deficiencies in the Confederation. But overriding all considerations was a pervasive fear among the nation's political leaders that the Confederation, as originally constructed, could not adequately protect American interests in a hostile world and that the excesses of the Revolutionary era threatened the interests of authority and stability in the name of popular liberty.

As the 1780s wore on, events pushed some of these national-minded elements into an almost revolutionary mood. Robert Morris's drive to strengthen the Confederation from within had stalled when the urgency of war was removed in 1783; all further attempts to remedy the inadequacy of the Articles by amendment failed. More important, the brief economic boom that followed peace collapsed into a commercial and financial depression in the mid-1780s, and inevitably merchants, financiers, and artisans began to think that their distress was related to the Confederation's weakness. As a result of the depression, the panic of conservatives over paper money and debtor legislation reached its peak. In the autumn of 1786, the conservatives' worst fears of the lower orders and anarchy seemed confirmed by the exaggerated accounts of Shays's Rebellion.

By this time, a concerted movement was under way to bypass the prescribed method for amending the Articles and to create a stronger government through constitutionally questionable means. The movement was initiated by a small group of national-minded people, particularly George Washington and James Madison in Virginia and Alexander Hamilton in New York. Unlike such older revolutionaries as Richard Henry Lee of Virginia and Samuel Adams of Massachusetts, these nationalists were less concerned with popular liberty than with social stability and economic growth, and less alarmed by central authority than by majoritarian tyranny. Washington shared the fears of anarchy held by other members of the upper classes, but his nationalism was more than a class prejudice. His views reflected his position as the pre-eminent personal symbol of American nationality, and he cared deeply about the strength, dignity, and perpetuity of the nation he had done so much to bring to birth.

Hamilton and Madison were younger men. After serving as Washington's aide-de-camp during the Revolution, Hamilton had become a highly successful lawyer in New York, where he had married into one of the leading families and had proved himself a staunch defender of property rights. But Hamilton was not primarily a servant of propertied interests. Instead he was obsessed with the need for vigor and strength in government and sought to ally wealth with government in the interest of strong government rather than of wealth.

Madison was a nationalist on more theoretical grounds. A close friend and correspondent of Jefferson and like him a member of the liberal wing of Virginia's planting gentry, the frail, youthful (36 in 1787), scholarly Madison, had combined the study of ancient and modern governments with a quiet but increasingly influential role in Virginia politics. His nationalism was a matter of intellectual conviction, stimulated by his association with Washington and buttressed by his wide reading and disinterested reflection on political problems. Although, until his death in 1836, he generously and accurately protested that the Constitution was not "the offspring of a single brain" but "the work of many heads and many hands," he, more than any other framer, was the father of that document.

In 1785, on Madison's initiative, a conference of commissioners from Virginia and Maryland met at Mount Vernon and Alexandria to consider improving navigation of the Potomac. Madison and Washington persuaded the commissioners that other states should be brought into the consultation, and the Virginia legislature invited all the states to send delegates to a convention at Annapolis in 1786 to deliberate on "a uniform system in their commercial regulations." When delegates from only five states appeared at Annapolis, Hamilton, a delegate from New York, persuaded the convention to send out a call for another convention in Philadelphia in May 1787, to "devise such further provisions as shall appear . . . necessary as to render the constitution of the federal government adequate to the exigencies of the union."

The call for the Philadelphia convention was grudgingly endorsed by the Confederation Congress with the explicit stipulation that any amendments it proposed must be endorsed by all the states as the Articles required. During the spring, delegates were selected by the legislatures of every state save debtor-dominated Rhode Island. With only a few exceptions, those who were satisfied with the Articles as they stood refused to serve as delegates, thus permitting people who were inclined to a stronger government to represent even those states where they were in a minority. The legislature of Hamilton's New York, dominated by his opponents, permitted him to be a delegate only as a member of a three-man delegation controlled by two staunch opponents of change. More typically, Richard Henry Lee and Patrick Henry, who "smelt a rat," pointedly stayed home, though they were chosen to serve by the Virginia legislature. Also conspicuously absent was the old and ailing Samuel Adams, who would in time reluctantly support the Constitution but preferred a "Federal Union of Sovereign States" to a "National Government." John Adams and Thomas Jefferson, who would both support ratification of the Constitution, were in Europe on diplomatic assignments and could not participate.

THE CONSTITUTIONAL CONVENTION

Except for scattered opponents, the convention was composed of delegates from the national-minded side of the political spectrum. In Hamilton's telling phrase, they were numbered among the Americans "who think continentally." Predominantly lawyers, merchants, and planters, the 55 male delegates were drawn principally from urban and seaboard areas and from the upper classes; no women were selected to serve as delegates. These men made an impressive showing of youth, education, ability, political experience, and wealth. Due to the circumstances of their selection, the crucial decision facing the convention — whether the government should continue as a decentralized confederated government with some additional powers to raise revenue and regulate commerce, or whether it should become a stronger, more centralized national government directly affecting the states and their citizens — was settled before the delegates met.

Had this not been the case, Madison could never have scored such a resounding victory for a national plan at the very outset of the convention. The Virginia delegation arrived in Philadelphia some days before the convention opened, and Madison had his fellow Virginians hard at work on a "Virginia Plan" that became the basis for the convention's early deliberations. By accepting the Virginia Plan as its basis for deliberation, the convention made the momentous decision that it would propose not simply amendments to the Articles but an entirely new frame of government. It also indicated that it favored a government radically different from the Confederation.

The two principal features of the Virginia Plan were its grant of sweeping powers to the central government and its requirement that representation in the national legislative body be in proportion to population. It was the second feature that raised the only fundamental disagreement in the convention's proceedings, for delegates from the small states rightly feared that basing representation on population would allow the large states to control the new government. Consequently the small-state delegates presented a "New Jersey Plan" to amend the Articles rather than to draft an entirely new constitution. The heart of the New Jersey Plan was the continuance of a one-house Congress in which each state would have one vote. By adhering to the form of the Articles, the small-state delegates were also proposing a confederated government of limited powers, though their plan did give Congress the power to levy import duties, regulate commerce, and admit new states. Yet it was the matter of representation rather than the question of nationalism that was at the bottom of the disagreement, and a compromise was finally effected by proposing a two-house Congress where representation in the lower house was apportioned by population and where the influence of the small states was safeguarded in an upper house composed of two senators from each state. Once the small states won this concession, their delegates showed less zeal in defending a confederated structure. From this point on, the convention was able to work out the detailed powers and structure of the new government without serious disagreement.

Though the delegates were predominantly nationalists and though many of them feared the influence of popular majorities, they were also political realists who recognized that whatever they proposed would have to be accepted by a society that was considerably more confederationist and democratic than the convention itself. Consequently, and to Hamilton's discomfort, the document that resulted from their deliberations was a compromise between the two poles of political thought. Its basic feature was the creation of a "federal" system in which powers and responsibilities were distributed between the state and national governments. While the powers given Congress were specified with the implication that only these powers could be exercised, the specified powers were quite ample. The new government was to have virtually unlimited authority to levy taxes, borrow money, regulate domestic and foreign commerce, conduct foreign relations, and maintain an army and navy. Moreover, the states were specifically forbidden to engage in diplomatic negotiations, maintain armies, or — closing the door on debtor legislation and paper money — "emit Bills of Credit, make any Thing but gold and silver Coin a Tender in Payment of Debts; pass any . . . Law impairing the Obligation of Contracts. . . ." Finally and most important, the new national government was to operate directly upon the citizens rather than upon the states, and the proposed national constitution and laws and treaties made in pursuance of it were declared to be "the supreme Law of the Land."

Following the eighteenth-century doctrine of separation of powers and fearful of a concentration of power anywhere in government, the convention was at pains to create, in addition to Congress, a strong and independent executive and judiciary so that the three branches would act as checks and balances on each other. The vesting of the executive function in a single and relatively strong president, independent of the legislative branch and eligible for re-election, was a remarkable departure from existing practices in the states and the Confederation. The president was given a veto over congressional legislation (unless repassed by two-thirds of both houses); he was to appoint judges and other officers (with consent of the Senate); he was given primary responsibility for foreign relations and the making of treaties (with the advice and consent of two-thirds of the Senate); and he was to be commander in chief of the armed forces.

The convention spent much of its time working out the methods for choosing the personnel of the legislative, executive, and judicial branches. Nearly all the delegates recognized that popular majorities must have a voice somewhere in the governmental structure they were planning, but they were equally anxious to erect ample safeguards against the workings of popular passions and temporary enthusiasms. Popular majorities were allowed direct sway in the House of Representatives, whose members were to be elected every two years by those who were qualified to vote for the popular branches of the legislatures in the respective states. But laws passed by the House of Representatives also had to be approved by the Senate, and the senators were to be chosen for six-year terms by the state legislatures. Even after passage by both houses of Congress, laws still needed the approval of the president, and the convention worked long and hard before devising a method of selecting the president that would leave him independent of state legislatures, Congress, and popular majorities. The result was that famous invention, the electoral college. Each state was to appoint, as its legislature directed, as many electors as it had members of Congress, and the electors were then to elect a president who was to serve for four years. Finally, the members of the judiciary were to be appointed by the president for life.

The system as a whole seemed admirably contrived to frustrate direct popular control of all branches of the government at any one time and to ensure that the various branches would pull in such different directions as to hobble effective government. The convention did not foresee that the rise of political parties would quickly subvert its intentions in both respects, and indeed the government under the Constitution would probably have proved unworkable if it had operated exactly as its architects intended that it should.

RATIFICATION

In September 1787, nearly four months after it convened, the convention lifted the veil of secrecy with which it had covered its debates and presented its handiwork to the country. Only then did people outside the convention discover that the delegates had vastly exceeded their authority. Not only had they drafted a substantially new framework for government, instead of a revision of the existing Articles, but they provided for its ratification by only 9 of the 13 states.

The work of a relatively small but vigorous and talented group of conti- nental-minded leaders who called themselves "Federalists" (rather than the more straightforward "Nationalists"), the Constitution won quick and deci- sive ratifications in the small states of Delaware, New Jersey, and Connect- icut, whose powerful neighboring states had taken advantage of them under the Confederation, and in the small and exposed frontier state of Georgia. Two states, Rhode Island and North Carolina, were so well satisfied with the virtually independent course they had been pursuing that they refused even to consider ratification until after the new government was in full operation.

The crucial struggles occurred in the great states of Pennsylvania, Mas- sachusetts, Virginia, and New York, which had been able to take care of themselves under the confederated system. Anti-Federalist delegates were probably in a majority when the ratifying conventions of several of these states opened — certainly overwhelmingly so in New York — but ratification finally carried in all of them. Rhode Island, the last to approve, did so in 1790. Federalist superiority in initiative, organization, and debate counted heavily in these close contests as did the strategy of agreeing to recommend whatever amendments the Anti-Federalist delegates wished to propose. Most of all, the Federalists had the advantage of a concrete proposal. Their opponents were forced, as one conceded, to ratify "this or nothing." Nor were Federalists opposed to unscrupulous tactics: in New York, Governor John Hancock was cynically won over by the implied promise of high national office; in Pennsylvania, Anti-Federalist legislators were physically dragged to their seats in a quorum-shy Assembly so that a ratification convention could be called. Thus not only was the Constitution adopted by extraconstitutional means, without the test of a mass plebiscite or even of Congressional ratification, but the Federalists' tactical advantages may well have given them victory over a potentially opposed but ineffectively organized majority in the country.

Allowing for the multitude of particular interests affecting people's attitudes toward the Constitution, there seems to have been a general pattern of division. The urban and seaboard areas were almost solidly in favor of the document, not just because particular interests were stronger here, but because in these wealthier, more commercial, more cosmopolitan areas, general commercial and elitist concerns were more prevalent. Conversely, the Constitution tended to be strongly opposed in the more provincial backcountry areas of small farms because of the greater prevalence of agrarian and democratic concerns. The numerically predominant small farmers, who comprised the backbone of Anti-Federalism during the ratification controversy, saw little need for stronger government.

The Federalist leaders tended to be the younger generation of nationalists — the John Jays, Alexander Hamiltons, James Madisons — who served their political apprenticeships with the emergent republican institutions of the independence movement and grew up with the Revolution. Many of their prominent critics, on the other hand, were the "old Revolutionaries" — the Richard Henry Lees, Patrick Henrys, Mercy Warrens — who came of political age combatting crown and Parliament and who often equated government with tyranny. There were exceptions, of course: Benjamin Franklin, 81 in 1787, was a strong supporter of the Constitution; Washington, the convention president, was 55. Certainly, the sides were not neatly drawn by generations. Yet among the leaders of the debate, age, or at least experience, was apparently a factor.

Until fairly recently, the Anti-Federalists were often described as small-minded, provincial obstructionists who in their petty, self-interested particularism lacked the continental vision of the Federalists. Recent scholarship, however, suggests that for all their political weakness and disunity, the Anti-Federalists should not be so easily dismissed. To be sure the Anti-Federalists were very often more state-centered, less cosmopolitan, and less educated than their opponents, and they were usually more suffused with the traditions of localism. Yet because they chose to align themselves against some of the nation's most formidable and revered political thinkers — the Founding Fathers: Washington, Franklin, Madison, Hamilton, Marshall, and Jay — it does not follow that they were "men of little faith," that they lacked virtue, or that their arguments were not well-founded.

Despite the centralizing pressures of the 1770s and 1780s, fears of concentrated governmental authority and loss of individual liberty remained central to popular American thought. It was in this tradition, then, that the Anti-Federalists opposed the Constitution. They were traditionalists, the conservators of a national heritage and were truer than the Federalists to the "wisdom of '76." Often their leaders, the old patriots, had been more committed to the struggle for independence than their Federalist opponents. In their fear of tyranny from centralized authority, in their fidelity to localism, in their belief that republicanism could survive only in a small and homogeneous society, the Anti-Federalists had their roots firmly planted in revolutionary assumptions. Some of them recognized the need for some revision of the Articles, but the Constitution, as they understood it, represented a profound departure. Patrick Henry, their principal spokesman, thought it "horribly frightful," "incompatible with the genius of republicanism," and "a revolution as radical as that which separated us from Great Britain." Richard Henry Lee believed that it turned back the clock, once again placing "Civil Liberty . . . at the mercy of Rulers." Yet if the Constitution did not "squint toward monarchy," it did create a strong executive office whose powers would, from time to time, be abused. Compared to some European nations, the regime crafted by the Constitution's framers was relatively decentralized. Yet in the context of the American experience, the Constitution represented, as the Anti-Federalists believed, a leap toward national consolidation and a radical erosion of state power.

Finally, it should be noted that the agrarian- and democratic-minded majority might have defeated the Constitution had it been effectively mobilized. The fact that the majority did not mobilize suggests that the opposition was not terribly intense. Politics beyond the local and state level was still a matter of indifference to most farmers. Only a small proportion of the eligible voters bothered to vote at all for delegates to the ratifying conventions, and when the Constitution went into effect, it was readily accepted by all elements of the population. Within little more than a decade, under a Constitution whose operations had been transformed by political parties that the framers did not envisage, the hitherto apathetic agrarian- and democratic-minded majority would come into its own.

CONFLICTING HISTORICAL VIEWPOINTS: NO. 2

How Democratic Was the Constitution?

American exceptionalism has been one of the basic presuppositions of our national experience. America was a land peculiarly blessed; its people were God's chosen people, the embodiment of the promise of human perfection.

In the words of John Adams, the nation's founding marked "the opening of a grand scheme and design in Providence for the illumination and emancipation of the slavish part of mankind all over the earth." More particularly, the Constitution was an instrument of heaven's will; its framers, Jefferson said, were themselves "demi-gods." Early students of American history were in full agreement. In fact, no article of American faith was more sacred to nineteenth-century nationalist historians than the document of 1787. In his History of the Formation of the Constitution *(2 vols., 1882), pious, patriotic George Bancroft concluded that the nation's fundamental law fulfilled the promise of the Revolution. It was inspired by the scriptures, he believed, and drafted with providential blessings. Much the same conclusion was reached by John Fiske, who portrayed the document as one of the supreme achievements of human intelligence. In full agreement with Bancroft, his older contemporary, Fiske viewed the Articles of Confederation as an unfit instrument for national government. In his* The Critical Period of American History *(1893), he described the half-dozen years following the Revolutionary War as "the most critical moment in all of the history of the American people." The period of national crisis passed, he believed, only upon the creation of a strong central government. To both Bancroft and Fiske, the Founding Fathers were men of noble purpose and unquestioned devotion to the national welfare.*

A later generation of scholars was more critical of both the Constitution and its framers. In his path-breaking study An Economic Interpretation of the Constitution *(1913), the progressive historian Charles Beard offered the then shocking argument that the Founding Fathers were not selfless patriots but self-serving plutocrats: "men whose property interests were immediately at stake." The product of their labor represented not the culmination of the democratic revolutionary spirit of 1776 but a counterrevolution. Thus, through the instrument of the Constitution, Beard averred, a few conservative men of property effected a coup d'état to protect their economic self-interest and check the growth of popular democracy. Samuel Adams and Patrick Henry could not have said it better!*

Although Beard confessed that his work was fragmentary and his conclusions tentative, his neo-Anti-Federalist interpretation won prompt and almost universal acceptance. Among the many latter-day Beardians, none did more to fill out and document the Columbia University scholar's interpretation than Merrill Jensen. In The Articles of Confederation *(1940) and* The New Nation *(1950), Jensen carefully supported Beard's contention that the Confederation government was not one of "stagnation, ineptitude, bankruptcy, corruption, and disintegration." In his view, the democratic radicalism that waxed with the Declaration of Independence waned with the Constitution. The framers engineered a "conservative counterrevolution" that served to "thwart the will of 'the people.'"*

More recently, Beard's critics have all but discredited his economic interpretations. Robert E. Brown (Charles A. Beard and the Constitution, *1955) and Forrest McDonald* (We the People, *1958), for example, have questioned Beard's use of the evidence and nearly all of his conclusions.*

Neither scholar accepted his class-conflict theories, and Brown argued co-
gently that the Constitution was an essentially middle-class democratic doc-
ument ideally suited for essentially middle-class democratic America. Other
scholars have offered different conclusions, and both Jackson Turner Main
(The Antifederalists, *1961) and Lee Benson* (Turner and Beard, *1960) have*
found elements of Beardian conflict in the alignment of mercantile capital-
ists versus agrarians during the period of struggle over the Constitution.
Yet most historians of the present generation (Main and Benson included)
agree that Beard's thesis is seriously deficient. As the intellectual historian
Gordon Wood writes in his important The Creation of the American Republic *(1969), the notion that the ideas and behavior of the founders were*
determined by material consideration is "so crude that no further time
should be spent on it." Wood does not reject the progressive view of the
Constitution as an intrinsically aristocratic document designed to curb the
democratic excesses of the Revolution. But he does suggest that the strug-
gle between Federalist and Anti-Federalist was actually a struggle over what
kind of democracy America would have — an elitist, nationally oriented
democracy or a popular, locally based democracy.

The founders, then, may not have been Jefferson's demigods nor Ban-
croft's agents of providential will, but modern scholars find little merit in
the Anti-Federalist charge that they were "avaricious adventurers" and par-
tisans of aristocracy. Rather, recent historians agree that the product of
their labors was basically democratic and that they themselves were peo-
ple of great stature and vision whose devotion to nation transcended pock-
etbook concerns. It should be noted, however, that democracy in this context
did not apply to blacks, the "slavish part" of John Adams's own nation, or
to women. The creative energies of the framers were lavished on the foun-
dation of a republic for white males, not on extending the benefits of lib-
erty to blacks or women. A half-century after ratification, when the abolitionist
William Lloyd Garrison proposed to burn the Constitution in the name of
liberty, he did so on the unassailable ground that it perpetuated slavery.
Although later generations of Americans celebrated the framers' work as a
charter for political freedom, it should not be forgotten that in 1787 it was
not such a charter for blacks, women, or native Americans.

FOR FURTHER READING

An excellent starting point for any study of the political and constitutional
significance of the American Revolution is R. R. Palmer's *The Age of the*
Democratic Revolution (2 vols., 1959–1964). Jack N. Rakove, *The Begin-*
nings of National Politics (1979) examines the Continental Congress, and
David P. Szatmary offers a fresh interpretation of *Shays' Rebellion* (1980).
The classic interpretation of the Constitution itself is found, of course, in
The Federalist (many editions), essays by Hamilton, Madison, and Jay. But
several modern-day studies — Clinton Rossiter, *1787: The Grand Conven-*
tion (1966); Calvin C. Jillson, *Constitution Making* (1988); and Forrest Mc-

Donald, *Novus Ordo Seclorum: The Intellectual Origins of the Constitution* (1985) — may prove more useful to the student. The second and third volumes of Irving Brant's biography of *James Madison* (6 vols., 1941–1961) give an excellent detailed view of both the Confederation period and the constitutional convention; Robert J. Morgan also provides a valuable look at *James Madison on the Constitution and the Bill of Rights* (1988). Robert Allen Rutland traces *The Birth of the Bill of Rights* (1983), and in *The Ordeal of the Constitution* (1966) explains the battle over ratification. Michael J. Lacey and Knud Haakonssen have collected essays that examine the Bill of Rights from a variety of perspectives in *A Culture of Rights* (1991). David Brion Davis's *The Problem of Slavery in an Age of Revolution* (1975) and Staughton Lynd's *Class Conflict, Slavery and the United States Constitution* (1968) offer differing perspectives on a common problem. Both E. James Ferguson in *The Power of the Purse* (1961) and Forrest McDonald in *E Pluribus Unum* (1965) develop the financial dimensions of union.

84

TABLE 2. PRESIDENTIAL ELECTIONS AND MAJOR POLITICAL EVENTS, 1789–1800

1789	**George Washington** elected without opposition.
1790–1791	Hamiltonian program enacted. Funding the national debt. Assumption of state debts. Bargain involving location of the national capital. First Bank of the United States. Excise taxes.
1792	**George Washington** reelected without opposition.
1793	Wars of the French Revolution begin. Washington's Neutrality Proclamation.
1794	Whiskey Rebellion.
1795	Jay's Treaty with Great Britain.
1796	Pinckney's Treaty with Spain. **John Adams** (Federalist) elected over Thomas Jefferson (Republican).
1797–1798	American commissioners to France insulted.
1798	Undeclared naval war with France begins. Alien and Sedition Acts.
1798–1799	Virginia and Kentucky Resolutions.
1800	Convention of 1800 resolves differences with France. **Thomas Jefferson** (Republican) elected over John Adams (Federalist).

7

★ ★ ★ ★ ★ ★

Federalists and Republicans, 1789–1800

THE NEW Constitution as written and ratified was merely a grand outline of government. An actual government was created only as the Constitution was put into practice, through adaptation and conflict, in the 1790s. During this stormy decade there were three major developments that lastingly affected the nature of the federal government. First, precedents were set with regard to the composition and functioning of the various branches of government. Second, the real and potential scope and authority of the new government were enormously broadened by Alexander Hamilton's vigorous program of exercising to the limit every power granted or even implied by the Constitution. Finally and most important, Hamilton's policies provoked a growing opposition around which a political party formed. By the decade's end a two-party system was well established, and it profoundly influenced how the new government operated.

LAUNCHING THE NEW GOVERNMENT

It was only natural that friends of the Constitution should be chosen to put it into effect. To no one's surprise, the first electoral college agreed unanimously on Virginia's George Washington for president. To provide geographical balance while avoiding the suspect Samuel Adams and John Hancock, the electors turned for vice-president to that sturdy patriot and nationalist, Massachusetts's John Adams. When the first Congress tardily assembled in New York's City Hall in April 1789, both houses were dominated by Federalists.

While the senators squabbled behind closed doors about titles and ceremonial procedures, James Madison was pushing through the House of Representatives a series of laws that would put the new government into practical operation. Income was provided by a tariff act levying import duties at a moderate rate, designed for revenue purposes only. An organization for the executive branch was provided by the creation of departments of state, treasury, and war. The Judiciary Act of 1789 specified that the Supreme Court should consist of six justices, that there should be a district court for each state, and that two Supreme Court justices sitting with a district judge should constitute an intermediate court of appeals. The act also provided for an attorney general and explicitly specified that any decision in the state courts that questioned federal, as opposed to state, powers could be appealed to the Supreme Court, thus authorizing the Supreme Court to pass on the constitutionality of state laws.

Finally, this first Congress considered the 78 amendments to the Constitution that had been proposed by the state ratifying conventions. Somewhat reluctantly, the House approved 17 of these, the Senate approved 12 of the 17, and by 1791, a sufficient number of states had ratified 10 of the 12. These first 10 amendments, now known as the Bill of Rights, guaranteed citizens that the federal government would not invade such rights as trial by jury and freedom of religion, speech, and the press. All proposed amendments that substantially modified the powers of the federal government had been carefully omitted from the approved list, and disgruntled Anti-Federalists could take only small comfort from the Tenth Amendment, which "reserved to the States respectively, or to the people" all powers not mentioned by the Constitution.

Meanwhile President Washington was enhancing the dignity of the new government through formal and ceremonial behavior that some critics thought too high-toned, perhaps too aristocratic, for a republic. In fact, some wished to address him as "His Elective Majesty" or "His Highness the President"; in the end the more democratic "Mr. President" was adopted. Also, during the first years of his administration, Washington contributed to the popularity of the new regime by taking exhausting tours through all parts of the country. The president influenced the course of events most by his appointments, especially of Alexander Hamilton as secretary of the treasury and Thomas Jefferson as secretary of state, enormously talented figures having antithetical convictions and personalities. Washington consulted with them regularly along with his secretary of war and attorney general, and soon the cabinet, nowhere mentioned in the Constitution, emerged as an important governmental institution.

THE HAMILTONIAN PROGRAM

Alexander Hamilton had no sooner taken office than he became the master spirit of the administration; indeed he thought of himself as Washington's prime minister. This ambitious and controversial man burned with a vision of national greatness. Aiming at a unified nation, he opposed the localistic tendencies of the states. Convinced that vigorous leadership by the able few, especially in the executive branch of the government, was the only way to

The Early Days of
the Republic

The site for the permanent capital of the new Republic was chosen in the middle area of the eastern seaboard. The plans for the city were drawn by the engineer Pierre L'Enfant. This engraving of Washington made in 1826 by J. W. Steel shows its undeveloped, rural aspect, with cows grazing in the foreground. *(Library of Congress)*

In a cartoon drawn in the mid-1790s, George Washington gazes down at the Federalist-Republican struggle. He says, "I left you a precious casket of choicest blessings [Peace & Plenty; Liberty & Independence] supported by three pillars — Desist my sons from pulling at them. Should you remove one, you destroy the whole." The man tugging at the Federalism column is saying: "This pillar shall not stand — I am determined to support a just and necessary war." The other man says, pulling at the Democracy support, "This pillar must come down — I am a friend of Peace." *(Library of Congress)*

The Louisiana Purchase from France doubled the land area of the new nation. This depiction of the historic purchase shows James Monroe and Robert Livingstone completing negotiations with Tallyrand, the French foreign minister, on April 30, 1803. *(Library of Congress)*

The optimistic tenor of the Republic's first days appears in this engraving showing an Allegory of America resting her shield to engage in art, education, agriculture, and naval commerce. This is from the title page of *The Universal Asylum and Columbian Magazine for 1790*. *(Library of Congress)*

American society was not classless. The wealthy and powerful followed European fashions and purchased goods from Europe. This detail from "The Tea Party," a painting by Henry Sargent, shows the dress and gracious living of the well-to-do. *(Courtesy, Museum of Fine Arts, Boston)*

During the early days of the struggle for independence from England, Americans of the Second Continental Congress passed the Articles of Confederation and Perpetual Union Between the States in 1777. Under this document the former colonies became a confederation of sovereign states. *(Library of Congress)*

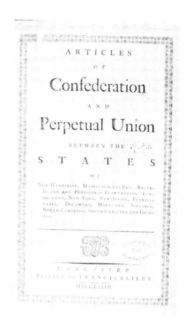

The growth of commerce and trade in the United States contributed to the expansion of the coastal cities. In the pre-mass production days, artisans were often entrepreneurs as well. *Nos. 168–172 Fulton Street, New York, showing the Shop and Warehouse of Duncan Phyfe,* 1816–17, is attributed to John Rubens Smith. From the left, the buildings are the workshop, shop, and warehouse of the famous furniture maker. *(The Metropolitan Museum of Art, Rogers Fund, 1922)*

As the nation grew, more and more people began to celebrate the anniversary of the adoption of the Declaration of Independence on July 4, 1776. In this painting, the 1819 Fourth of July celebrants congregate for the festivities, which at this time included not only fireworks but commemorative sermons. *(Historical Society of Pennsylvania)*

The freedom of the seas and cessation of impressment of American seamen by the British navy became rallying points for the War of 1812. In this painting by John Woodside, a sailor loosed from shackles crushes the crown with his foot. *(American Heritage)*

build a powerful nation, he distrusted human nature and feared what he viewed as the turbulence and irresponsibility of the democratic masses. Astutely aware of the relationship between political power and economic power, he was determined to promote the country's rapid economic growth and to forge political and economic ties between the government and the rich and well-born.

Hamilton was far from satisfied with the Constitution as an instrument for national power and economic growth. Yet he recognized that it was the best that could be secured, and he came into office resolved to strengthen it by an expansion of its provisions and by vigorous administration. Seizing from Congress the initiative for public policy, he outlined in a series of four reports a brilliant, tightly integrated program for the achievement of his objectives.

Hamilton first proposed that the long unpaid continental debt, having a face value of over $50 million, he funded at par — that is, that the old and greatly depreciated securities be called in and exchanged for new federal bonds on which interest would be regularly paid and which upon maturity would be redeemed at full value. This would not only dramatically restore American public credit, but would at the same time bolster the private credit of American entrepreneurs and make it easier for them to obtain the European capital needed for a rapidly growing economy. Gilt-edged federal bonds could form the basis for investment capital. Moreover, the whole class of wealthy investors (or speculators) in continental securities would be greatly enriched, for many of them had obtained their securities from the original holders for as little as 20 or 25 cents on the dollar. On all these grounds, funding would have the political effect of attaching the wealthy to the idea of a strong federal government.

Hamilton next proposed that the federal government assume, in similar fashion, over $20 million in unpaid debts incurred by the various states during the Revolution. This would have the advantage of attaching the large class of state creditors to the federal government rather than to the states, thus strengthening the prestige of the former at the expense of the latter.

Funding and assumption of debts required additional revenue, and Hamilton recommended that this be raised by increasing tariff duties and by levying a direct excise tax on spirituous liquors. He frankly advocated the latter tax both as a means of increasing the government's power to collect a tax and of demonstrating that power to the fiercely independent whiskey-making farmers of the interior.

The capstone of Hamilton's financial system was his proposal for a national bank. The bank was to be chartered for 20 years as a mixed public-private corporation controlled by private investors who were to purchase four-fifths of the $10 million worth of capital stock. Investors could pay three-fourths of their stock subscriptions in the form of federal bonds and one-fourth in gold or silver coin (specie). On the basis of this capital the bank was to issue specie-redeemable bank notes for loans to borrowers. The fact that these notes were to be receivable for all dues to the government would tend to keep up their value. Such an institution, Hamilton argued, would provide an ample and uniform circulating medium, a source of credit for businesses, and a profitable investment for capitalists. More particularly it would convert into fluid and expandable capital the funded Continental and state securities. In all these ways, it would be another instrument for binding the wealthy to the federal government. A final advantage of the bank, Hamilton believed, was that it was nowhere authorized in the Constitution; it could be chartered only under a "broad construction" of that instrument and would help to establish a doctrine of "implied powers."

One major element in Hamilton's economic vision remains to be mentioned. As a pioneer student of what today would be called the economic growth of underdeveloped countries, he was far ahead of his time in recognizing the importance of promoting manufacturing. A major factor in his financial proposals was the desire to provide capital for industrial development and make the new nation less dependent on foreign markets. The last of his four great reports was devoted wholly to this subject, calling for tariff rates that would give "infant industries" a competitive advantage in the domestic market until they could become well established.

To win congressional support for these proposals Hamilton fought with every political weapon at his command. The more agrarian-minded sections of the country had taken immediate alarm, and the first battle came over funding the Confederation debt. Critics objected particularly to the windfall profits of speculators who had acquired Continental securities at greatly depreciated rates. Indeed the opposition was so strong in Virginia that Madison parted with Hamilton, proposing that current holders be paid at only the depreciated rate with the remainder going to the original holders. Nevertheless, Hamilton's will prevailed. The commercial-minded Federalists in the first Congress passed the measure as originally proposed.

Assumption of state debts aroused even stronger opposition, especially from states like Virginia that had already paid off many of their own debts, and again Madison was in opposition. This time the measure was stalled, until Hamilton adroitly connected it with the simultaneous controversy among New York, Pennsylvania, and the southern states over the permanent location of the national capital. At a dinner with Hamilton, Jefferson agreed that he and Madison would draw off some of the opposition to assumption and that in return the national capital would be moved for 10 years to Philadelphia and then permanently to a 10-mile-square tract to be selected by Washington on the Potomac River between Virginia and Maryland.

Hamilton's revenue proposals met their strongest opposition not in Congress but among backcountry farmers who violently resisted the tax on whiskey, their only easily transported and salable product. By 1794 this resistance culminated in a Whiskey Rebellion in Pennsylvania, and only when Washington sent an army of some thousands into the disaffected area were the armed mobs dispersed and order restored.

The serious constitutional objections to the national bank gave even Washington pause, and before signing the bill he requested written opinions from members of his cabinet. Embracing a doctrine of implied power, Hamilton pointed out that the Constitution authorized Congress to "make all laws which shall be necessary and proper for carrying into Execution" the specifically enumerated powers. "Necessary" should be construed as meaning "*needful, requisite, incidental, useful, or conducive to,*" and he argued that powers "ought to be construed liberally in advancement of the public good." Jefferson, an opponent of centralized, concentrated national authority, on the other hand, argued from a "strict construction" point of view, contending that all powers not expressly granted were reserved by the Tenth Amendment to the states or the people. Restricting "necessary" to the narrowest sense, he asserted that the bank was unconstitutional. Washington, after some temporizing, followed the loose constructionism of Hamilton and signed the bank bill, thus foreshadowing his future political alignment with the Hamiltonians.

Hamilton's proposals for encouraging manufacturing were the only part of his program that failed in Congress. Manufacturing was still in an infant state in the country, most of it carried on by independent artisans and in people's homes, and there was no strong interest group to back Hamilton's plans. Indeed, the wealthy mercantile capitalists who were his strongest supporters on other measures were opposed to tariff barriers that would impede the flow of international trade.

On the whole, Hamilton had been successful, and his policies gave to the new government a vigor and direction that profoundly affected its future development. Combative, opinionated, and often imperious, Hamilton also had helped provoke a rising opposition from agrarian-minded people. By 1791 there was a group in Congress opposed to Hamiltonian policies, and Madison and Jefferson began to organize resistance to the New Yorker's influence. American politics was polarizing along lines of ideology and economic interest, and some observers already spoke of a Republican or Anti-Federalist interest in contrast to the Federalist interest of the Hamiltonians and the followers of the more moderate John Adams. Despite the confusion of names and some overlapping membership, the two political groupings are not successors to the pro- and anti-Constitution factions of the later 1780s. Some original Federalists, such as Madison, became latter-day Anti-Federalists, or Republicans, and some opponents of the Constitution, Patrick Henry, for example, became Federalists once the party system developed. (At Washington's re-election in 1792, this nascent Republican party — also known as Democratic-Republican and Jeffersonian — was strong enough to garner 50 electoral votes for New York's George Clinton for vice president against 77 votes for John Adams.) Though Washington disliked political controversy and tried to remain above the partisan storm, he found Hamilton's ideas more congenial than Jefferson's and may properly be called a Federalist.

THE WARS OF THE FRENCH REVOLUTION

The outbreak of the French Revolution in 1789 was greeted with enthusiasm by most Americans for it confirmed their faith that their own Revolution had blazed a trail to liberty that all humanity would eventually follow. But widespread "Bastille fever" lasted only so long as the revolution in France remained relatively moderate. As the great upheaval moved into a new and more somber phase, American ardor cooled and public opinion divided sharply. The people who tended toward Federalism in domestic politics were shocked by the execution of Louis XVI and the wholesale guillotining of political opponents. When the revolutionary agitation spread to other countries, followed by French revolutionary armies, conservative Americans were driven into hysterical fears of mob rule, atheism, and Jacobinism at home. On the other hand, more democratic-minded Americans, those who tended toward Republicanism in domestic politics but often deplored the worst excesses of the "reign of terror," remained steadfast in their support of the goals of the French Revolution. Jefferson, for one, did not applaud the beheadings, but he believed that "the liberty of the whole earth" depended on the triumph of *liberté, égalité,* and *fraternité* in France. To Jefferson and his followers, the conservative reaction was proof that their Federalist opponents were really monarchists.

The French Revolution precipitated a great European war, lasting with brief interruptions from 1793 until 1815 and pitting France against a series of European coalitions headed by Great Britain. American leaders of all persuasions agreed that their infant nation should avoid becoming directly involved on either side, but there were sharp differences in sympathies. The Hamiltonians favored the British, partly because they preferred British conservatism as opposed to French radicalism and partly because the large trade with Great Britain enriched the merchant class and provided 90 percent of the tariff revenues essential to Hamiltonian financial policies. Jefferson and his friends, more sympathetic to French aims, argued that the country owed its independence to the Franco-American alliance of 1778, which was still in force, and urged a neutrality that would be benevolent toward France.

Actually France did not want to invoke the alliance to bring the United States into the war as a belligerent. The powerful British navy was sweeping French merchant ships from the seas, and the French hoped that if the United States remained neutral, American merchant ships could supply her with foodstuffs and raw materials. Britain, too, as she devoted more of her resources to war, relied increasingly on American shipping. As a result, commercial interests and producers of exports in the United States entered upon a period of unparalleled prosperity.

Washington's proclamation of American neutrality in 1793 made considerable sense economically, but it did not begin to solve all the problems created by the European war. Existing American grievances against Great Britain over the northwest posts, incitement of the northwestern Indians, and discrimination against American trade were compounded in 1794 when Great Britain moved to cripple the newly flourishing American commerce on the high seas. Determined to starve France into submission, the British navy suddenly seized some 300 American ships under newly promulgated rules that forbade neutrals to carry grain or flour to France, to carry any French-owned goods whatever, or to engage in trade with the French West

Indies. Adding insult to injury, British naval commanders began stopping American merchant ships and forcibly taking off crew members thought to have deserted from the British navy, including some American citizens.

Despite a storm of indignation, Hamilton was determined to avoid a break with Great Britain at all costs. Jefferson had already resigned in disgust at Hamilton's domination of the administration and interference in the affairs of the State Department, leaving no one in the cabinet strong enough to oppose the iron-willed treasury secretary. The only diplomatic weapon against the British the United States had was the threat to join the Armed Neutrality of smaller European trading nations that was forming to resist British restrictions on international trade. Chief Justice John Jay was sent to London to negotiate, but Hamilton undercut his mission by assuring the British minister that the United States would not join the Armed Neutrality.

As a result Jay had to accept whatever terms the British offered. The British did agree to pay indemnities for seized American shipping and to withdraw by 1796 from their posts within the northwestern boundary of the United States. In return, Jay had to agree that the United States pay old claims of British merchants against American citizens and tacitly accept the restrictive British definitions of the rights of neutrals in international trade. Not a word was said about British impressment of American sailors, British interference with the northwestern Indians, or indemnity for the slaves carried away by British armies.

Hamilton's outraged opponents charged that these terms were a humiliating surrender to British power; in the violent debate over Jay's treaty during 1795, the emerging line of division between Federalists and Republicans finally crystallized. The only alternative to accepting the treaty, argued the Hamiltonians, was war with England. Ratification of the treaty by the Senate guaranteed a return of commercial prosperity and gave the young nation a further period of freedom from European embroilments, during which it could further strengthen its independence and institutions.

In another area of diplomacy, the Washington administration was able to capitalize on Spain's involvement in the European wars to achieve a brilliant diplomatic triumph. When Spain shifted in 1795 from the British to the French side and when the Jay Treaty appeared to align the United States with Great Britain, the Spanish authorities recognized that their possessions on the southwestern border of the United States had become exceedingly vulnerable. Consequently, the American minister Thomas Pinckney had little difficulty negotiating a treaty, ratified in 1796, that granted all the American demands: the fixing of the Florida boundary at the 31st parallel, free navigation of the Mississippi and a right of "deposit" (the right to bring goods down the Mississippi and land them while awaiting oceangoing ships) at New Orleans for American citizens, and a Spanish promise to restrain the Indians along the frontier.

Thus by the end of Washington's second term, the Jay and Pinckney treaties had eased America's difficulties with two of the three European powers with which the United States was dangerously involved. Washington's policy of preserving American neutrality had strengthened the nation's independence and yet afforded it opportunities to capitalize on the involvements of European nations. Whether this policy could be pursued in the face of difficulties with a third European power, France, was the major problem facing Washington's successor, John Adams.

THE TRIALS OF JOHN ADAMS

Washington's determination to retire at the end of two terms inopportunely deprived the Federalists of their greatest political asset just as the Jay Treaty controversy unfolded. Consequently the election of 1796 was the first hard fought and closely contested presidential election. Hamilton, the "High Federalist," had made too many bitter enemies to be a successful candidate; his ultracommercial and elitist views were too extreme for many Federalist voters. Vice President John Adams, to whom the party leaders turned, represented a more moderate Federalism. The Republicans, almost without discussion, accepted Jefferson, spokesman for the agrarian-minded majority, as their candidate. After a vituperative campaign, Adams narrowly edged Jefferson, 71 electoral votes to 68. According to electoral college procedure, Jefferson became vice president, thus dividing the Adams administration. Once friends and allies, Jefferson and Adams soon became antagonists; they were only reconciled late in life, largely through Abigail Adams.

At the time of Adams's election, the French were enraged by the Jay Treaty. When they ordered seizure of American ships carrying British goods, the Hamiltonians took exception, reversing the stand they had taken when the British stopped American ships. Resisting Hamiltonian pressure, however, Adams sent a special commission of three men to Paris to try to settle the difficulties. When French officials treated the commissioners insultingly and set impossible conditions, including the demands of French agents "X, Y, and Z" for a bribe of $250,000, the commissioners allegedly cried, "Millions for defense, but not one cent for tribute." And the war spirit again flamed high in the United States. By the spring of 1798, President Adams and Congress were making preparations for war, and an undeclared naval war broke out between French and American vessels on the high seas. Yet Adams was never quite swept away by the war fever, and in early 1799, against bitter Hamiltonian opposition, he resolved to make one last effort for peace. Another three-man commission was sent to France and this time an agreement was reached that recognized American principles of neutral rights and abrogated amicably the Franco-American alliance of 1778.

John Adams must be credited with courage and disinterestedness for single-handedly resisting the war hysteria at the cost of his own popularity and the political success of his party, but there was one respect in which he went along with the Hamiltonian extremists. As in other periods of national crisis, the populace was suspicious of political dissenters and foreigners, and the Federalists regarded the Republicans as disloyal — sympathizing with, if not acting as agents of, the nation's enemies. (The ideas of free speech, a free press, and the legitimacy of partisan opposition were not yet firmly established.) In the name of national security, Adams and the Federalists capitalized on the war hysteria and the furor caused by the XYZ Affair by pushing through Congress in 1798 four measures designed in large part to crush the political opposition. Known collectively as the Alien and Sedition Acts, three of these laws lengthened from 5 to 14 years the minimum residence requirements for new citizens (a great many of whom were pro-Republican) and authorized the president to deport or imprison any alien he thought dangerous. The fourth, the Sedition Act, prescribed fines up to $5,000 and imprisonment up to five years for persons who opposed the government's measures, who promoted riots or unlawful assemblies, or who uttered, wrote, or published "any false, scandalous, and malicious" statements against the government or its officials.

No aliens were deported under these extraordinary measures, although many left the country in fear of prosecution. But partisan Federalist district attorneys and judges used the Sedition Act to secure indictments against 15 Republican newspaper editors; 10 were convicted, one of them a Vermont congressman who had printed that Adams possessed an "unbounded thirst for ridiculous pomp, foolish adulation, and selfish avarice." The congressman sought re-election while in jail and won handily.

No one was more alarmed by the Alien and Sedition Acts than civil libertarian Thomas Jefferson. To arouse popular protest, he drafted a set of resolutions and sent them to Kentucky where they were adopted by the legislature. Meanwhile, Madison secured adoption of similar resolutions by Virginia lawmakers. Claiming for the states the power to determine the constitutionality of federal law, these Kentucky and Virginia resolutions of 1798 took the position that the Alien and Sedition Acts violated the First Amendment and were therefore null and void. Although largely ignored by the other states, these resolutions became part of a tradition of southern state-rights thought that would ultimately threaten the Union.

THE "REVOLUTION" OF 1800

The Kentucky and Virginia resolutions opened the campaign for the return match between Adams and Jefferson in the presidential election of 1800. Again there was a close, hard fought contest. The Republicans had been greatly weakened by the charge of Francophilism during the war hysteria, but with the passing of the threat of war, the reaction against the Alien and Sedition Acts gave hope of a Republican comeback. Moreover, the Federalists were weakened by the increasingly rancorous split between the Adams and the Hamilton wings of the party. The death in December 1799 of Washington, the party's chief political asset and unifying presence, compounded their problems, as did popular resentment of the taxes levied to support the war-preparedness program. This time Jefferson edged Adams, 73 electoral votes to 65. Nevertheless, the election had to be decided in the House of Representatives because Jefferson's vice presidential running mate, Aaron Burr, received as many electoral votes as Jefferson. The Constitution did not as yet specify separate balloting for the two highest offices. Ironically, although the Federalist majority in the House favored the unscrupulous Burr, the "high Federalist" Hamilton gave his support to Jefferson, who won on the 36th ballot. The procedural imperfection in the Constitution was corrected in 1804 with the ratification of the Twelfth Amendment.

This "revolution of 1800" inaugurated no revolutionary change in public policy, nor even a revolutionary shift in the balance of strength between the emerging parties. In fact, it was hardly a revolution at all. But the working of the constitutional system had been transformed beyond the intention of the framers by the growth within it of a system of two opposing political parties, representing divergent constituencies, holding divergent ideologies, and proposing divergent policies. The potentially overwhelming majority of the Republicans was not yet fully mobilized for political action in pursuance of its democratic- and agrarian-minded objectives. But already that party had overcome the great initial advantages of its competitor and won a majority. Meanwhile the Federalists, though often out of tune with the awakening majority and insensitive to popular yearnings for equality and personal liberty, had given the new government a vigorous start, had avoided international war, and had turned over a thriving and intact country to the Republican party of Thomas Jefferson. Thus the principle of peaceful competition and transfer of power between parties was established.

FOR FURTHER READING

A good analysis of the political thought of the 1790s can be found in Joyce O. Appleby's *Capitalism and a New Social Order* (1984). The rise of the legitimate opposition is perceptively traced in Richard Hofstadter's *The Idea of a Party System* (1969). John C. Miller's *The Federalist Era* (1960) is a brief and sympathetic overview of the Federalists, while Stanley Elkins and Eric McKitrick offer a more comprehensive look at *The Age of Federalism* (1993). John R. Alden's *George Washington* (1984) and James T. Flexner's *George Washington and the New Nation* (1970) are excellent studies. Manning J. Dauer distinguishes between two wings of the Federalist party in *The Adams Federalists* (1953). Recent biographies of the second president include Joseph J. Ellis's *Passionate Sage* (1993) and John Ferling's *John Adams* (1992). Jacob E. Cooke has provided a brief and readable biography of *Alexander Hamilton* (1982). On the Republican side, Noble Cunningham has analyzed the development of the Republican party organization in *The Jeffersonian Republicans* (1957), and Lance Banning focuses on the evolution of party ideology in *The Jeffersonian Persuasion* (1978). John F. Hoadley has suggestively analyzed the *Origins of American*

Political Parties, 1789–1803 (1986), and sociologist Seymour M. Lipset in *The First New Nation* (1963) has made a suggestive comparison between the problems faced by American leaders in the 1790s and the problems faced by leaders of the new nations of the twentieth century. James M. Smith in *Freedom's Fetters* (1956) focuses on the Alien and Sedition Acts, and Thomas P. Slaughter explores *The Whiskey Rebellion* (1986). Charles R. Ritcheson's *Aftermath of Revolution* (1969) offers a bold interpretation of early British policy toward the United States; Daniel G. Lang explains *Foreign Policy in the Early Republic* (1985); and William C. Stinchcombe examines *The XYZ Affair* (1980).

TABLE 3.   PRESIDENTIAL ELECTIONS AND MAJOR POLITICAL EVENTS, 1800–1823

1800	**Thomas Jefferson** (Republican) elected over John Adams (Federalist).
1803	*Marbury* vs. *Madison*. John Marshall's Supreme Court declares a law of Congress unconstitutional. Louisiana Purchase.
1804	**Thomas Jefferson** (Republican) re-elected over Charles C. Pinckney (Federalist).
1804–1806	Lewis and Clark expedition.
1805–1807	Mounting seizures of American shipping under British Orders in Council and Napoleon's Decrees.
1807	*Chesapeake-Leopard* affair. Embargo Act.
1808	**James Madison** (Republican) elected over Charles C. Pinckney (Federalist).
1809	Nonintercourse Act replaces Embargo Act.
1810	Macon's Bill No. 2 replaces Nonintercourse Act.
1811	Recharter of First Bank of the United States defeated. Power of northwestern Indians broken at Tippecanoe.
1812	**James Madison** (Caucus Republican) re-elected over DeWitt Clinton (Independent Republican).
1812–1815	War of 1812.
1814–1815	Treaty of Ghent.
1816	**James Monroe** (Republican) elected over Rufus King (Federalist).
1817	Rush-Bagot Agreement with Great Britain demilitarizes the Great Lakes. Andrew Jackson invades Spanish Florida.
1818	Convention of 1818 settles outstanding differences with Great Britain.
1819–1821	Transcontinental Treaty with Spain acquires Florida.
1820	**James Monroe** (Republican) re-elected without opposition.
1823	Monroe Doctrine enunciated.

8

★ ★ ★ ★ ★ ★

The Jeffersonian Republic in a Threatening World, 1800–1823

THOMAS JEFFERSON wisely recognized the political foolhardiness, if not the practical impossibility, of trying to erase the legacy of Hamiltonian measures that he inherited. The national bank was allowed to run its course undisturbed until its 20-year charter expired in 1811, and the funded federal debt continued to be honored. Yet there was a significant shift in the tone and direction of public policy. The government had just moved to the new Washington City. In sharp reaction to the formality and ceremony that his more aristocratic predecessors had cultivated, the egalitarian Jefferson invested the muddy little capital on the Potomac with a studied casualness, an almost ostentatious simplicity. This lack of pretension symbolized his deliberately negative policy: to avoid ambitious measures, to keep the federal establishment as plain and simple as possible, to practice the most frugal economy, and to reduce as rapidly as possible the federal debt that Hamilton had apparently designed as permanent.

In taking this line, Jefferson was not only following his own agrarian and democratic preconceptions, but also proving himself a shrewd reader of the country's mood. The Hamiltonian system, for all its brilliant success, had been premature, resting on the transitory and fortuitous ascendancy of a commercial-minded minority that was out of tune with the bulk of the population. Even in the Federalist stronghold of New England, religious and sectional considerations had contributed more to that party's strength than commerical-mindedness, and the Adams brand of Federalism was more popular than the Hamilton brand. Despite a flourishing overseas commerce that was gradually pulling more farmers and planters into producing staples for market, the country as a whole remained wedded to the vision of a simple, unprogressive, democratic utopia, dominated by self-sufficient and, therefore, independent and virtuous farmers. Jefferson's reasonable behavior in office and the eloquence of his statements and policies in behalf of the agrarian, democratic ideal won him overwhelming political strength, even in New England.

During these Jeffersonian years Americans appeared to believe that their utopian republican order might endure without change forever. They failed to realize that history will not leave societies, much less utopias, alone. The only problems that most of them saw were those arising out of the continuing international conflict. These were indeed to be severe problems for Jefferson and his successor Madison and would lead ultimately to war. Yet it was not war that was to undermine the republican utopia, but the unsuspected forces of westward expansion and economic change that were already gaining momentum.

VESTIGES OF FEDERALISM

Jefferson's disciplined majorities in Congress had moved promptly to repeal the whiskey tax, the unpopular war-preparedness taxes, and the parts of the Alien and Sedition Acts that had not already expired. Those imprisoned under the latter measures were freed, and their fines were refunded. The only serious battle over remnants of Federalism arose in connection with the judiciary.

The federal courts were staffed entirely by Federalists serving for life, and some judges had conducted themselves with flagrant partisanship. In the last days of the Adams administration, the Federalists had sought to strengthen their judicial bastion with an act establishing a series of new courts, and President Adams had spent his last hours in office signing commissions for the "midnight judges" and other officials to staff the new courts. Adams had made his most important contribution to perpetuating Federalist principles a month earlier by appointing as Chief Justice of the Supreme Court John Marshall, a Virginian of the Washington rather than the Jefferson-Madison stamp, whose nationalistic ideas were to dominate the Court from 1801 until 1835.

The Republicans had no sooner assumed power than they repealed the act establishing the new courts, and Jefferson ordered Secretary of State James Madison to withhold the commissions of Adams's midnight appointees. The stage was set for a showdown when one of these appointees applied to the Supreme Court for a *writ of mandamus* ordering Madison to deliver his commission. Chief Justice Marshall's famous decision in the case of *Marbury* vs. *Madison* was handed down in 1803. Marshall knew that he had no means of forcing Madison to deliver the commission so he skillfully sidestepped a direct confrontation with the administration while he gained an advantage in another quarter. Declaring that the petitioner was entitled to his commission, he contended nevertheless that the Supreme Court was not empowered to act in this kind of case. It had been given such jurisdiction by the Judiciary Act of 1789, but Marshall argued that in this respect the Judiciary Act contradicted the constitutional definition of the Supreme Court's jurisdiction. Therefore, said Marshall, this section of the Judiciary Act was unconstitutional and consequently void. The Court for the first time asserted the power, nowhere explicitly given it, to invalidate an act of Congress on constitutional grounds.

Even before Marshall's decision, the Republicans had begun a campaign to neutralize the Federalism of the judiciary. Incensed by the prosecutions under the Sedition Act and fearful of keeping any branch of the government from popular control, Jefferson favored making the judiciary amenable to political influence. This he thought might be accomplished by congressional impeachment of the more notorious judges. The Republicans had little difficulty getting one drunken and incompetent district judge removed from office. In a key case, however, they failed to get enough votes to impeach Supreme Court Justice Samuel Chase. This failure preserved the principle of an independent judiciary and left Chief Justice Marshall free to develop the Supreme Court into a fortress of nationalistic and anti-Jeffersonian influence.

AN EMPIRE FOR LIBERTY

Early in Jefferson's administration, the exigencies of international war again presented the United States with a splendid diplomatic opportunity. Napoleon had just forced Spain to return Louisiana (in Spanish hands since 1763) to France, hoping to use it as the granary for a growing French empire in the Western Hemisphere. Under Spanish control, Louisiana had been no great threat to the United States, but the prospect of having Napoleonic France astride the Mississippi with an economic stranglehold on the whole interior of the country was another matter. Promptly, Jefferson sent James Monroe to aid the American minister in Paris, Robert R. Livingston, in securing American interests at the mouth of the Mississippi. If possible, they were to purchase the isle of New Orleans, that small portion of Louisiana that lay east of the lower Mississippi. (See map on page 109.)

By the time the negotiations opened in 1803, the collapse of the French expeditionary force in the West Indies and the resumption of the European war after a brief truce had caused Napoleon to abandon his plans for a French empire in America. To the astonishment of the American negotiators, the French offered to sell not only New Orleans but the whole of Louisiana, the entire western watershed of the Mississippi. A price of $15 million was quickly agreed upon, although the Americans were exceeding their instructions. When the news reached Washington, Jefferson, the strict constructionist, worried briefly about the lack of specific constitutional authorization for such purchases of territory, but his philosophical doubts were dissipated in his pragmatic enthusiasm for so vast an extension of his agrarian "empire for liberty." Advising Congress to ratify quickly lest Napoleon change his mind, Jefferson seemed to embrace the Hamiltonian doctrine of implied powers.

Even before the Louisiana Purchase was consummated, Jefferson had evinced his interest in the western country by beginning preparations for the exploration led by Meriwether Lewis and William Clark. Between 1804 and 1806, Lewis and Clark's party ascended the Missouri River to its sources, crossed the Rocky Mountains, and descended the Columbia River to the Pacific, returning with a wealth of information about the vast domain the United States had acquired.

During these years, a strong tide of migration was running westward out of the original states; the line of regular settlement had not yet reached the Mississippi River. The first of the new states (Vermont, 1791; Kentucky, 1792; Tennessee, 1796; and Ohio, 1803) were becoming populous common-wealths, while the French-Spanish settlements around New Orleans were attracting sufficient immigrants from the older states to enter the Union as the state of Louisiana in 1812.

Thomas Jefferson and his party showed a special solicitude for the agrar-ian, democratic West. One demonstration of this solicitude was the provision made that a percentage of the public land proceeds from the new state of Ohio would be used to construct a great National Road from Cumberland, Maryland, on the Potomac River across the mountains to Wheeling, Vir-ginia, on the Ohio. From there, the National Road was eventually extended through Ohio and Indiana and surveyed as far as St. Louis.

The new western states returned Jefferson's solicitude with overwhelming support for the Republican party. And so, increasingly, did the other states. In 1804, Jefferson was elected to a second term by a resounding victory over Charles Cotesworth Pinckney, 162 electoral votes to 14.

THE PERILS OF NEUTRALITY

During Jefferson's second administration the European war entered a more desperate phase. Napoleon's authority was extending over the whole of con-tinental Europe, while the British were achieving unchallenged supremacy on the high seas. As the great land power and the great naval power moved into their final mortal struggle, each increasingly sought to cripple the other through economic warfare, and Americans, the leading neutral traders, were caught in the middle.

Out of self-interest and principle the United States had asserted an ad-vanced doctrine of neutral rights, claiming the right to trade unmolested with all belligerents. This doctrine had been tenable in connection with the limited warfare of the sixteenth and seventeenth centuries, and it was sup-ported by the code of international law that won considerable acceptance during that period. But the wars of the French Revolution brought a new kind of general warfare, precursor of the total war of the twentieth century, ranging populations against populations. This new warfare was waged by mass armies with sweeping ideological and nationalistic objectives, in place of the earlier small professional armies seeking limited national goals.

Under these circumstances, it was not realistic to expect belligerents to respect the doctrines of neutral rights that the United States sought to maintain. The Federalists had earlier recognized the realities of the world power situation in accepting Jay's Treaty as an alternative to war. Faced with these same realities, Jefferson was just as anxious as the Federalists had been to avoid American involvement in the war but more reluctant to compromise American principles of neutral rights. Believing that the belligerents needed American trade too much to risk war with the United States, he embarked on the difficult task of using American commerce (the strength of which he overestimated) as a weapon to coerce the belligerents into respecting neutral rights.

During Jefferson's first administration, American shippers had been able to pile up such tremendous profits as to more than offset their losses from seizures under the temporarily relaxed British and French restrictions. But in 1805, in the *Essex* case, the British admiralty courts outlawed the most lucrative part of this trade, involving goods shipped from the French West Indies to France by way of the United States. This was but the first in a series of British decisions blockading Europe to stem the flow of commodities useful to the French war effort. As a result, seizures of American shipping mounted alarmingly. Even more intolerable to American pride was an increase in British impressments of sailors from American ships.

Congress responded in 1805 by barring certain British goods from American ports, and the Jefferson administration sought to use this Nonimportation Act as a counter in negotiations in London. The British were willing to relax their restrictions on the French West Indian trade, but since they refused to renounce altogether the right of impressment, Jefferson would not submit the resulting treaty to the Senate for ratification. British indignities culminated in 1807 when the British naval vessel *Leopard* opened fire on the unsuspecting American naval vessel *Chesapeake*, stopped her, and at cannon's mouth impressed four seamen.

Like Adams before him, Jefferson had to resist the clamor for war, meanwhile pushing through Congress the Embargo Act of 1807. This extreme measure of economic coercion forbade American ships to sail for Europe. Jefferson hoped, of course, to force the British to terms by denying them desperately needed American goods and shipping. Unfortunately the effects of the embargo were felt more severely by American commercial and exporting interests than they were by the British. New England, its economy prostrate and its people bitter, moved back into the Federalist orbit. Finally even Jefferson concluded, just before he left office in the spring of 1809, that the embargo could no longer be sustained. Congress repealed the act, and it was left to James Madison to seek some better solution to the prickly problem of neutral rights.

MADISON TRIES HIS HAND

By the time of Madison's election, French depredations on American commerce were becoming as serious as those by the British. Napoleon had responded to the British blockade of the Continent with a series of decrees declaring the British Isles blockaded. Though he did not have the naval power to enforce a blockade, he could and did order the seizure of American ships reaching French ports after having submitted to British regulations. Such seizures reached wholesale proportions early in the Madison administration.

Shifting from one expedient of economic coercion to another, Madison and his congressional followers tried supplanting the embargo with a Nonintercourse Act (1809), freeing American shippers to trade with all nations except France and England and promising to resume trade with whichever of these nations would first remove its restrictions. Profits of trade were so high, however, that American shippers preferred to take their chances on the British and French trade even under the restrictions, and in 1810 Congress supplanted the Nonintercourse Act with a measure known as Macon's Bill No. 2. This overingenious measure reopened the whole world to American trade but declared that whenever either of the major belligerents rescinded its restrictions on neutral shipping, nonintercourse would be reinvoked against the other.

American embarrassment was compounded by the pathetic eagerness of the Madison administration to seize upon any indication that its policy of economic coercion was working. Under the Nonintercourse Act, the president used favorable negotiation with a too pliable British minister as a pretext for announcing resumption of trade with Great Britain, only to have to eat his words when the British minister's work was disavowed in London. Napoleon exploited Macon's Bill No. 2 with even greater cynicism. A carefully ambiguous French promise to rescind the obnoxious decrees against neutral shipping hoodwinked Madison into reinvoking nonintercourse against Great Britain, whereupon the French resumed seizing American ships.

Thus by 1811, the pacific, agrarian-minded diplomacy of economic coercion had been tried in every way that could be imagined, all to no avail. The nation had never seemed so powerless to avert indignities, and the only alternatives seemed to be humiliating submission or war.

THE WAR OF 1812

Submission was utterly unacceptable to a remarkable group of vigorous young men who were elected to the Congress that convened in December 1811, and who came to be known as the War Hawks. Led by the captivating Henry Clay of Kentucky and the intellectually impressive John C. Calhoun of South Carolina, the War Hawks represented a new generation of Repub-

lican politicians who were eager to wrest leadership from the tired hands of
Madison and his dispirited companions of the Revolutionary generation.

These new Republicans were nationalistic, not only in their patriotic love
of country but also in their freedom from the agrarian localism that animated
the companions of Jefferson. This was especially true of Clay, whose Kentucky Bluegrass constituency had been drawn into flourishing hemp production for the international market by way of New Orleans, and Calhoun,
whose South Carolina up-country was undergoing a heady transformation
into a land of cotton plantations. Such areas of recent economic boom shared
the cosmopolitanism, progressivism, and nationalism of the older commercial-minded areas and might be characterized as agrarian-commercial in
spirit; they were increasingly emanating a new style of Republican
nationalism.

It was no accident that the advocates for the agrarian-commercial areas
were War Hawks in 1811 and 1812. In the older, strictly commercial areas
of the Northeast, merchants and shipowners could run the risk of British
and French seizures and still make great profits; they opposed both the Republican measures of economic coercion and the talk of war. But in the agrarian-commercial enclaves of the South and West, exhilarating booms had
been stalled by the disorganization of international trade. As loyal Republicans, people in these areas had been willing to give the policies of economic
coercion a trial, but their patience had run out. Only war could save the
national honor and enable the march of progress and prosperity to resume.

Embarrassingly, Great Britain and France had been equally obnoxious,
and the United States could hardly take on both. There were special reasons
for hostility to Great Britain. The British officials in Canada were thought to
have encouraged Indian unrest in the Old Northwest and the organization
of an ominous Indian confederacy, headed by Tecumseh and his brother the
Prophet, to oppose the advance of American settlement. Though a frontier
army destroyed Tecumseh's power at Tippecanoe in 1811, the bumptious
Republicans of the Ohio Valley clamored for the conquest of Canada.

Similarly southwestern Americans were calling for the conquest of Spanish Florida, and Spain was again allied with Great Britain in the European
war. Through Spanish Florida ran the rivers on which the people of the
Georgia, Alabama, and Mississippi country depended for trade. The Spanish
authorities were also suspected of encouraging Indian hostility, and their
territory was a haven for the runaway slaves of the Americans. The United
States asserted a doubtful claim under the Louisiana Purchase to West Florida, roughly the territory between Mobile Bay and New Orleans. Already
by 1810, the Madison administration had taken advantage of a "revolution"
by immigrants from the United States to annex part of this area. War with
Great Britain would provide an opportunity to complete the conquest of
Florida.

Thus the stalling of economic booms in several agrarian-commercial areas,
resentment of British tampering with the Indians, and a desire for Canada
and Florida made the war fever especially intense in a great arc running

along the frontier from northern New England out through Kentucky and Tennessee to South Carolina and Georgia. Yet more important than any of these specific grounds for war was the widespread desire, especially among younger Republicans of the War Hawk stripe, to avenge the national honor and dignity. The callous impressments of American sailors made Great Britain the inevitable enemy.

By the spring of 1812, the Madison administration, not knowing what else to do, was ready to go along with the agitation for war. In June, on the President's recommendation, a declaration of war was pushed through a seriously divided Congress. Two days before the declaration, the British government in London decided to repeal all its restrictions on neutral trade. The Republican diplomacy of economic coercion had finally accomplished its purpose. The moralistic Republican diplomacy that had escalated issues of commercial rights and neutral rights to a question of national honor had left no alternative to war.

The War of 1812 was a military debacle. But for British preoccupation with Napoleon, it would have been an utter disaster. Feeble administration in Washington and feebler generalship in the field brought defeat after defeat. Grandiose western boasts about the easy conquest of Canada eventuated in the surrender of the American army at Detroit. In 1814, the defeat of Napoleon enabled the British to pay serious attention to the American war. One invading army easily captured Washington and burned the public buildings. Another, marching down from Canada to cut the country in two along the line of the Hudson, would have succeeded if its timid general had not been unduly discouraged by the success of a small American flotilla in maintaining naval control of Lake Champlain along his line of march. A final formidable force, fresh from victories over Napoleon, was sent to seize New Orleans with the aim of wresting much of the West from the United States. This seasoned army was annihilated by Andrew Jackson and his western militia in the only significant American triumph of the war. Americans were able to take pride in the naval victories of individual ships, but these could not prevent the mighty British navy from establishing unquestioned control of the seas along the American coasts.

Much of the American weakness arose from internal dissension. Southerners had little enthusiasm for the conquest of Canada, and Northerners had little for the conquest of Florida. The whole war was bitterly opposed in commercial areas, especially New England. New England banks and capitalists would not lend money to rescue the bankrupt federal treasury, the New England governors refused to supply troops, and in December 1814, a convention of the New England states met at Hartford to seek redress against the tyranny of the federal government. Some participants advocated the secession of New England, but the more moderate majority contented itself with proposing constitutional amendments that would protect the interests of their section.

The war had hardly started when the Madison administration began efforts to end it, but it was 1814 before a group of British and American commissioners got down to negotiating in earnest at Ghent in Belgium. The treaty they finally agreed on in December simply restored the state of things existing at the beginning of the war without mention of neutral rights, impressment, or any of the other questions that had been in dispute between the two countries. The United States escaped without loss of territory only because the British were too war weary at the end of their long struggle with Napoleon to go on fighting. Indeed, had the British defeated Jackson as expected at New Orleans in January 1815, two weeks after the peace terms were agreed upon at Ghent, they would probably have insisted on territorial concessions before ratifying the treaty.

THE CENTURY OF SECURITY

However ignominious the War of 1812 seemed at the time, the independence of the United States was not really secure until it had been fought and, by great good luck, the country had survived. Thus began a century such as no other western nation has ever had the good fortune to enjoy, a century in which the United States would develop free from any external threat.

This security was guaranteed primarily by British domination of the seas. By the end of the War of 1812, Great Britain was ready to accept the permanence of the United States and to look for advantage in encouraging trade between the two countries. Seeing great commercial opportunities throughout the Americas, British ministries observed with satisfaction the crumbling of the Spanish Empire, the last great colonial empire in the New World, and resisted any efforts by other European powers to extend their influence across the Atlantic.

This happy turn in British-American relations was signaled by the amicable settlement of the outstanding questions between the two countries shortly after the War of 1812. The Rush-Bagot Agreement of 1817 provided for demilitarization of the Great Lakes, and in the Convention of 1818, American fishing rights in Canadian waters were specified, the northern boundary of the United States was set at the 49th parallel from the head of the Mississippi to the Rocky Mountains, and the two countries agreed to joint occupation of the Oregon country beyond the Rockies for a period of ten years. In 1827 the joint occupation agreement was extended indefinitely until such time as either nation should give a year's notice for terminating the arrangement.

The Anglo-American rapprochement facilitated another diplomatic achievement of this period: the liquidation of American difficulties with Spain through the acquisition of Florida. After acquiring West Florida as far east as the Pearl River (the area now a part of the state of Louisiana) through "revolution" in 1810, the Madison administration took advantage of the war to annex, in 1813, another chunk extending beyond Mobile Bay east to the Perdido River (the coastal areas of the present states of Mississippi and Alabama). Following the war, Spain was wracked by political turmoil at home and revolution in her South American colonies. Forays on American territory by Florida Indians intensified southwestern demands for annexation and furnished the pretext that Spain was not living up to her obligations under Pinckney's Treaty. When Andrew Jackson was sent to pacify the Indians along the Florida border in 1817, he moved on into Florida and seized the whole northern Gulf Coast area.

The administration in Washington could not sanction this rash and unauthorized occupation, but Secretary of State John Quincy Adams (son of President John Adams) finally persuaded his Cabinet colleagues that Jackson should not be censured. Instead Adams told the Spaniards that the incident revealed their inability to maintain their treaty obligations along the Florida boundary, indicating the propriety of ceding Florida to the United States. Under this implied threat of forcible seizure, Spain yielded. By a treaty signed in 1819 but not ratified until 1821, Florida was ceded to the United States in exchange for the sum of $5 million. In the process, the Americans won undisputed control of the territory to the Rocky Mountains as well as a window on the Pacific. Sometimes called the Transcontinental Treaty, this remarkable agreement defined the boundary between the United States and the Spanish possessions to the southwest as running from the Gulf of Mexico up the Sabine River (the western boundary of the state of Louisiana), then west and north of the Rockies, then west along the 42nd parallel to the Pacific coast. The Florida treaty was consummated during the administration of James Monroe, who had succeeded Madison in 1817.

During his presidency, Monroe defined America's diplomatic position of hemispheric separation and avoidance of foreign entanglements. Called the Monroe Doctrine, the policy was declared in the president's last message to Congress in December 1823. He asserted that the American continents were no longer open to colonization by European powers, and he warned against any European interference in the revolutionary new nations of Latin America and against extension of European political systems into the Americas. In return for such nonintervention, the president pledged the United States to noninterference in the "internal concerns" of Europe. An expression of self-confident American nationalism, Monroe's unilateral declaration recognized the existence of spheres of influence and, by implication, claimed one in Latin America for the United States.

In part, recent scholarship suggests, the document was the product of domestic politics, of Secretary of State John Quincy Adams's concern with the forthcoming presidential elections. But international considerations very likely predominated. The noncolonization declaration was prompted by an expansion of the spheres of Russian activity down the northwest American coast from Alaska, and in 1824, the Russians agreed to limit their interests to the area north of 54°40', leaving the United States and Great Britain as the only claimants of the Oregon country between that line and the Spanish-Mexican boundary at 42°.

The *nonintervention* statement in the Monroe Doctrine was prompted by the fear that major European powers might unite to subdue Spain's rebellious American colonies and by the growing American commercial interests in Latin American markets. Great Britain also opposed European takeover and intervention in Latin America, so earlier the British foreign secretary had suggested that the United States join his country in opposing such action. But Secretary of State Adams and Monroe decided that the United States should act independently. But, in fact, it was British seapower that enforced the policy, not American. The doctrine had little effect in the short term. Though irritated by this "arrogant" American "blustering," the European powers had no enthusiasm for the reconquest of Spanish America against British opposition. But the doctrine did clarify the American view of the relationship between the Old World and the New, and it expressed the U.S. claim of dominance in the Western Hemisphere. Although it had no standing in treaty arrangements or international law — and was forgotten after its declaration for a generation — the Monroe Doctrine remains a cornerstone of twentieth-century American foreign policy.

CONFLICTING HISTORICAL VIEWPOINTS: NO. 3

What Caused the War of 1812?

The American war cry of 1812, "Free trade and sailors' rights," moved the eccentric Virginian John Randolph to quip: "Men shall not live by bread alone, but mostly by catchphrases." The phrase nevertheless appealed to the people of Randolph's generation, who believed that the second Anglo-American war was fought for national honor and neutral maritime rights. With their president, James Madison, they traced the origins of conflict to "the continued British practice of violating the American flag on the great highway of nations, and of carrying off persons sailing under it." Actually, in his war message to Congress, Madison had mentioned other causes as well, but the maritime interpretation captured the American imagination. Throughout the century, lay persons and scholars alike believed that British commercial interference lay at the heart of the conflict. Historians as diverse as John Bach McMaster (History of the People of the United States, 8 vols., 1883–1913) *and Alfred T. Mahan* (Sea Power in Its Relation to the War of 1812, 1905) *stressed impressment of sailors, interruption of trade, and the Royal Navy's blockade. Even Henry Adams* (History of the United States, 9 vols., 1889–1891), *who found the exclusive emphasis on maritime matters oversimple, offered only a slightly modified version.*

Following World War I, however, a generation of scholars, disillusioned by the failures of American wartime idealism, looked for causes less lofty than patriotism and principle. For example, Louis Hacker (Mississippi Valley Historical Review, *March 1924), then an economic determinist, identified conflict in the War Hawks' lust for Canadian land. Julius Pratt* (The Expansionists of 1812, 1925), *on the other hand, emphasized southern yearnings for the Floridas and a western desire to drive Britain from Canada as a solution to the Indian problem. A third scholar, George Taylor* (Journal of Political Economy, 1931), *linked westerners to seaboard grievances by noting that the farmers of the interior, hardly less than New England merchants, were economically dependent on foreign trade.*

More recently, pocketbook and sectional considerations have fallen from favor. After World War II, during a period of domestic conservatism and

Cold War, a number of scholars returned to arguments of national honor and free seas. Bradford Perkins (Prologue to War, 1961), Reginald Horsman (The Causes of the War of 1812, 1962), and Norman Risjord (William and Mary Quarterly, April 1961), with varying degrees of emphasis, led us back to the maritime causes stressed by nineteenth-century historians. Indeed, most historians today agree that England's policies of impressment and commercial restriction left its former colonies with but two alternatives: submission or war. As Risjord put it, "War was the only alternative to national humiliation and disgrace."

FOR FURTHER READING

Henry Adams's *History of the United States During the Administrations of Jefferson and Madison* (9 vols., 1889–1891) is a classic of American historical writing. Much material that has come to light since Adams wrote is utilized in two distinguished multivolume biographies: Irving Brant, *James Madison* (6 vols., 1941–1961), and Dumas Malone, *Jefferson and His Time* (6 vols., 1948–1981). Merrill D. Peterson's *Thomas Jefferson and the New Nation* (1970) is an excellent one-volume biography; Marshall Smelser's *The Democratic Republic* (1968) views Jefferson as a "Whiggish moderate"; Noble Cunningham's *In Pursuit of Reason* (1987) examines Jefferson's political career; Forrest McDonald's *The Presidency of Thomas Jefferson* (1976) offers a latter-day Hamiltonian critique; and Leonard Levy's *Jefferson and Civil Liberties* (1963) savagely explores "the darker side" of the sage's life. Noble Cunningham has written a study of *The Jeffersonian Republicans in Power* (1963); Drew McCoy's *The Elusive Republic* (1980) examines the political economy of Jeffersonian America; and Richard E. Ellis's *The Jeffersonian Crisis* (1971) carefully analyzes judicial politics and reform in the young republic. David H. Fischer's *The Revolution of American Conservatism* (1965) probes Federalist efforts to adapt to a more popular style of politics; Robert L. Clinton explains *Marbury v. Madison and Judicial Review* (1989); and Linda K. Kerber's *Federalist in Dissent* (1970) assesses Federalist ideology in the period of Republican ascendancy. For the Lewis and Clark expedition and western development during the Jeffersonian era, see Stephen Ambrose's *Undaunted Courage* (1996) and Gary E. Moulton's edition of *The Journals of the Lewis and Clark Expedition* (7 vols., 1986–1991). On the coming of the War of 1812, see J. C. A. Stagg's *Mr. Madison's War* (1983) and Roger Brown's *The Republic in Peril: 1812* (1964). Donald R. Hickey's *The War of 1812* (1989) is a good general history of the conflict. The Treaty of Ghent and postwar diplomacy are splendidly delineated in Samuel Flagg Bemis's *John Quincy Adams and the Foundations of American Foreign Policy* (1949); Dexter Perkins's *A History of the Monroe Doctrine* (1955) is the standard account of that subject; and Ernest R. May's *The Making of the Monroe Doctrine* (1975) emphasizes the role of domestic politics in external policy. R. David Edmonds explains *Tecumseh and the Quest for Indian Leadership* (1984), while Laurel Thatcher Ulrich, in *A Midwife's Tale* (1990), uses the richly detailed diary of one woman to paint a vivid portrait of the lives of women in the early republic.

MAP 3:   WESTWARD EXPANSION, 1800–1860

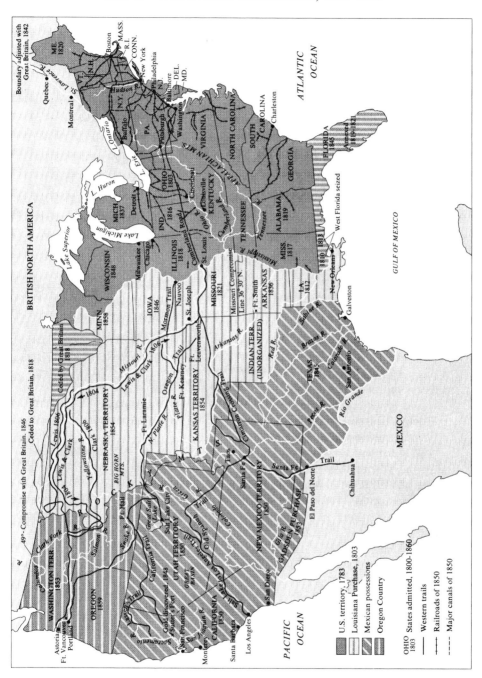

9

★ ★ ★ ★ ★ ★

The Market versus the Agrarian Republic, 1800s–1850s

THE CENTURY of Security into which the Republican leaders ushered the country was also a century of exceptional growth and development in the United States. Freedom from all entanglements with the Old World, except a free and peaceful trade, was deemed essential to the simple, and therefore virtuous republic that Jefferson and his colleagues sought to perfect. Yet this freedom and security helped to foster a spirit of enterprise and rapid change that undermined the agrarian ideal.

The spirit and direction of American life became so strikingly different after the War of 1812 that the period around 1815 must be regarded as a major turning point in American history. The change was not quite so abrupt as it may appear — war has a way of temporarily damming up latent tendencies in a society and accelerating others so that they all seem to burst forth at the end of the conflict and as a result of it. In this case, economic changes were primary.

THE MARKET REVOLUTION

The American economy has developed through three main stages: the staple-exporting, national market, and industrial stages. The economy of the colonial period was a *staple-exporting economy*, in which people either concentrated on production of tobacco, grain, and other staples for overseas markets or on the carrying trade, or were largely self-sufficing in their economic activities. About the middle of the eighteenth century, population flowed heavily into the interior where poor transportation prevented staple production, and the self-sufficing sector of the economy began to grow relative to the staple-exporting and, therefore, commercial sector. This development set the stage for the struggle between commercial-mindedness and agrarian-mindedness in the last quarter of the century.

From the viewpoint of economic development, the important thing about the staple-exporting economy was its static quality, its lack of any tendency to self-acceleration or change. The overseas markets for American staples were seriously disturbed by the Revolution, and with the steady growth of the self-sufficing sector toward the end of the century, the economy was becoming, if anything, more set in its ways. This unprogressive, staple-exporting economy with its sizeable self-sufficing sector supported the stable agrarian utopia of Thomas Jefferson.

How, then, did this economy become a dynamic *industrial economy?* The "industrial revolution" that brought factories, large-scale enterprises, and rapid technological change did not really gain full momentum in the United States until after the Civil War. But the critical shift in the pace, direction, and spirit of the economy had occurred decades before as a result of the "market revolution," which brought most American economic activity into the orbit of an intricately intermeshed national market system. Between the *staple-exporting economy* of the eighteenth century and the *industrial economy* of the late nineteenth century there intervened a *national market economy*, which did not until the 1850s become significantly industrial.

The essence of the market revolution was a vast extension of the division of labor or, in other words, specialization of economic activities. Areas and individuals who had formerly been self-sufficing or who had engaged in mixed enterprises began to concentrate on the one product or service they could produce most efficiently, selling it for money and then buying with that money the other goods and services they needed. Areas and individuals engaged formerly in only barter or limited local trade were inexorably drawn into a national and international market system, linked together by the mysterious mechanisms of money and credit. Overnight the resulting gains in efficiency and productivity jolted the formerly static economy into rapid growth. And it was in this atmosphere of rapid growth and ready profits that an economically conservative population became deeply infected with the spirit of enterprise, progress, and economic individualism.

The market revolution seemed to spring full blown from the War of 1812. With a staple-starved Europe paying high prices for American products, a long dammed-up flood of European imports pouring into American harbors, and settlers swarming over the newly opened lands of the West, the country was swept into an unprecedented four-year boom (1815–1818). Lured by high profits and easy credit into venturing their all on enterprises ranging from farms to steamboats, countless Americans were drawn for the first time into the money-market nexus. This spectacular boom ended in the even more spectacular bust of 1819 and the depression of the 1820s, to be followed by another boom-bust cycle in the 1830s.

The short-term boom-bust cycle of 1815–1819 arose immediately out of war and peace, but it had roots in the market revolution and in the greater interdependence of the economy that the market revolution produced. The market revolution itself was rooted in certain long-term developments that began before, and continued long after the War of 1812. One of these was the accumulation of investment capital from the high profits of the American carrying trade during the Napoleonic Wars. Others will be discussed in the following sections.

THE ADVANCE TO THE MISSISSIPPI

A major stimulus to the growth of the American economy after 1815 was the rapid settlement and economic development of the West up to, and across the Mississippi River. Much of this area was not open to settlement until William Henry Harrison destroyed the Indian power in the Old Northwest and Andrew Jackson crushed the Creeks and Cherokees of the southwestern areas during the War of 1812. Following the war, the broken tribes yielded to repeated demands for additional cessions of territory. In the 1820s, John C. Calhoun, Monroe's secretary of war, inaugurated a policy of resettling the remaining Indians beyond the Missouri River, and by the middle 1830s, this objective had been substantially accomplished.

With the return of peace in 1815, a flood of settlers poured west to take up rich lands under the liberal Harrison Land Act of 1800. A tract of as little as 160 acres could be bought for $2.00 an acre, with a minimum down payment of 50 cents an acre and four years to pay the remaining $1.50. Overnight, great plantations appeared on the fertile river lands of Alabama and Mississippi as planters from the worn soils of eastern Virginia, the Carolinas, and Georgia moved west with slaves, stock, and plantation gear. Along the line of the Mohawk Valley and the Great Lakes came a torrent of refugees from the stony hill farms of northern and western New England, blanketing the productive plains of northern Ohio, Indiana, and Illinois with townships, churches, and school houses on the New England pattern. The older western states of Kentucky and Tennessee became thickly settled, and from them and from farther south and east a stream of immigrants moved into southern Ohio, Indiana, and Illinois, establishing a pattern of life that differed from the New England-based style in the northern sections of those states.

During the boom years, this migration attained staggering proportions. Annual federal land sales, which had risen from 67,800 acres in 1800 to over 500,000 acres in 1813, abruptly shot to 1,306,400 acres in 1815 and reached a peak of 3,491,000 acres in 1818. Even during the depressed 1820s, the tide continued to run strongly. The population of the country beyond the Appalachians doubled between 1810 and 1820 and again between 1820 and 1830. In quick succession, five new states came to be: Indiana (1816), Mississippi (1817), Illinois (1818), Alabama (1819), and Missouri (1821). The typical western migrant was no solitude-loving Daniel Boone, but a person of enterprise, bent on self-improvement through shrewd investment, hard work, and a ride on a rising market. The market revolution in its early stages fostered the western boom that stimulated migration, and the great migration in turn accelerated the market revolution.

COMMERCIAL AGRICULTURE

The most important feature of the market revolution was the spectacular expansion of commercial agricultural production, with cotton leading the way. The development in England during the latter part of the eighteenth century of machinery that could manufacture cotton cloth cheaply had created a heavy demand for cotton. Cotton production was restricted for a time by the difficulty of separating the fibers from the seeds, but after Eli Whitney perfected in 1793 a gin that performed this task, cotton plantations mushroomed across the interior of Georgia and South Carolina. Checked for a time by the embargo and the War of 1812, the cotton boom roared ahead with the return of peace and the opening of the rich southwestern lands to cultivation. Production rose from 146,000 bales in 1814 to 209,000 bales in 1815 and 349,000 bales in 1819. Within a few years after 1815, a wide belt extending from North Carolina around to Louisiana had been converted into the world's largest cotton-producing area, and cotton was the country's leading export.

Unlike the staple-exporting sector of the colonial economy, the new cotton sector was intimately tied to the national as well as the international market system. The bulk of the cotton shipped from New Orleans, Mobile, and Charleston went to Europe, much of it by way of northeastern ports, especially New York. The crop's proceeds paid for European imports that found their way back to all parts of the United States through northeastern mercantile houses. Importations from Europe were financed to a great extent through the services of merchants in the Northeast in shipping and selling the South's cotton crop, through the South's purchases of northeastern manufactures, and through the foodstuffs and livestock shipped by the farmers in the Northwest to southern cotton planters. For some decades after 1815, the ever-mounting cotton exports were the most important factor in the economy's growth.

Cotton production was merely the biggest segment of an expanding commercial agriculture. Tobacco cultivation in the old tidewater area of Virginia and Maryland never recovered from its post-Revolution slump, but new tobacco belts developed along the North Carolina-Virginia border and in sections of Kentucky, Tennessee, and Missouri. Not until the 1840s, however, did tobacco production flourish and become highly profitable. Rice culture benefited from improved seed selection and methods of cultivation, but did not expand beyond its long-established locale in the coastal region of South Carolina and Georgia. The development of an improved variety of ribbon cane fostered a booming sugar-plantation economy in Louisiana following the War of 1812; hemp, used especially for baling cotton, afforded a similarly profitable commercial crop for areas in Kentucky and Missouri.

While the great export staples were concentrated in the South, other sections were not lacking in an extensive commercial agriculture produced at first for the national market. Areas of commercial wheat production expanded steadily west from Pennsylvania's Susquehanna Valley to New York's Mohawk and Genesee valleys to Ohio, Indiana, and Illinois. In the decade after 1815 a mounting stream of wheat, flour, corn, pork, beef, and livestock began pouring from the Old Northwest into the East and South. Cincinnati became the country's leading center of flour milling and meat packing, and by the 1840s the flood of cheap wheat and flour from the fertile Northwest was becoming a major item in American exports to Europe.

Farmers on the less productive soils of the Northeast, forced out of cereal and meat production by the cheap western products, turned to producing perishables — fruits, vegetables, poultry, and dairy products — for the growing eastern cities. Improved breeds of wool-bearing sheep and increased demand from an expanding woolens industry made wool production a profitable enterprise in many parts of the Northeast as well as the Northwest.

Thus within a brief space of time, mainly following the War of 1812, countless self-sufficing or general farmers had responded to the lure of cash returns held out by a mushrooming national and international market system and were concentrating on those staples that they could produce most efficiently. Little of this would have occurred, however, had it not become possible to transport bulky products cheaply from one part of the country to another.

THE ONSET OF INDUSTRIALIZATION

Commercial agricultural products did not represent the only bulky items requiring transportation; as the century wore on, manufactured items grew in volume. But during the first quarter of the nineteenth century, despite the early appearance of cotton textile mills and iron works in New England and Pennsylvania, most American manufacturing was still of the domestic variety — spinning, weaving, shoemaking, hatmaking, and countless other enterprises carried on in the homes, mills, or small shops of artisans who marketed their goods locally. Thereafter, though independent craftsmen survived longer in some trades than in others, household manufacture declined rapidly, as factory growth, development of modern transportation, and a spreading market economy sped the transition from hand to machine production.

The movement from domestic manufactures to the factory system came first to the Northeast. Lacking the fertile soil required for successful, large-scale agriculture and blessed with ready access to raw materials, a growing home market, and an abundance of water power, Yankee merchant-investors (particularly New Englanders) turned easily from commerce to manufacturing. Thus, the American factory had its beginning in 1790 at the cotton-spinning mill of Almy, Brown, and Slater in Pawtucket, Rhode Island. The mill, powered by waterwheel, was based on British technology pirated by the gifted mechanic and immigrant Samuel Slater, and produced cotton yarn for markets throughout New England and the middle states. Soon there were a number of these small enterprises putting out their yarn to individuals to be woven into cloth on hand looms in their homes. When imports of English cloth were cut off during the War of 1812, the infant American textile industry expanded to meet the demand.

In Waltham, Massachusetts, in 1813, Francis Cabot Lowell's Boston Manufacturing Company introduced the first successful American power loom and built the world's first self-sufficient textile plant, which brought all steps in cotton cloth production under one roof. The rapidly expanding firm marketed its coarse sheeting nationally and soon opened factories in the new town of Lowell, where women operated the machines. The "Lowell System" employed unmarried Yankee farm girls in their late teens and early twenties, who lived in comfortable but tightly regulated surroundings. The women worked long hours (72 per week) for low wages ($2.50 to $3.00 per week, less room and board). Never the "philanthropical manufacturing college" it was often called, the Lowell experiment in industrial paternalism was briefly imitated and widely celebrated. But it was shortly abandoned by cost-conscious managers, who turned in the 1840s to cheaper, more compliant, and abundant, unskilled immigrants for laborers.

Periodic depressions (1819, 1837, 1857) caused working conditions to worsen steadily not only in Lowell, the "Manchester of America," but throughout New England's textile industry. As competition for jobs mounted with the rising numbers of immigrants, and demand for cotton cloth fluctuated with the business cycle, managers came to regard workers as commodities to be bought at the lowest price. Production rates increased, factories became more dangerous places to work, hours were extended, and wages were slashed below already low levels. By the 1840s the drab and blighted factory town, once thought to be a post–Civil War development, was already a fixture of New England life. A substantial urban industrial class — including not only women but a growing number of children — was already inured to the rigorous demands of machines. Even as Alexis de Tocqueville was celebrating the principle of equality in America, the cities of the Northeast were marked by growing inequality between classes, especially as the pre-industrial artisan class began to decline to wage-earner status.

The textile factory system found ready application: first in woolen goods and then by the 1850s in clocks, firearms, farm implements, footware (rubber and leather), glass, iron, sewing machines, and other consumer goods. Deriving power successively from the waterwheel, the water turbine, and after 1860 the steam engine, these industries were based on the nation's uniquely rich natural resources and on borrowed British technology, particularly machine-tool technology. But Yankee ingenuity must not be discounted. Much of the nation's initial industrial success, perhaps even its ultimate economic leadership, can be traced to early mastery of manufacturing principles essential to mass-production. Based on the late eighteenth-century innovations of Delaware flour miller Oliver Evans and Massachusetts inventor Eli Whitney, the so-called American system of continuous-process manufacture (assembly-line production) and interchangeable parts became the model of the industrial world.

THE CONQUEST OF DISTANCE

So important were the dramatic improvements in transportation facilities in the early nineteenth century that some historians have called the market revolution a transportation revolution. Like the great westward migration, the transportation revolution was part cause and part effect of the broader market revolution.

During the colonial period, production for market had been confined to areas along navigable waterways, and at the beginning of the nineteenth century, almost the only other transportation was by wagon or pack team over primitive dirt roads. As late as 1816, a ton of goods could be shipped 3,000 miles from England for what it cost to transport the same goods 30 miles overland in America. The cost of moving a bushel of wheat from Buffalo to New York City in 1817 was three times the market value; the cost of moving corn was six times the market value for corn; and the cost for oats was twelve times the market value. Cheaper transportation was an obvious prerequisite to a national market economy.

The first attempts to solve the problem were through improved roads. In 1794 a company chartered by the Pennsylvania legislature opened between Lancaster and Philadelphia the first major turnpike, or graded and paved road on which tolls were charged. So dramatically did it lower wagoning rates and stimulate commercial development and so profitable did it prove that a wave of turnpike construction followed. By the War of 1812, most major cities in the Northeast were connected by turnpikes; after the war the turnpike craze reached its peak and spread into the West. One major turnpike led west from Baltimore to Cumberland, Maryland; from here, the federal government began constructing the National Road. By 1818 this great highway had reached Wheeling, Virginia, on the Ohio River, and by 1833 it extended to Columbus, Ohio. The National Road quickly became a major artery of east-west trade, while elsewhere the turnpikes reduced transportation costs and brought previously isolated areas into the market.

More important than better roads, especially in the West, was the introduction of the steamboat. From the early days of settlement, flatboats going down the Ohio and Mississippi rivers to New Orleans had transported some production to market, but this mode of transportation was extremely slow even downriver while upriver shipping by oar-driven keelboat was so slow, backbreaking, and expensive as to inhibit any extensive commerce. A new era was predicted when Robert Fulton operated the first commercially successful steamboat, the *Clermont*, on the Hudson River in 1807. By 1812, a few forerunners of the classic shallow-draft sternwheeler had appeared on the Mississippi. The development of western steamboating came with a rush at the end of the war, and by 1820 there were 60 steamboats on the Mississippi-Ohio system (by 1860 there would be more than 1,000) and others on the river systems of Alabama and Mississippi. Steamboat freight rates were only 5 to 10 percent of what keelboats had charged to haul goods upriver and only 25 to 30 percent of what it had cost to flatboat goods down river; there were also gains in shipping time. Able to operate far up the network of tributaries that laced the West, the shallow-draft sternwheeler made possible the commercial production of cotton, wheat, and other bulky commodities in widespread areas that could not otherwise have entered the national market.

While the steamboat was accelerating commercial development in the West — and nourishing such river cities as Cincinnati, Louisville, and St. Louis — another transportation development was providing a direct water link between East and West. In 1817 the New York legislature, prodded by Governor DeWitt Clinton, authorized the construction of a canal from Albany on the Hudson River west along the Mohawk Valley to Buffalo on Lake Erie, and by 1825 the 364-mile Erie Canal was completed. Traffic on the new canal was so heavy that tolls equaled its construction cost within nine years. Given cheap water communication with New York City and Europe, a flood of commodities from the Great Lakes region soon flowed eastward along the canal, meeting a return flow of eastern and European goods destined for the entire West.

The success of the Erie Canal (operating today as the New York State Barge Canal) prompted Pennsylvania to build a competing system linking Philadelphia with Pittsburgh on the Ohio, and in the 1830s and 1840s the states of the Old Northwest completed a series of canals connecting the Great Lakes with the Ohio and the Mississippi rivers.

The development of a railroad network in the 1840s and 1850s gave added efficiency to a transportation system that had already succeeded in bringing most parts of the country within the orbit of the irresistible market. Baltimore began constructing its railroad west toward the Ohio River in 1828, and in the next decade several thousand miles of short lines were built. Not until the 1850s, however, did the railroad boom reach its height. In this decade the great trunk lines connecting East and West were completed, and by 1860 the country had more than 30,000 miles of railroad.

In a parallel development, Samuel F. B. Morse perfected the electric telegraph, which revolutionized the nation's communication system. Often literally parallel, wires were strung beside the railroad tracks wherever practical. The innovation spread rapidly, carrying news, building markets, and transforming business and financial patterns. By 1860 there were 50,000 miles of telegraph wire in use.

Measuring the economic benefits of these changes in transportation and communication is impossible, but their impact was vast. In 1815 it took more than 50 days to ship a cargo from Cincinnati to New York by keelboat and wagon. By 1850 the same commodities could be shipped from and to the same cities by barge in 18 days, and by railroad in 6 to 8 days. Overland freight rates by wagon ranged from 30 to 70 cents per ton per mile in 1815. By the 1850s the cost dropped: 2–9 cents per ton-mile by railroad, and about 1 cent per ton-mile by canal barge. Similarly, a message sent overland from the nation's midsection to the West Coast could take six months by wagon, a month by stage coach, 7 to 10 days by the fabled (and briefly operated) Pony Express, and scarcely an instant by magnetic telegraph.

ENTERPRISE AND PUBLIC POLICY

The transportation revolution, the market revolution, and the onset of industrialization would have come much more slowly if the Americans of the early republic had followed the *laissez-faire* notions of political economy that are often mistakenly ascribed to them. Instead, as the market advanced and the spirit of enterprise quickened, entrepreneurs demanded that their governments ally themselves with private interest to speed progress.

The most notable alliance of public and private enterprise at the state and local level was in the field of transportation, where progress demanded undertakings too vast for individuals or even groups of individuals. The early turnpike companies raised much of their capital from stock subscriptions by the states and towns through which they ran. The great canals, including the Erie, were built directly by state tax money, while other states spent large sums of public revenue on improving navigable rivers. Congress financed the first telegraph line, the Washington–Baltimore line, before turning it over to private enterprise in 1847; the first transcontinental telegraph line, completed in 1861, was subsidized generously by the federal government. Public aid to transportation reached its peak in the construction of railroads; many were subsidized by local, state, and federal grants, and a few were built entirely with state money. How many million dollars of public funds spent on these projects is not known, but the revolutionizing transportation and communication networks could certainly not have grown so without governmental aid.

The turnpike, steamboat, and railroad companies were the forerunners of the modern corporation. These early corporations were born out of the theory of "mixed enterprise" — the idea that government should ally itself with private enterprise to accomplish ends beneficial to the public. In the simple days of the staple-exporting economy, all enterprise had been carried on by individuals or partnerships. Economic combinations of many individuals or their capital in large enterprises were thought to be dangerous to the public interest and were frowned upon by the law. Only where some great public purpose was to be accomplished were these corporations thought to be justified, and then only when chartered by special act of a legislature.

Such corporate charters usually facilitated the raising of capital by granting the privilege of "limited liability," making stockholders in the corporation (unlike members of partnerships) liable for debts of the corporation only to the extent of the stock they held. Charters also usually granted, either explicitly or implicitly, monopolies or semimonopolies — for example, when a company was given the exclusive right to develop a certain transportation route. Thus the early corporate charter was thought of as a privilege conferred by government in order to enlist private enterprise for the accomplishment of a public purpose.

The corporate device found much of its early use not only in transportation but in banking, and the rapid growth of banking was another major factor in the acceleration of economic development. The banking system before the War of 1812 had consisted of the Hamiltonian national bank, chartered by Congress, and a small number of private banks that were called *state banks* because they were chartered by state legislatures. In theory at least, stockholders bought stock in these banks by paying in gold and silver. On the basis of this specie capital, the banks made loans; the interest they collected from their borrowers provided profits that could be paid back to the stockholders as dividends. What made the banks extremely profitable was the fact that they could safely lend out more than their capital. Instead of lending specie, a bank gave borrowers *bank notes*, or pieces of paper resembling modern paper money, each bearing a promise that the issuing bank would redeem the note on demand with a specified sum of specie. These bank notes then circulated as money in the vicinity of the bank and, as long as people had confidence in the bank, were not returned for redemption in specie. Thus the bank could safely print, lend, and collect interest on considerably more bank notes than it had specie to cover.

Though at first conservatively managed and restrained by the national bank, the state banks were potentially capable of expanding the supply of credit and investment capital almost infinitely and, thus, of stimulating feverish economic activity. This began to happen when the national bank's demise in 1811 and the war's economic stimulus prompted enterprising politicians and businesses to secure legislative charters for a large number of new state banks designed to operate on more generous and lucrative principles than their predecessors. The bank mania reached its peak after the war, and the rapid multiplication of banks and bank credit contributed greatly to the boom-and-bust cycle of 1815–1819. Bust was again followed by boom, and the expansion of bank credit reached even greater heights than in the 1830s. In spite of the violent short-term fluctuations that the banks fostered, they also contributed greatly to the spectacular, long-term prosperity of the economy through their active stimulation of its growth.

REPUBLICAN NATIONALISM

The spirit of enterprise was strong in the new generation of Republican leaders who had pushed Madison into war in 1812 and who dominated a transformed Republicanism after the war. Federalism, despite a momentary comeback in embargo days, was so weakened by the steady swelling of the Republican electorate and so discredited by secession discussion at the Hartford Convention before the war that in 1816 only three states voted for the Federalist presidential candidate. To succeed Madison, the Republicans picked James Monroe, the last prominent Virginian of the Revolutionary generation, and in 1820 Monroe was re-elected without opposition.

Monroe himself retained some of Jefferson's agrarian-minded and strict-constructionist scruples and rejoiced that the death of Federalism had ushered in an "Era of Good Feelings" when parties should no longer be necessary. In truth, the younger men surrounding the president had moved, in the enterprising atmosphere of the boom years, so far toward the nationalist and commercial-minded views of the Federalists that Federalism had become superfluous. Monroe's State Department was headed by the ardent nationalist John Quincy Adams, who had deserted his father's party over the embargo issue. Monroe's Secretary of the Treasury, William H. Crawford of Georgia, worked for a new national bank. Presiding over the War Department was John C. Calhoun, vigorous champion of a strong army, protective tariffs, and federal road and canal construction. And in Congress, the dominant figure was Speaker of the House Henry Clay, who for a generation would symbolize a broad program of federal action — he would call it the "American System" — to aid enterprise and speed progress.

These people were preaching Hamiltonianism shorn of its elitist overtones. The onrushing market revolution was democratizing business, and the rapid spread of the entrepreneurial spirit through all levels of society made the new Republican nationalism more dynamic than the old Federalist nationalism of conservative merchants and financiers.

The war was no sooner over than several problems growing out of wartime developments were attacked in the spirit of Republican nationalism. The overexpansion of state banks had led to a financial crisis early in the war. Outside New England, the overextended banks had had to "suspend specie payments" (stop redeeming their bank notes in gold or silver coin on demand), and their notes had depreciated; the resulting financial chaos had contributed greatly to the government's difficulties in carrying on the war. To get the federal government out of its financial troubles and to furnish a sound paper currency and credit system as a basis for orderly business growth, the younger Republicans pushed through Congress in 1816 a charter for a Second Bank of the United States.

This institution, with headquarters in Philadelphia and branches elsewhere, was to have a capital of $35 million as compared with the $10 million of Hamilton's national bank. It was to be the depository for all federal funds, and its bank notes were declared receivable for all sums due the government. The bank was to serve public purposes by making loans to the government and also by regulating the state banks, aiding them to resume specie payments at the earliest possible moment, and thereafter keeping them on a sound basis by sustaining them in periods of financial stringency and by restraining them in periods of boom. Power to do this came from the bank's large capital base and from the fact that it was constantly receiving large quantities of state bank notes in its role as federal depository. By promptly presenting these notes to the state banks for redemption during booms, it could force them to curtail their issues, while by expanding its own loans and note issues during bust periods, it could ease any pressure on the state banks. Yet this was to be essentially a private, profit-making institution with the government subscribing only one-fifth of its capital and designating only one-fifth of its directors.

Beginning operation in 1817, the Second Bank helped secure a general resumption of specie payments and then succumbed to the boom spirit itself. Inefficient and often dishonest officers so overextended the bank's own loans and note issues that it lost all power to restrain the expanding state banks. The inevitable reaction, the Panic of 1819, was much more severe than it might otherwise have been because the national bank suddenly reversed its policy and saved itself by ruthlessly applying pressure against its debtors and the state banks. Not until Nicholas Biddle became the bank's president in 1823 did it begin to realize its great potential as a balance wheel and regulator for the economy as a whole.

A second problem growing out of the war was the desperate situation of American industry. As we have seen, the War of 1812 — by cutting off imported European goods — stimulated a rapid growth in this manufacturing activity. But when the war had ended, British manufacturers dumped on the American market their stored-up surplus of products at cut-rate prices, an act that threatened the promising American manufacturing establishment with sudden death.

In the mood of generous nationalism that followed the war, Republican members of Congress from all areas responded to the plight of the beleaguered northeastern manufacturers by passing the first tariff act designed primarily to protect American producers from foreign competition. The Tariff of 1816 required foreign imports that competed with such leading American manufactures as cotton, woolen cloth, and iron to pay import duties ranging around 20 to 25 percent of their value. Additional protection was granted to iron and textiles in 1818 and 1819.

One great ambition of the national-minded Republicans was frustrated by the lingering constitutional doubts of Presidents Madison and Monroe. In the closing days of his administration, Madison vetoed as unconstitutional Calhoun's Bonus Bill of 1817, a measure reserving $1.5 million, which the new national bank paid the government for its charter, for beginning a great national system of roads and canals. Although he recognized that internal improvements were necessary to encourage national expansion and to cement the national union, Madison's strict-constructionist background asserted itself. While Calhoun found justification for the measure in the "general welfare" clause, Madison reluctantly concluded that without a constitutional amendment, federal expenditures for internal improvements were unlawful. With this judgment, his successor, solemn, middle-of-the-road James Monroe, agreed fully.

JUDICIAL NATIONALISM

In the congenial atmosphere of Republican nationalism following the War of 1812, the Federalist nationalism of Chief Justice John Marshall and the Supreme Court he dominated came to full fruition. Having asserted the court's authority on constitutional questions in *Marbury* vs. *Madison* back in 1803, Marshall now used this authority in a series of remarkable decisions to establish his Federalist and nationalist views on questions of property rights, constitutional interpretation, and federal and state powers.

In *Dartmouth College* vs. *Woodward* (1819), the Supreme Court overruled an attempt by the New Hampshire legislature to change the college's colonial charter. Marshall's court had already made itself the defender of property rights against state legislatures in an earlier case, and now Marshall declared that charter rights, too, were sacred. This decision was to become increasingly significant with the growing importance of chartered corporations in American economic life.

The biggest corporation of Marshall's day, the Second Bank of the United States, was involved in his most far-reaching decision, *McCulloch* vs. *Maryland* (1819). This case arose from Maryland's attempt to tax out of existence the bank's branch at Baltimore. The power to tax was the power to destroy, he argued, and no state could be allowed to destroy an instrument of the federal government. Perhaps the most important part of this decision was Marshall's argument, based on the doctrine of implied powers, that Congress had acted constitutionally in chartering the bank. Here he echoed Hamilton's argument to President Washington at the time the first national bank was chartered, maintaining that if the end Congress sought to attain was sanctioned by the Constitution, then "all means which are appropriate, which are plainly adapted to that end" are constitutional.

Among various other decisions affirming federal over state powers, one may be singled out as particularly important. In *Gibbons* vs. *Ogden* (1824), the court invalidated a monopoly that New York had granted over steamboat service between New York and New Jersey. In giving Congress the power to regulate interstate commerce, Marshall declared, the Constitution meant that *only* Congress should have such power. Furthermore he defined interstate commerce so broadly as to include the carrying of passengers or any other variety of commerce between states. Marshall's sweeping extension of the commerce clause not only invalidated the New York monopoly as an invasion of Congress's exclusive power to regulate, but also laid the basis for the great future extensions of federal regulatory powers. The antimonopoly implications of Marshall's decision in *Gibbons* vs. *Ogden* were carried further by Marshall's Jacksonian successor, Chief Justice Roger B. Taney. In *Charles River Bridge* vs. *Warren Bridge* (1837) Taney diminished the vested rights of monopolistic corporate charters in a decision that created the opportunity for a more venturesome corporate capitalism to open up new markets.

Thus in the first flush of the market revolution, the spirit of enterprise and nationalism seemed pervasive in American life — in the entrepreneurial undertakings of countless citizens, in the states' efforts to hasten progress through transportation projects and corporate charters, in the tariff and banking legislation of Congress, in the diplomacy of President Monroe's doctrine, and in the Supreme Court's decisions. The only jarring note seemed to be the doubts of old-fashioned Virginia presidents about federal appropriations for roads and canals, and even this slight barrier to progress would be removed when one of the younger, national-minded Republicans entered the White House in 1825. Yet an unprogressive, agrarian society had not — could not have — changed so totally and quickly as this one momentarily appeared to have done. Two decades of crisis and conflict were to elapse before Americans would be at ease in the new world of enterprise.

FOR FURTHER READING

A good introduction to American economic history is Stuart Bruchey's *The Roots of American Economic Growth, 1607–1861* (1965). Other general surveys for this period include Douglass C. North's somewhat technical but rewarding analysis of *The Economic Growth of the United States, 1790–1860* (1961); Thomas C. Cochran's *Frontiers of Change* (1981); and Charles Sellers's *The Market Revolution* (1991). These may be supplemented with detailed accounts of specific aspects of the economic revolution in the following: George R. Taylor, *The Transportation Revolution, 1815–1860* (1960); Christopher Clark, *The Roots of Rural Capitalism* (1990); Robert Albion, *The Rise of New York Port, 1815–1860* (1939); Robert W. Fogel, *Railroads and American Economic Growth* (1964); Paul Wallace Gates, *The Farmer's Age* (1960); and Ronald Shaw, *Erie Water West: A History of the Erie Canal* (1966). Useful community studies include Steven Hahn and Jonathan Prude's collection of local studies on *The Countryside in the Age of Capitalist Transformation* (1985); Jonathan Prude's *The Coming of Industrial Order: Town and Factory Life in Rural Massachusetts, 1810–1860* (1983); Thomas Dublin's *Women at Work: The Transformation of Work and Community in Lowell, Massachusetts* (1979); and Anthony Wallace's *Rockdale: The Growth of an American Village in the Early Industrial Revolution* (1978). For western development, see Frederick Jackson Turner's *The Frontier in American History* (1920), Ray A. Billington and Martin Ridge's *Westward Expansion* (1982), and Richard White's *"It's Your Misfortune and None of My Own"* (1992). Malcolm Rohrbough's *Land Office Business* (1968) and *The Trans-Appalachian Frontier* (1978) are important works on early white settlement of the West. Reginald Horsman's *The Frontier in the Formative Years* (1970) is a skillful synthesis of developments on the Old Northwest and Old Southwest frontiers. *Flush Times of Alabama and Mississippi* (1853) by Joseph Baldwin is an absorbing contemporary account of the boom years in the Old Southwest. George Dangerfield's *The Era of Good Feelings* (1952) is an account of the political history of the era of Republican nationalism.

TABLE 4. PRESIDENTIAL ELECTIONS AND MAJOR EVENTS, 1816–1828

1816	**James Monroe** (Republican) elected over Rufus King (Federalist). Tariff of 1816, the first deliberately protectionist tariff act.
1816	Second Bank of the United States chartered. Madison vetoes Calhoun's Bonus Bill for internal improvements.
1817–1825	Erie Canal constructed.
1818	National Road reaches the Ohio River.
1819	*Dartmouth College* vs. *Woodward.* John Marshall's Supreme Court defends charter rights against state legislation. *McCulloch* vs. *Maryland.* John Marshall's Supreme Court upholds the constitutionality of the national bank. Panic of 1819 forces a general suspension of specie payments and inaugurates a long and severe economic depression.
1820	Land Act of 1820. Lower land prices and abolition of credit system. Missouri Compromise. **James Monroe** (Republican) re-elected without opposition.
1824	Tariff of 1824. Higher protection. *Gibbons* vs. *Ogden.* John Marshall's Supreme Court extends the federal power to regulate interstate commerce. **John Quincy Adams** (Republican) elected over Andrew Jackson, William H. Crawford, and Henry Clay (all Republicans).
1826	Anti-Masonic movement begins.
1828	Tariff of Abominations. Extremely high protective duties. **Andrew Jackson** (Democratic Republican) elected over John Quincy Adams (National Republican).

10

★ ★ ★ ★ ★ ★

Depression Decade: Sectionalism and Democracy, 1819–1828

THE PANIC of 1819 was the first severe economic crisis that affected the American people as a whole. Part of an international economic dislocation following a long period of war, it was especially intense in the United States because of the reckless expansion of banks, credit, and entrepreneurial investment that preceded it. When the prices of cotton and other commodities suddenly plummeted on the world markets, countless Americans faced the loss of their homes, farms, workshops, and other property because they could not meet the debts they had incurred to finance their ventures. The banks suspended specie payments, and bank notes, the only circulating medium, skidded toward worthlessness in their holders' hands. Merchants went bankrupt, city workers lost their jobs, and the economy ground to a standstill. The paralysis maintained its grip through the early 1820s, and not until after mid-decade did prosperity return.

The economic effects of the Panic were no more momentous than its psychological and political effects. In rapid succession, the American people had been drawn from the settled ways of the old agrarian order into a national market economy of dizzying prosperity, unlimited optimism, and headlong change; then they were suddenly plunged into privation and despair. The shock of this experience made the 1820s a decade of soul-searching and tension. The postwar mood of generous nationalism evaporated as sections and interest groups became narrowly concerned with their own welfare and jealous of rival sections and interest groups. There was a striking revival of Jeffersonian orthodoxy as prodigal agrarians gave up the fleshpots of the market and resolved to return to the old ways of frugality and honest toil. Class antagonisms sharpened as impoverished farmers and urban workers blamed political and business leaders — above all, the banking fraternity — for the disaster. And finally, there was a growing interest in politics, a dissatisfaction with the political leadership that had allowed hard times to come, and a demand for new leaders who would be more responsive to the popular will and use government to relieve the distress.

POLITICAL SECTIONALISM

The resurgence of sectional rivalries was dramatically demonstrated by the heated congressional controversy in 1820 over admitting Missouri as a slave state. Slavery had been a source of conflict in the constitutional convention and on several later occasions, but it had not yet become a major issue. The Quakers had been bearing testimony against human servitude for some time, and by 1804 every state north of Delaware had provided for the ultimate emancipation of slaves within its borders. But there was no strong general movement against slavery as a moral and political evil, for most persons of goodwill, both North and South, continued to indulge Jefferson's hope that it would eventually disappear everywhere through the gradual operation of economic and moral forces.

Thus when northern members of Congress sought to amend the Missouri admission bill to require the gradual emancipation of Missouri slaves, they were acting less from moral repugnance at the institution than from a revival of the traditional northeastern resentment at southern political domination. Much of the South's political power was derived from the constitutional provision that three-fifths of its slaves be counted in apportioning congressional representation and electoral votes. Northeasterners seized upon the Missouri question as a means of blocking the extension of this political injustice throughout the Louisiana Purchase. Southern members of Congress, on the other hand, reacted violently to this attack on their vulnerable system of labor. Admission of Missouri as a free state would upset the even balance between slave and free states and destroy the protection that this gave the South in the Senate against any future antislavery measures.

A Missouri Compromise was finally reached because of the simultaneous movement to make the geographically separate eastern appendage of Massachusetts (now Maine) a separate state. Maine was admitted as a free state, Missouri was admitted as a slave state, and no further slave states were to be created from that part of the Louisiana Purchase lying north of latitude 36°30′ (the latitude of the southern boundary of Missouri).

What many northern members of Congress had in mind when they opposed the admission of any more slave states was illustrated at this same session of 1820 by the fate of a bill to extend further tariff protection to the hard-pressed manufacturers. Representatives from slave-holding states voted almost five to one against this measure in the House and provided most of the votes that killed it in the Senate. By 1824, when the manufacturers tried again for higher duties, the South was opposed 57 to 1 in the House. This time the Northeast was heavily in favor, the only opposition there coming from representatives of international merchants and shippers, who resisted any diminution of international trade. Western representatives provided the margin by which the tariff bill squeaked through Congress, because western farmers had become convinced that the growth of manufacturing might create a flourishing home market for their unprofitable products. The Tariff of 1824 raised duties on textiles to 33.3 percent, sharply increased the rate on iron, and won rural support with duties on raw wool and hemp.

RELIEF AND DEMOCRACY

Manufacturers were not the only ones who had learned from the doctrines of Republican nationalism to look to government for aid. Thousands of western settlers were now unable to complete their payments for public lands under the credit system inaugurated by the Land Act of 1800. In response to their outcries, Congress forgave interest charges, extended payment periods, and allowed delinquent purchasers to retain an amount of land proportionate to the payments they had made. At the same time the Land Act of 1820 abolished the credit system and lowered the minimum price of public lands from $2.00 to $1.25 an acre. The minimum tract that could be purchased had recently been reduced to 80 acres, and all these changes enabled a settler to buy a farm for as little as $100 cash.

But people looked to the state governments for relief from the most desperate problem created by the Panic, the disappearance of money and the collapse of the pyramid of debt that had been built up during the boom. People could neither collect debts owed them nor pay the debts they owed, property could not be sold, and a sweeping liquidation through foreclosures and bankruptcies threatened many Americans.

Legislatures, especially in the hard-hit South and West, responded to the demands of their aroused constituents by various schemes to circumvent the constitutional prohibition against issuing paper money or making anything except gold and silver legal tender. Some states established "banks" or "loan offices" to print state-backed paper money for loan to desperate debtors. Usually these measures were coupled with "stay laws" requiring creditors who refused to accept the state-backed paper money to delay executions on their debtor's property. Relief was also provided through "property laws" whereby a "disinterested" jury composed of the debtor's neighbors set a minimum value below which property could not be forcibly sold to satisfy a debt.

The violent political struggles over debtor relief laws and the closely related banking question accelerated the drift toward a more democratic political system in many states. A few socially complex states like New York and Pennsylvania were already far along the road toward a well-developed two-party or bifactional system in which evenly matched candidates campaigned against each other, aided by party newspapers and stable party organizations expert in the techniques of garnering votes. Under such circumstances, voter interest and participation were high, and public policy was responsive to majority wishes.

In most of the country, however, widespread interest in politics had appeared only sporadically before the 1820s. Having little sense that government — at least the remote state and national governments — affected them much anyhow, most people were willing to leave politics to those well-to-do and socially superior men in their communities who had something to gain from political power, whether land grants or bank charters or simply offices. This resulted in a *personal-factional* political system in which a group of leaders allied through personal or family ties normally maintained unchallenged predominance in a county or other district. In the legislatures, representatives from the various local oligarchies formed shifting alliances, again based on personal or family ties.

This system was sanctioned by Jeffersonian political theory. Jefferson had never maintained that the people as a whole should decide public policy, but only affirmed that the people were wise enough and virtuous enough to select the wisest and most virtuous among them as political leaders. Candidates pretended that they did not seek office and certainly did not electioneer; they only reluctantly consented to serve when called upon by their fellow citizens. The voters did not tell their chosen representatives — who were, of course, always male — what to do once elected, and certainly the representatives did not seek votes by promising to do thus and so. Instead, according to Jeffersonian theory, these unusually wise and virtuous men should be left free to reach wise and virtuous decisions through rational debate and compromise with each other in legislatures and Congress.

The personal-factional system was best adapted to homogeneous communities where conflicts of interest were not very important. It mustered enough genuine wisdom and disinterestedness to function satisfactorily until the market revolution began multiplying the number of specialized economic roles and competing interest groups in the community, while at the same time making people more conscious of the connection between enterprise and public policy. This caused no difficulty during the boom years when there seemed to be enough for everybody. But the Panic made people suddenly aware of their separate and competing interests at the very moment that they began looking to government for mutually contradictory kinds of aid. With debtors clamoring for stay laws and loan offices while creditors denounced them, the Jeffersonian notion of a harmony of interests served by wise and virtuous leaders could no longer be sustained. Voters wanted to know where candidates stood on questions of vital concern to them, and the more alert politicians began telling the voters what they thought a majority wanted to hear.

As elections began to be transformed into popular referenda on public policy, discontent with the established political leadership appeared. The main target of popular resentment was the banking system, which was blamed for causing the collapse by its reckless overexpansion of credit. While the banks were refusing to pay their own debts by not redeeming their notes in specie and while the depreciation of bank notes was the most conspicuous source of loss to the whole community, the banks were fore-closing on the property of their debtors, continuing to pay dividends, and extending special accommodations to their favored borrowers. The state banks managed to shift some of the resulting resentment to the national bank, against which they had similar complaints. But in the eyes of many newly aroused voters, the blame belonged to the banking system as a whole, along with the politicians and business people who had fostered and profited from it. Moreover, these same politicians and business people were often leading the opposition to debtor relief.

As voters came to the polls in increasing numbers to repudiate the established leaders, a new style of democratic politics began to supplant the personal-factional system. The new-style democratic politicians not only promised what the voters wanted, but also portrayed themselves as fighting the battle of the plain people against a group of unscrupulous aristocrats. The old loose and shifting factional groupings in state politics began to stabilize as "democratic" and "aristocratic" alignments. In Kentucky, and to a lesser extent in some other southern and western states, something very like a two-party system developed out of the violent conflict over debtor relief.

In the East, where debtor relief was not such a pressing problem, other issues led to similar results. In New York, DeWitt Clinton capitalized on some high-handed maneuvers by the long entrenched "Albany Regency" candidates to make a smashing political comeback as gubernatorial candidate for the "People's Party." In the same state in 1826, the disappearance and presumed murder of a man who had revealed the secrets of the Masonic order caused an astonishing anti-Masonic outburst, which became a political movement and eventually a short-lived political party. Since Masonic lodges were usually composed of the most prominent men in their communities and since many dominant politicians were Masons, the anti-Masons attacked the order as an aristocratic conspiracy against the rest of the community.

The urban counterpart of anti-Masonry was the labor movement that began to flourish late in the 1820s. By fostering larger and more specialized units of production, the market revolution was making it more difficult for artisans to follow the traditional progression from apprenticeship through the wage-earning journeyman status to independent proprietorship. The depression and unemployment highlighted the insecurity of the permanent wage-earning status in which more and more workers were finding themselves. Journeyman workers organized labor unions and called strikes against the 10-hour day. On the political front, they joined with small entrepreneurs, whose middle-class status was likewise threatened, to form workers' parties in Philadelphia and New York City. Under the banner of "Equal Rights," these parties advocated free public education, opposed imprisonment for debt, and agitated against banks and other monopolies through which a favored few could exploit the many.

Amid the frustrations and conflicts of the 1820s, the long drift toward popular sovereignty in the United States was reaching its culmination. From the beginning of settlement, the cheapness of land and the demand for labor had created an atmosphere of universal opportunity and rough social equality that was quickly reflected in the quasi-democratic political institutions of the colonies. The Revolution, consigning the destiny of Americans to their own hands, had cut off elitist tendencies and firmly established the ideal of equal political rights, but only for white males. In the following decades, state after state had alleviated restrictive male suffrage requirements and other denials — often more symbolic than real — of the Revolutionary ideal. Meanwhile, the egalitarian tendency of American life had been reinforced by the process of western settlement, and the new western states had been free to adopt constitutions reflecting the increasingly democratic tone of the country.

Yet it remained for the market revolution to democratize enterprise, to give a final push to the egalitarian tendency, and to arouse a hitherto apathetic electorate to the importance of public policy and politics. The boom-bust cycle made this popular political awakening more abrupt than it might otherwise have been. Appearing first at the local and state levels, the new-style democratic politics began to manifest itself at the national level in the presidential election of 1824.

THE ELECTION OF 1824

An institutional symbol of the established personal-factional system was the presidential caucus. Every four years, the Republican senators and representatives met in caucus at Washington to designate their party's presidential candidate, and since 1800 the caucus designation had been tantamount to election. As the election of 1824 approached, the foreordained choice of the caucus was William H. Crawford of Georgia, Monroe's secretary of the treasury and a favorite in areas that had been relatively immune to the postwar boom and the Republican nationalism accompanying it. He ran as the candidate of a resurgent Jeffersonianism.

This time, however, the caucus system itself was challenged by the sectional and personal rivalries that had rendered Monroe's second term anything but an "Era of Good Feelings." Secretary of State John Quincy Adams was the choice of New England, Speaker of the House Henry Clay was the favorite of the West, and Secretary of War John C. Calhoun found his backers in the South. All these anti-Crawford candidates, in fact, were champions of Republican nationalism. Calhoun led them in attacking the caucus as undemocratic, and their supporters' refusal to attend it resulted in Crawford's being nominated by only a minority of the Republican congressmen.

The beneficiary of these rivalries was Andrew Jackson, hero of the Battle of New Orleans. Although not thought of initially as a serious candidate even by his home state (Tennessee) politicians, "Old Hickory" demonstrated remarkable appeal. Though no one knew where the general stood on public issues, to those disenchanted with the old leaders it was enough that he was a popular hero — the people's man against the established leadership.

When the election took place, Jackson had the most popular and electoral votes, but none of the candidates won a majority. The Constitution directed that the House of Representatives, voting by states, should choose among the three highest candidates. This eliminated Clay, low man in electoral votes; Crawford was also removed from serious contention by a physical collapse; and Calhoun had withdrawn before the election. Clay had the opportunity to wield his great influence in the House on behalf of either Jackson or Adams. He chose Adams, who was narrowly elected.

THE TRIBULATIONS OF THE SECOND ADAMS

John Quincy Adams was among the ablest and most patriotic presidents but was also one of the least successful. Partly through circumstances and partly through insensitivity to public sentiment, he defied and was overwhelmed by the most powerful political currents of the 1820s.

The Jackson supporters regarded Adams's election as a flouting of the people's will. But when he appointed Henry Clay as secretary of state, traditional stepping-stone to the presidency, their fury knew no bounds. The cry of "Bargain and Corruption" rang throughout the land, touching off a four-year campaign to vindicate popular sovereignty by placing Jackson in the White House.

Adams compounded his difficulties by underestimating the depression-bred reaction against Republican nationalism. Adams and Clay sought to build a National Republican party, based on a coalition of the Northeast and the Ohio Valley and dedicated to Clay's "American System" of protective tariff, national bank, and internal improvements. In addition, the president's first annual message called for a national university and federally sponsored scientific research and exploration, while cautioning Congress against being "palsied by the will of our constituents."

The Adams-Clay program outraged the neo-Jeffersonian Crawford supporters, now led by New York's Martin Van Buren, and drove them into alliance with the Jackson and Calhoun factions. Calling itself the Democratic Republican party, this Jacksonian coalition for four years blocked the president's program in Congress and harassed him in every way possible. The only significant legislative product of these four years was a tariff act passed in 1828. With both parties trying to win presidential votes by juggling complicated tariff schedules, this "Tariff of Abominations" pushed duties on both manufactured and agricultural products to absurdly high levels and satisfied almost no one.

The presidential election of 1828 was marked by the return of the two-party system to national politics and by an abusiveness on both sides that was unmatched since the last closely contested two-party election in 1800. Questions of public policy were hardly discussed, the real issue being whether the people's man Jackson should prevail over the seasoned statesman and old-style political leader Adams. This was enough to produce a substantial increase in the number of voters and a substantial majority for Jackson.

FOR FURTHER READING

Murray N. Rothbard focuses on *The Panic of 1819* (1962). The best general account of the 1820s is Frederick Jackson Turner's *The Rise of the New West, 1819–1829* (1906), but see also George Dangerfield's *The Awakening of American Nationalism, 1815–1828* (1965). Although it deals only with the southern states, Charles S. Sydnor's *The Development of Southern Sectionalism, 1819–1848* (1948) is also suggestive. Glover Moore has carefully examined *The Missouri Controversy, 1819–1821* (1953). Some idea of the political transformations going on in the states in the 1820s may be gained from Shaw Livermore, Jr.'s *The Twilight of Federalism* (1962); from Thomas E. Jeffrey's *State Parties and National Politics* (1989); and from Charles Sellers's *James K. Polk, Jacksonian: 1795–1843* (1957). The entire political career of John Quincy Adams is splendidly narrated by Samuel Flagg Bemis in *John Quincy Adams* (2 vols., 1949–1956), while Mary W. M. Hargreaves focuses specifically on *The Presidency of John Quincy Adams* (1985). Robert V. Remini has written a lively scholarly account of *The Election of Andrew Jackson* (1963).

TABLE 5. PRESIDENTIAL ELECTIONS AND MAJOR EVENTS, 1828–1840

1828	**Andrew Jackson** (Democratic Republican) elected over John Quincy Adams (National Republican). Tariff of Abominations.
1830	Jackson vetoes the Maysville Road Bill. Indian Removal Act.
1831	*Cherokee Nations* vs. *Georgia.*
1832	Tariff of 1832 remedies worst abuses of the Tariff of Abominations but fails to satisfy South Carolina Nullifiers. Black Hawk War ends Indian resistance in Northwest. Jackson vetoes Second Bank of the United States recharter bill. **Andrew Jackson** (Democratic-Republican) re-elected over Henry Clay (National Republican). South Carolina nullifies tariff laws.
1833	Compromise Tariff gradually reduces all tariff duties to 20%. Force Act authorizes president to use military to enforce the laws. Jackson transfers the federal deposits from the national bank to selected state-chartered deposit banks.
1835	Seminole resistance to removal begins.
1836	Jackson issues Specie Circular requiring specie for purchase of federal lands. Distribution Act distributes the federal surplus among the states. **Martin Van Buren** (Democrat) elected over William Henry Harrison, Daniel Webster, and Hugh Lawson White (all Whigs).
1837	Panic of 1837 forces a general suspension of specie payments and initiates a severe and prolonged economic depression. Van Buren proposes the independent treasury system.
1838	New York Free Banking Act is a forerunner of general incorporation laws: one of the many efforts by the states to reform and regulate banking. Cherokee removal to Oklahoma.
1840	Independent treasury system finally approved by Congress after three years of debate. **William Henry Harrison** (Whig) elected over Martin Van Buren (Democrat).

11

★ ★ ★ ★ ★ ★

The Jacksonian Era, 1828–1840

WITH Andrew Jackson's inauguration, the forces of egalitarianism swept over the federal government. Though Jackson had risen to become master of a large plantation and one of his state's leaders, he had never abandoned the egalitarian habits of his earlier surroundings in small-farmer North Carolina and frontier Tennessee. On Inauguration Day, he opened the White House reception to an unruly mob of the high and the low, shocking the older official society but unmistakably announcing the new regime's conviction that common people were as good as aristocrats.

The same point was made with more substantial effect by Jackson's extension of the "spoils system" and his frank advocacy of "rotation in office." The new president was accompanied to Washington by a host of new-style democratic politicians demanding office as a reward for their support. Jackson took the position that any honest citizen could discharge the duties of a government office as well as any other. Furthermore, public offices should not be the property of their holders for life. They should be passed around, with a preference shown for friends of the administration that the people had elected. The numerous removals and appointments that Jackson made on these principles somewhat impaired the efficiency of government service but also made it more representative of, and responsive to the country as a whole. Moreover, the spoils system helped make possible the new-style political parties through which the popular will could be translated into public policy.

Jackson was the first president to operate on the principle that the people themselves should decide public policy. Arguing that the president was the only federal official elected by the people as a whole, he was supremely certain that his policies represented the popular will. So great was the popular confidence he inspired that the people, or a majority of them, usually agreed.

By assuming this role of democratic tribune, Jackson greatly increased the power of the presidency relative to Congress. All his predecessors combined had vetoed only 9 congressional measures, usually on the grounds that they were unconstitutional. Old Hickory used the veto 12 times, against legislation he thought inexpedient as well as legislation he thought unconstitutional. By taking his differences with Congress to the voters, he was highly successful in making recalcitrant legislators compliant or in replacing them.

JACKSONIAN POLICIES

Though the people's candidate had been elected, it was by no means clear what policies a people's administration would follow. Jackson himself had little political experience, and it was supposed that much would depend on whether Calhoun or Van Buren controlled the administration and became the heir for the presidential succession. Calhoun wanted to base the Jacksonian Democratic-Republican party (which gradually came to be called simply the Democratic party) on an alliance between the South and the West, which would reduce tariffs for the South and liberalize federal land policy for the West. A most embarrassing issue for Calhoun's plans was that of internal improvements, which the West favored and the South increasingly opposed.

Van Buren, on the other hand, wanted to resurrect the old Jeffersonian coalition between southern planters and the "plain Republicans" of the Northeast. Such a coalition could unite on neo-Jeffersonian grounds to oppose internal improvements (New York wanted no federally financed competition for its Erie Canal) and the national bank (New Yorkers resented the bank as a Philadelphia institution that gave New York City's rival an undeserved financial dominance). The one issue dangerous to Van Buren's plans was tariffs, over which northerners and southerners were disagreeing with mounting vehemence.

Although the Calhoun supporters seemed to have the upper hand in the party, Jackson's inauguration produced a sudden reversal. Calhoun's friends were almost frozen out of the cabinet, while Van Buren himself was made secretary of state. Van Buren astutely used information that Calhoun, while a member of Monroe's cabinet, had advocated punishing Jackson for his rash invasion of Spanish Florida. The New Yorker was aided, too, by the "Eaton imbroglio," when the socially prominent women of Washington tried to ostracize the somewhat disreputable wife of Jackson's old friend and Secretary of War John Eaton. Calhoun's wife, Floride, was among the ladies who angered the president by snubbing Peggy Eaton, while the widower Van Buren was free to treat her with conspicuous gallantry. Relations between Jackson and Calhoun steadily deteriorated until the South Carolinian was finally driven from the party.

Jackson found Van Buren more congenial than Calhoun, both personally and in political outlook. Though Jackson came to Washington without a very well-thought-out position on the major issues, he did have some deeply rooted political instincts that he trusted implicitly. These determined his administration's policies. His instinctive egalitarianism has already been noted. Joined to this was an instinctive neo-Jeffersonian agrarian-mindedness.

Jackson himself had once engaged in extravagant land and commercial speculations based on credit. The bankruptcy that ended these operations and the long struggle to pay off his debts and regain solvency through farm-ing were experiences decisive for his political outlook. Thoroughly chas-tened, advocating the virtues of agriculture, hard work, and economy, abhorring debt, and fearing the get-rich-quick atmosphere fostered by easy credit, he interpreted the boom-bust cycle of 1815–1819 as reproducing his own personal experiences on a national scale. Consequently, when he as-sumed the presidency, his one clearly defined objective was to administer a simple, economical government and to pay off the national debt as rapidly as possible.

Jackson's mood agreed more with Van Buren's neo-Jeffersonianism than with the Republican nationalism that had heretofore been Calhoun's trade-mark. The influence that this gave Van Buren became most apparent over an improvements matter. The advocates of a nationwide federal road system managed to push through Congress the Maysville Road Bill in 1830. Though this bill only provided that the federal government should buy stock in a company building a turnpike from Maysville to Lexington in Kentucky, it was regarded as the test measure for the whole internal improvements pro-gram. Such expenditures would delay Jackson's cherished project for paying off the national debt, and Van Buren had little difficulty persuading him that the measure should be vetoed. The veto message not only condemned the Maysville project, but suggested that all federal expenditures for internal improvements were perhaps either unwise or unlawful — showing that the Jacksonians favored not only frugal government but limits on federal powers. Though the veto did retard for several decades the dream of a nationally financed transportation network, the effect of the Maysville veto was more symbolic than practical. Jackson himself authorized some $10 million in im-provement bills, including some for local projects.

THE TARIFF AND NULLIFICATION

Clearly, Jackson and Van Buren were not ready to assault all the works of Republican nationalism. To undertake a thorough downward revision of the Tariff of Abominations would be to delay payment of the public debt and to disrupt the North-South alliance that Van Buren sought to perfect. Conse-quently, the president urged his first Congress to handle the question with "utmost caution," and the resulting tariff revisions of 1830 hardly touched the more abominable features (the outrageously high duties) of the system.

At this point South Carolina exploded. No state had enjoyed a more un-interrupted prosperity from colonial days to 1819 than South Carolina. Rice, indigo, and sea island cotton first had created a wealthy ruling class in the low country, and then the upland cotton boom had spread comparable riches through the rest of the state. No state, except perhaps Kentucky, was harder hit or more permanently damaged by the depression of the 1820s. The disruption of business coincided with the rise of more efficient cotton-producing areas in the Gulf states, and to make matters infinitely worse, a growing anxiety over the slavery issue made South Carolina particularly sensitive about state rights. South Carolina's reaction to its economic prostration was the more violent because a long period of heady prosperity had preceded it and because no state had developed a prouder or touchier group of political leaders.

Until the depression, the Republican nationalism of Calhoun and his friends had been ascendant in South Carolina. The hard times enabled a rival state-rights faction to blame Calhoun's favorite policies for all the state's woes. By the mid-1820s, the state-rights advocates had stirred up a storm of resentment against the protective tariff and were close to winning political control of the state. Calhoun and his friends were forced to retreat from Republican nationalism as rapidly and unobtrusively as possible. When Congress passed the Tariff of Abominations in 1828, the Calhoun supporters confounded their state rights rivals by outdoing them in violent agitation against protection and by adopting an even more radical version of the state rights doctrine.

The famous Doctrine of Nullification was announced in the South Carolina Exposition and Protest of 1828, secretly written by Calhoun and issued as a report of a legislative committee. The Nullifiers maintained that the Constitution was a compact among states that retained their essential sovereignty and had delegated only limited and clearly specified powers to the federal government. The states themselves were the only proper judges of whether their common agent, the federal government, had exceeded the powers delegated to it by the constitutional compact. If a state judged that some federal law was a violation of the compact, it could declare it null and void, whereupon the federal government must desist unless and until three-fourths of the states, through the amending process, explicitly granted it the nullified power.

The South Carolinians counted on the Jackson administration to push tariff reform, and only after failure to do so in 1829–1830 did Calhoun's friends begin a campaign in the state for actual nullification. The Jacksonian Congress responded by eliminating some of the worst excesses of the Tariff of Abominations in 1832, but the rates were still decidedly protectionist. Meanwhile, Calhoun had openly broken with Jackson and put himself at the head of the Nullifiers; the Nullifiers won the two-thirds majority in the state legislature necessary to call a state convention; and in November, 1832, the state convention declared the tariff laws null and void and forbade their enforcement in South Carolina.

When Congress met in December, Jackson called for thorough tariff reform but at the same time announced his determination to enforce all federal laws throughout the land, by military means if necessary. This situation produced the Compromise Tariff of 1833. Snatching from the Jackson party the credit for tariff reform, Clay and Calhoun united to push through a measure by which all tariff rates were to be reduced by gradual steps over a 10-year period to a uniform rate of 20 percent. Congress also complied with Jackson's demand that it simultaneously pass a Force Act, authorizing him to use the armed forces to uphold the laws. The South Carolina convention then reassembled and rescinded its nullification of the tariff laws, but got in the last word by nullifying the Force Act.

The seemingly inconclusive outcome should not obscure the important long-range effects of this dangerous crisis. The fact that the Nullifiers could claim victory — the tariff had been reformed — heightened their uncompromising attitude toward the federal government and gave them complete dominance over South Carolina. From this time on, the state and its magnetic leader Calhoun sought to unite the South in radical resistance to "federal tyranny," and the incessant agitation from this source was a major factor in producing the eventual secession of the southern states.

In the shorter run, nullification and disunion were discredited. Every other southern legislature denounced the South Carolina doctrine, the aged Madison denied that it derived from the Kentucky and Virginia resolutions of 1798, and the country as a whole responded enthusiastically to the nationalistic sentiments that Jackson expressed in opposing the Nullifiers. In fact, Jackson's zeal for preserving the Union led him to embrace a nationalistic interpretation of the Constitution that greatly embarrassed Van Buren and other state-rights Jacksonians. Heretofore the state-rights idea had been associated with democratic-mindedness in American politics, but now that the people's candidate was in the White House proclaiming federal pre-eminence over the states, federal power seemed less threatening. Perhaps the most significant result of the nullification crisis was the decline of state-rights sentiment in the face of a rising democratic nationalism.

INDIAN REMOVAL

Jackson was not always a single-minded champion of federal prerogatives, as indicated by his handling of claims of the Cherokee nation, one of the Five Civilized Nations. A practical westerner and renowned Indian fighter who was not inclined to romanticize the "noble savage," the Tennessee president winked at Georgia's expropriation of Cherokee lands in defiance of a federal court ruling. In *Cherokee Nation* vs. *Georgia* (1831) and *Worcester* vs. *Georgia* (1832), the Marshall court sided with the Indians and invalidated the state's claim to Cherokee territory. But Jackson refused to enforce the ruling, reportedly saying, "John Marshall has made his decision, now let him enforce it."

That which followed — the enactment of the Indian Removal Act of 1830 and the relocation at gun point of these Native Americans to territory beyond the Mississippi — is one of the darker chapters in the nation's history. Amid scenes of indescribable suffering, some 4,000 of the 16,000 refugees died in 1838 and 1839 of cold, hunger, and disease along the 800-mile-long route known in Cherokee memory as the "Trail of Tears." One witness, the young Frenchman Alexis de Tocqueville, watched as "the wounded, the sick, newborn babies, and the old men on the point of death" passed near Memphis and feared he could never forget the "solemn spectacle." By 1839, three more of the remaining Five Civilized Nations — Choctaw, Chickasaw, and Creek — had been forcibly removed to the West under congressional authorization. In 1843, the fifth nation, the Seminoles of Florida who under the leadership of Osceola had resisted removal efforts since 1835, were all but exterminated by federal troops. Meanwhile, the Black Hawk War (1832) had ended effective Indian resistance to white settlement in the Old Northwest.

Through relocation, about 100,000 Indians were forced onto western lands that were pledged to them "forever." Their evacuation opened some 100 million acres of fertile eastern agricultural land to land-hungry whites. In return, they received $68 million, 32 million acres, and empty promises of federal protection from future white encroachment. Emerging as it did at the peak of the nullification crisis, the federal restraint implicit in Jackson's Indian policy may have confused some Jackson watchers. But Southerners, Westerners, and land speculators were delighted to find a president who shared their views of the Indian's place in an expanding nation. In fairness to Jackson — who, as nearly all historians agree, was no champion of Native American rights — the policy of dispossession and relocation that he so vigorously enforced was begun well before his election. Moreover, given the social values of the age and a context of growing conflict between Indian nations and eastern states, it did not appear an unreasonable solution to the "Indian problem." Convinced that assimilation was impossible and that autonomous Indian enclaves were impractical, if not unconstitutional, Jackson seems genuinely to have believed that his was a "just and humane policy" that placed the Indian "beyond the reach of injury or oppression." That it proved to be none of these things is indisputable; that other, more enlightened alternatives were open to him is less certain.

THE BANK WAR

Simultaneously with the nullification controversy, another great conflict had begun to take shape, this one between Andrew Jackson and the Second Bank of the United States. Jackson's experience with debt and depression had made him distrustful of all banks. On the bank question, his democratic-mindedness merged with his agrarian-mindedness to produce the conviction that banks fostered an unhealthy atmosphere of speculation, created boom-and-bust cycles, and transferred wealth from the many to the few. The national bank was open to special objection because it concentrated so much power in private hands and because it violated the Jeffersonian principles of strict construction and limited government. Jackson's views in all these respects reflected the resurgent agrarian-mindedness and neo-Jeffersonianism produced by the depression, as well as the antibank animus of the emerging workers' movement.

Actually, since Nicholas Biddle had become president of the bank in 1823, it had acted to restrain the numerous state-chartered banks from the tendencies Jackson feared, and most businesses and politicians had become convinced that the bank was indispensable to a soundly growing economy. Yet the opponents of banking in general saw the national bank as the head of the whole odius system and as the only part of the system that the federal government could readily reach. As a new boom gathered strength in the early 1830s, they were aided by an incongruous ally — entrepreneurial democracy.

As in the boom years following the War of 1812, the glittering promise of profits held out by a rapidly expanding market economy was creating a host of new entrepreneurs. For these business people, easy credit was the key to success, and the more reckless of the state-chartered banks became the citadels of the entrepreneurial spirit. By restraining the state banks from overexpansion, the national bank curtailed the profits and dimmed the prospects of the state banks and their borrowers. Consequently, the new entrepreneurs, the more speculative elements of the economy, regarded the bank as an aristocratic and repressive institution, representing established wealth and using its privileged position to hobble newcomers who attempted to join the race for success.

Both the entrepreneurs and the agrarian-minded had been heavily attracted to Jackson's Democratic party. Both groups opposed the bank on somewhat egalitarian grounds, but their common hostility to Biddle's institution could not indefinitely conceal the fact that their ultimate objectives were diametrically opposed.

When Jackson became president, Biddle was already thinking about getting a bill passed to renew the bank's charter, which was due to expire in 1836. Jackson dismayed the bank's supporters when he questioned its constitutionality and expediency in his first message to Congress. Their dismay turned to alarm when it became clear that Jackson would be a candidate for re-election in 1832. The old Adams-Clay alignment, calling itself the National Republican party, was planning to run Clay against Jackson, and Clay was urging Biddle to press for recharter before the election. Clay argued that this would force Jackson to approve a recharter bill, for a veto would be a damaging issue against him in the election. Biddle finally agreed, and in July 1832 a recharter bill passed Congress by substantial majorities.

Jackson promptly returned the measure to Congress with a veto message declaring the bank unconstitutional and demagogically denouncing the foreign ownership of much of the bank's stock. At the heart of his message was an eloquent paragraph expounding the Jacksonian social philosophy. The president granted that natural inequalities existed in every society. "But," he said, "when the laws undertake to add to these natural and just advantages artificial distinctions, to grant titles, gratuities, and exclusive privileges, to make the rich richer and the potent more powerful, the humble members of society — the farmers, mechanics, and laborers — who have neither the time nor the means of securing like favors to themselves, have a right to complain of the injustice of their government."

Jackson's hostility to the bank was genuine, but his veto message was at least in part designed to make the bank an election issue. The bank supporters did not have the votes in Congress to override the veto, but they confidently expected that both the veto and its author would be repudiated in the ensuing presidential election. When the returns were in, Jackson's estimate proved to be the shrewdest as he won 219 electoral votes to Clay's 40.

Yet the bank was far from dead. Jackson rightly feared that Biddle was determined to use the bank's great economic and political power to push a recharter bill through Congress over his veto. Equally determined to cripple the bank, the president resolved to remove the government's mounting deposits from its vaults. Federal receipts were booming along with the economy, the national debt had been paid off, and a federal surplus of millions of dollars was beginning to accumulate. These surplus federal deposits greatly extended the bank's lending ability, profits, and power. It took the administration a year to find a way of removing surplus deposits from the bank. After discharging two consecutive uncooperative secretaries of the treasury and after protracted negotiations with nervous state bankers, Jackson announced in September 1833 that henceforth the Treasury would deposit the federal funds in selected state banks, so-called deposit banks or pet banks.

Enraged by the removal of deposits, Biddle recklessly threw the full economic power of the national bank against the government. Deposit removal and Jackson's hostility made some contraction of the bank's loans necessary, but Biddle resolved to force such a severe loan contraction and to create such widespread distress that Congress would be compelled to restore the deposits and eventually recharter the bank. As a result, the "Panic Session" of Congress was under intense pressure during the winter of 1833–1834 to restore the deposits to relieve the country from mounting bankruptcies, unemployment, and distress. But Jackson's antibank majority held firm. Biddle was finally forced to relax the pressure, and the bank's doom was sealed — partly because Biddle's panic helped to prove Jackson's case against the bank's immense power.

BOOM AND BUST AGAIN

The destruction of the national bank was only a Pyrrhic victory in the Jacksonians' larger campaign to reform banking in general. Jackson and many of his principal followers were "hard-money" people who wanted all bank notes driven from circulation, leaving only gold and silver coin as a circulating medium. Their attack on the national bank was only the first step in their deflationary, agrarian-minded program, and they hoped to use the state-bank deposit system to reform the state banks. The deposit banks would be required, as a condition for receiving the deposits, to cease issuing notes in denominations under $5 or accepting such notes in their transactions with other banks. Gradually the prohibition would be extended to notes under $10 and then $20. Driving small notes from circulation would create a steady demand for specie for small transactions, and all banks would have to reduce their loans and note issues in order to have enough specie on hand to meet the demand.

But this scheme did not have time to get under way before it was overwhelmed by a massive inflation. The Jacksonians had destroyed the national bank's stabilizing influence on the economy just at the moment when powerful inflationary forces were pushing the country into a boom even more wildly speculative than the one that followed the War of 1812. With the national bank's restraining influence removed, the state banks expanded their loans, note issues, and profits; new state banks were chartered by the hundreds; the deposit banks themselves got out of control; and the wave of inflation and speculation rolled ominously higher toward its inevitable cresting and crash.

The hard-money supporters could only shout futile warnings. Their Jeffersonian constitutional scruples prevented them from attempting direct federal regulation of the state banks. Regulation at the state level was equally impossible because the uneasy alliance between hard-money (or agrarian-minded) Democrats and enterprise-minded Democrats began breaking down as soon as their common enemy, the national bank, was finally defeated.

Nevertheless, in 1836, Jackson attempted a drastic remedy with his Specie Circular. The flood of bank notes had stimulated an especially frantic speculation in public lands, and the Circular directed that thenceforth lands must be paid for in specie or specie-redeemable bank notes. Coming too late, the Specie Circular succeeded only in putting a strain on the vastly overextended structure of credit. The strain was increased by the Distribution Act that Jackson had reluctantly signed a few weeks before. Congress had decided to distribute the bulging federal surplus (approaching $40 million) among the states; the federal deposit banks were suddenly called upon to transfer vast sums to the state treasuries. Finally, in the spring of 1837, only weeks after Jackson left office, a financial crisis in England set off a wave of bankruptcies in the United States. The banks suspended specie payments, and the Panic of 1837 brought the whole towering pyramid of credit crashing down.

Jackson's hand-picked successor Van Buren was left to cope with a severe and prolonged depression. Aligning himself with the hard-money wing of the Democratic party, Van Buren proposed that the government sever its connections with all banks and keep its funds in its own "independent treasury" offices. He further proposed that the government accept and pay out only gold and silver coin, which would have some deflationary effect by creating a constant demand for specie. But in the main the proposal meant that the federal government would wash its hands of responsibility for the economy. Because of the split between hard-money and soft-money Democrats, Congress wrangled over the independent treasury throughout Van Buren's term. The bill was finally passed in 1840.

Meanwhile, the depression had forced most state legislatures to attempt some kind of banking reform. A few states prohibited banks entirely, others gave a monopoly of the banking business to a state-owned or mixed public-private bank, and most states adopted stricter regulations to prevent an overextension of credit by private banks. New York's widely imitated Free Banking Act of 1838 sought to provide state regulation and at the same time to divest banks of the monopolistic special privileges they enjoyed through their legislative charters. Foreshadowing general incorporation laws for all kinds of enterprises, the act provided that anyone who complied with certain regulations could engage in the banking business. Thus by the early 1840s, the country had reached a practical compromise on the banking question: banks would continue to stimulate economic growth, but they would be restrained through free competition and state regulation rather than through a national bank.

The long and hotly contested struggle over banking was important in two respects. On the most obvious level, it reflected the efforts of an economy newly swept forward by the market revolution to develop a credit and currency system that would sustain growth and broaden opportunity without causing disastrous boom-and-bust cycles. At a deeper level, it reflected the psychological ambivalence of a conservative, agrarian society toward the world of rapid change and growth into which it had suddenly been thrust.

The boom-bust cycle experience made its mark on the people. During the first great boom, 1815–1819, the country as a whole succumbed with uncritical enthusiasm to the new spirit of enterprise. The depression of the 1820s produced an equally decided reaction in the other direction — against banks, easy credit, paper money, and entrepreneurial ambition. Thus the return of prosperity and the second great boom, 1834–1837, evoked more ambivalent reactions. Some Americans again saw unlimited opportunity and clamored for unlimited credit; others, the neo-agrarians who remembered the 1820s, championed hard money, took seriously Jackson's Bank Veto plea for equal-rights, and contrasted the self-interest of privileged corporations (especially banks) with old republican virtues. The great depression of 1837 and its long aftermath increased neo-agrarian fears of the collusion of legislatures and corporations. New midwestern state constitutions of the 1840s placed restrictions on both legislative and corporate power. Ideological differences, dating to the conflicts of Jefferson and Hamilton, remained, despite the new politics of the second party system.

THE NEW POLITICS

Just as the Jacksonian era saw the evolution of financial institutions and practices to serve the emerging spirit of enterprise, so did it see the evolution of political institutions and practices to serve the emerging spirit of egalitar-

ian democracy. The basic feature of the new politics was the two-party system, which had flourished briefly and imperfectly around 1800 and which
re-emerged to reach its full development only in the 1830s.

Carrying to the national level the new-style democratic politics that had
emerged in the states during the 1820s, the Jacksonians created a strong
political party and forced their opponents to imitate their organization and
techniques for wooing a mass electorate. The anti-Jacksonians were at first
an ill-organized coalition of Clay-Adams National Republicans, Nullifiers,
and — out of hostility to the Van Buren organization in New York — the
democratic-minded anti-Masons. These elements were unable to unite to
stem the Jacksonian tide in the presidential election of 1832, but they were
already beginning to learn the lessons of Jacksonian politics. In fact the anti-
Masons had anticipated the Democrats in calling a national party convention
representing the grass-roots elements of the party to replace the discredited
caucus method of nominating candidates.

A powerful, unified opposition party developed only in 1833–1834 when
Jackson's removal of deposits caused the defection of many business-minded
Democrats and enabled his opponents to unite on the platform of resistance
to executive tyranny. Taking the name *Whigs* to identify themselves with
earlier defenders of liberty, they stood for sound business enterprise and a
program of Republican nationalism. Though the Whigs drew increasing support from all sections and classes, they appealed especially to the wealthier
and more established members of the business community, to the manufacturing interests, and to the larger southern planters whose staple crops involved them extensively in the commercial network. Calhoun's Nullifiers
cooperated with the Whigs for a few years, but after 1837 returned to the
Democratic party.

In 1836 the new Whig party sought to capitalize on political sectionalism
by running three presidential candidates, hoping to throw the election into
the House of Representatives. But the magic of Jackson's popularity was
sufficient to win his candidate, Van Buren, a slim majority over all three
Whigs. The Whigs' day finally came in 1840 when the Democrats were discredited by the depression and when the Whigs outdid the Democrats at
the game of democratic politics. Running the popular old Indian fighter William Henry Harrison as the people's candidate against the "aristocratic" Van
Buren, the Whigs whipped up enthusiasm with monster rallies, torchlight
parades, songs, and log-cabin symbolism to win a sweeping majority.

The presidential election of 1840 also produced by far the largest outpouring of voters yet seen. Only 27 percent of the estimated eligible voters
had voted for president in 1824; the Jackson-Adams contest of 1828 had
raised the figure to 56 percent; but the contest of 1840 brought out 78 percent of the eligible electorate, a proportion that may never have been
equaled since. This dramatic rise in political interest was a result of the full
development of the two-party system. By 1840 the two parties were almost
equally strong not only at the national level but also in every section, in
most of the states, and in a majority of counties. This meant closely contested

elections for all offices from sheriff to president with no efforts being spared to woo hesitant voters. Each party maintained an elaborate network of stridently partisan newspapers in Washington, the state capitals, and countless villages and towns. Rival orators stumped every neighborhood for months before every election. Competing systems of party committees at county, state, and national levels issued a constant stream of broadsides and pamphlets, organized parades and rallies, and made sure that no voter stayed away from the polls on election day. This incessant political activity not only brought voters to the polls in droves, but also made politics a leading form of American recreation, while providing the population with a massive political education.

But the parties were as much affected by the voters as they affected the voters. The new-style democratic politicians of both parties developed an acute sensitivity to shifts in public opinion and became expert in building coalitions that would yield a majority or near-majority. The Whigs continued to appeal more strongly to business interests, the well-to-do, manufacturers, and large planters, while the Democrats attracted smaller farmers, workers, and frontier areas. But both parties needed additional support to achieve a majority, and both quickly learned the techniques for constantly adjusting their positions to changing public moods. As a result the parties tended not to differ sharply in normal times and to maintain a nearly even balance of strength. From Jackson's day to our own, with only brief interruptions, this two-party system has remained a reasonably sensitive instrument for translating majority opinion into public policy while moderating the sharpness of conflict among the diverse groups that compose American society.

CONFLICTING HISTORICAL VIEWPOINTS: NO. 4

What Was Jacksonian Democracy?

In his Life of Andrew Jackson *(3 vols., 1860), the nineteenth-century historian James Parton concluded that the seventh president was "a patriot and a traitor.... A democratic autocrat. An urbane savage. An atrocious saint." On this note of paradox, scholarly investigation of Jacksonian politics began, and the Jacksonian era remains among the most controversial in American history.*

Parton, the earliest and most distinguished nineteenth-century Jackson scholar, represented the patrician school of historians. Sons of affluent and often aristocratic eastern families, deeply suspicious of popular democracy and the common folk, these early historians viewed Jacksonianism as the degradation of American government. Jackson, they affirmed, was an illiterate backwoods barbarian, the agent of the unwashed and ignorant masses.

Soon after 1900, a generation of reform-minded scholars challenged this decidedly conservative interpretation. Countering the anti-democratic beliefs of the patricians with pro-democratic views, these progressive historians celebrated Jackson as the champion of the popular will. Thus, in his distinguished Life of Andrew Jackson *(2 vols., 1911), John Spencer Bassett praised the rustic Tennessee president for his "brave, frank, masterly lead-ership" of a broad democratic movement. Although generally agreed on the nature of Jacksonian democracy, the progressives often argued about its origins.* In The Frontier in American History *(1920) and* The United States, 1830–1850 *(1935), Frederick Jackson Turner emphasized the influence of frontier democracy in the development of Jacksonianism. In Turner's view, Jacksonian Democracy was a sectional, rather than a class, movement. It was inspired and sustained, he believed, by the pioneer societies of the new states of the West and Southwest. To Arthur M. Schlesinger, Jr., on the other hand, Jacksonianism was "a problem not of sections but of classes." In his* Age of Jackson *(1945), the younger Schlesinger included eastern wage earners as well as western farmers among the Old Hero's supporters. The movement, he argued, pitted "noncapitalist groups, and laboring men, East, West, and South" against "capitalist groups, mainly Eastern."*

By the 1950s and 1960s the critics of the progressive interpretation, par-ticularly of Schlesinger's labor thesis, were numerous. Bray Hammond (Banks and Politics in America, *1957) and Edward Pessen* (Jacksonian Amer-ica, *1969), for example, denied that Jackson's was a working-class move-ment. Arguing that his supporters were not common people at all but incipient entrepreneurs, Hammond characterized the Jacksonians as "newer, more aggressive businessmen" who clashed with "an old and conservative merchant class." According to Pessen, Old Hickory was anti-labor, and workers opposed him at the polls. Marvin Meyers* (The Jacksonian Persua-sion, *1957) and John W. Ward* (Andrew Jackson, Symbol for an Age, *1955), on the other hand, fastened on symbolism and psychology to explain the Jacksonian phenomenon. In differing though complementary studies, these scholars concluded that in Jackson, Americans found not a champion of class or section but the embodiment of old-fashioned republican virtues. The ultimate refutation of the Schlesinger interpretation, however, came from Lee Benson, who argued in* The Concept of Jacksonian Democracy *(1961) that Jacksonianism existed only as a figment of the historical imag-ination. Benson's argument that ethnic and religious differences were more important than class or section in determining voting behavior seemed to invalidate the need for the concept of Jacksonian Democracy altogether.*

While Benson's ethnocultural thesis attracted numerous followers and de-stroyed forever any notion that Jacksonian Democracy had a purely class or sectional basis, over the last two decades scholars have sought to restore some meaning to the concept of Jacksonian Democracy by focusing on the ways Jacksonian politics were a response to the social, economic, and cul-tural changes of the era. Harry L. Watson has synthesized much of this re-cent work in his Liberty and Power *(1990). Watson argues that Jacksonian politics represented "a serious policy debate about the future of the Re-public and the nature of its society," as Whigs and Democrats offered dif-ferent positions on how best to respond to the most sweeping change of the day, the emerging market revolution. At the same time, while "ethnocul-tural tensions" affected voters' choices, such conflict did not necessarily override concern about more substantive economic and social issues. Other scholars, while also emphasizing the centrality of the market revolution to Jacksonian politics, have noted that political change during the era sometimes came from actors outside the formal party system, such as the working-class radicals of New York City during the 1830s, brilliantly detailed in Sean Wilentz's* Chants Democratic *(1984).*

While the Old Hero is no longer the focus of studies of Jacksonian America, debate over the nature of the political party system launched by his election in 1828 continues to rage.

FOR FURTHER READING

Robert V. Remini's *Andrew Jackson* (3 vols., 1977–1984) is both a comprehensive and flattering portrait. Glyndon Van Deusen's *The Jacksonian Era* (1959) provides a generally Whiggish overview of the entire period. John Ashworth's *"Agrarians" and "Aristocrats"* (1983), Ronald P. Formisano's *The Transformation of Political Culture* (1983), and Harry L. Watson's *Jacksonian Politics and Community Conflict* (1981) describe party formation in the Jacksonian era. Robert V. Remini has analyzed *Andrew Jackson and the Bank War* (1967); James Roger Sharp's *The Jacksonians Versus the Banks* (1970) follows the controversy in the states; and Edward Pessen's *Riches, Class, and Power Before the Civil War* (1973) provides a valuable social portrait of the era. In *The Political Culture of the American Whigs* (1979), Daniel Howe considers some of the nation's most influential political losers; in *Prelude to Civil War* (1966), William Freehling observes the nullification controversy in South Carolina; and Charles Wiltse focuses on *John C. Calhoun: Nullifier, 1828–1839* (1949). Other important biographies of Jackson's contemporaries include Merrill D. Peterson, *The Great Triumvirate: Webster, Clay, and Calhoun* (1987), and Robert V. Remini, *Henry Clay* (1991). Ronald N. Satz outlines *American Indian Policy in the Jacksonian Era* (1975); the consequences of those policies may be traced in Thurman Wilkins's *Cherokee Tragedy* (1970) and Arthur DeRosier's *Removal of the Choctaw Indians* (1970). Bernard W. Sheehan's *Seeds of Extinction* (1973) thoughtfully analyzes the evolution of pre-removal white attitudes; and in *Fathers and Children* (1975), Michael Rogin ranges widely, draws upon both Marx and Freud, and explains the dispossession of the Indians. Richard White examines the *Roots of Dependency* (1983) for the Choctaws and compares their experience with that of two other tribes — the Pawnees and the Navajos — removed from their lands later in the century. A firsthand impression of Martin Van Buren can be gained from his *Autobiography* (published in the *Annual Report of the American Historical Association*, 1918); and Donald B. Cole examines *Martin Van Buren and the American Political System* (1984). The analyses of Jacksonian America by European observers are highly illuminating. The classic is Alexis de Tocqueville's *Democracy in America* (2 vols., 1835–1840). Also fascinating are Michael Chevalier, *Society, Manners, and Politics in the United States* (1839); Francis J. Grund, *Aristocracy in America* (1839); Harriet Martineau, *Society in America* (1837); and Frances Trollope, *Domestic Manners of the Americans* (1832).

12

★ ★ ★ ★ ★ ★

Romanticism, Reform, Slavery, 1800s–1850s

THE COUNTRY had no sooner developed a two-party system for reflecting the majority will while moderating conflict than it ran head-on into the one conflict that could neither be resolved by majority will nor be moderated: the conflict over slavery. The age of enterprise and egalitarianism that produced the two-party system had also brought Americans to their highest pitch of confidence about the possibilities for individuals and for optimism about the future of their society. It was a reforming age, abounding in schemes for wiping out the remaining blemishes that marred the full perfection of humanity. It was a utopian age, spattered with perfectionist communities and looking forward to the early perfection of the whole society. Such an age was bound to find intolerable the most glaring affront to the liberal principles of the Declaration of Independence. Yet slavery of blacks was so deeply rooted as a social and economic institution that the slaveholders, though themselves heirs of the American liberation tradition, could not surrender it.

ROMANTICISM

Underlying the reformist spirit of the age was a new configuration of ideas and attitudes called *Romanticism*. A vast and complicated movement in the intellectual and literary history of the western world, Romanticism took different forms and suggested different conclusions for different countries, periods, and individuals. As used here, the term denotes the central tendencies of thought in the United States in the first half of the nineteenth century.

Romanticism grew out of the eighteenth-century Enlightenment and was akin to it. Both movements assumed that the world was designed for human happiness, emphasized human ability, and had little concern for the rights of women. In America at least, both movements led in the direction of optimism, individualism, and liberal political principles. But Romanticism was a reaction against the Enlightenment's mechanical view of the natural world and its emphasis on intellect. Where Enlightenment thought ascribed human competence to the ability through reason to understand the natural laws by which a watchmaker Creator regulated both the physical and moral universes, Romanticism distrusted intellect and valued human emotional and intuitive qualities. Regarding the natural world as the embodiment of a divine spirit, Romanticism held that the natural and the spontaneous were good and that the highest truth was derived not through reason but through the instantaneous spiritual intuition of the individual.

American Romanticism reached its most sophisticated and self-conscious form in the Transcendentalism of Ralph Waldo Emerson and the New England intellectuals who shared his belief in a philosophical system that exalted the spiritual over the natural, the intuitive over the empirical. Most of Emerson's contemporaries were probably unaware of Transcendentalism or Romanticism as an explicit body of doctrine, but the pervasive Romantic assumptions were apparent in every aspect of American life. The overwhelming theme of popular literature and the popular stage was the primacy of feeling over intellect. In more serious writing, James Fenimore Cooper celebrated the moral perfection and superior wisdom of the "natural" but untutored woodsman Leatherstocking and the "noble savage" Chingachgook, and from a Romantic standpoint, Nathaniel Hawthorne *(The Scarlet Letter, The House of the Seven Gables,* and *The Blithedale Romance)* and Herman Melville *(Moby Dick* and *Billy Budd)* explored the problem of evil and some darker implications of Romantic doctrine. Landscape painters of the Hudson River School, notably Thomas Cole and Asher B. Durand, sought to capture on canvas the emotion of the "sublime" evoked by the unspoiled majesty of American river valleys and mountains. Architects turned from the intellectually satisfying simplicity, harmony, and proportion of the eighteenth century's colonial or Georgian style to exotic and more titillating models — Gothic, Moorish, and Egyptian. Even in laying out gardens and parks, Americans abandoned formal patterns and tried to reproduce nature in its wild state, as in Frederick Law Olmsted's design for Central Park in New York City.

The influence of Romanticism extended far beyond intellectuals, writers, and artists. Jacksonian egalitarianism was reinforced by some widely accepted Romantic assumptions. The Enlightenment's emphasis on reason and education, with its insistence that reason was more highly developed in some people than in others, had prevented even the more liberal people of the eighteenth century from endorsing full egalitarianism and popular sovereignty. Thus, Jefferson had relied on a "natural aristocracy" to rule, trusting the people to elect the natural aristocrats to office, yet not trusting the people to dictate public policy. But when intuition rather than reason was seen as the source of truth, the situation changed. The Romantic doctrine of democracy was expounded most boldly by the Jacksonian politician and distinguished historian George Bancroft: "If the sentiment of truth, justice, love, and beauty exists in every one, then it follows, as a necessary consequence, that the common judgment in taste, politics, and religion is the highest authority on earth." Indeed, by Jackson's time, the semiliterate farmer who lived simply and close to nature was often regarded as being superior in virtue and wisdom to a city dweller whose "natural" impulses had been stifled by the artificialities of education and culture.

Jackson's enormous popularity may be attributed in considerable measure to the prevalence of such attitudes. The contest between Jackson and John Quincy Adams in 1828 was widely interpreted as pitting a natural man of virtue, a product of the American frontier, against the well-educated, highly cultured (and therefore suspect) Adams, who had the additional disadvantage of having spent much of his early life in the artificial surroundings of an overcivilized and decadent Europe. To Harvard-trained John Quincy Adams, Jackson was "a barbarian who could not write a sentence of grammar and hardly could spell his own name." But the people found in him the embodiment of all the natural wisdom of the common folk. In the presidential election of 1840, the Whigs turned the tables by using, in naked parody, the Jacksonian political formula. Deftly exploiting a hard-cider and log-cabin symbolism, they presented William Henry Harrison, "the Ohio Plowman," as the representative of the "hardy yeomanry" whose "primitive" qualities contrasted sharply with the city-slicker airs of the Jacksonian candidate, Martin Van Buren. The voters who responded enthusiastically to these appeals had never heard of Romanticism as a body of doctrine, but the smashing victory they gave Harrison at the polls demonstrated their unconscious conversion to some key Romantic assumptions.

ROMANTIC CHRISTIANITY

Apart from political behavior, extensive popular acceptance of Romantic assumptions was most evident in religious behavior. Well into the nineteenth century, the story of religion in the United States was a story of the gradual erosion of the originally dominant Puritan-Calvinist strain of Protestant Christianity. In an increasingly self-reliant, optimistic, and individualistic society, it continually became more difficult to sustain a view of life that emphasized the awful sovereignty of God, the sinfulness and helplessness of humanity, and the necessity for salvation by God's miraculous and arbitrary grace.

Under the impact of the eighteenth-century Enlightenment, some members of the more sophisticated classes had abandoned the inscrutable, omnipresent God of the Calvinists for Deism's remote and kindly Creator. Others had moved in the same direction more gradually, retaining the outward forms and language of orthodox Christianity but coming to believe that a reasonable God was favorably disposed toward all people, that people were sufficiently endowed with reason to be capable of goodness, and that the objective of a religious life ought to be goodness in this world rather than

God's arbitrary salvation in a world to come. Such opinions spread rapidly even among the direct descendants of seventeenth-century Puritanism, the New England Congregationalists. However, violent controversy broke out between the liberal and orthodox factions. By the end of the century, the liberal Congregationalists — representatives of the often wealthier, better educated "rational" wing of American Protestantism — were breaking off to form separate churches and taking the name Unitarians. Replacing the God of Vengeance with the God of Benevolence, Unitarians stressed the basic goodness of human beings and the mercy of God. Heavily influenced by Enlightenment thought, they rejected trinitarianism and what they thought to be the irrational side of Christian orthodoxy for a doctrine of God in one person.

Though Unitarianism and even its more popular offshoot, Universalism, remained minority movements — too intellectual, perhaps too optimistic for the great mass of Americans — religious orthodoxy was unquestionably at a low ebb in the last quarter of the eighteenth century. The mighty orthodox counteroffensive, the Great Awakening of the 1730s and 1740s, had spent its force; the Revolution had brought with it the spiritual and moral laxity usual in wartime; Deism was growing popular and militant; and the orthodox themselves had become listless and had begun to acquiesce in compromises with the spirit of the age.

It was under these circumstances that the orthodox clergy resorted to the emotional techniques of the Great Awakening to launch another vigorous counteroffensive known as the Great Revival, or the Second Great Awakening. Really a series of revival movements beginning around the turn of the century, the Great Revival kept the country in religious ferment for 25 years, obliterating the last traces of Deism and bringing a majority of Americans into the Protestant churches. America did not return to Calvinism, for in the process of capturing America, Protestant Christianity was itself captured and transformed by the Romantic optimism and individualism of American culture.

One phase of the Great Revival began with spectacular open-air camp meetings led by James McGready in Kentucky. These week-long extravaganzas of religious enthusiasm spread rapidly over the West and spawned a host of poorly educated but effective revivial preachers, including famed Methodist circuit rider Peter Cartwright. These traveling revivalists left in their wake many new churches, which were mainly of such evangelical and popular groups as Baptists and Methodists who won converts at the expense of the often staid Presbyterians, Congregationalists, and Episcopalians.

Meanwhile President Timothy Dwight of Yale and his protégé Lyman Beecher were showing the conservative clergy in the East how to use a more restrained revivalism as a technique for combating Unitarianism and maintaining the hegemony of orthodox Congregationalism. At the same time, the Congregationalists were cooperating with the Presbyterians in a joint campaign to evangelize the frontier areas of western New York and the Old Northwest. The revival movement and the western missionary effort both culminated in the 1820s in the spectacularly successful evangelism of Charles Grandison Finney, "father of modern revivalism" and precursor of later religious spell-binders like Dwight Moody, Billy Sunday, and Billy Graham. A former lawyer, Finney combined emotional intensity with some shrewdly devised new techniques: cottage prayer meetings preceding his protracted revival meetings, the full participation of women, the "anxious bench" where sinners sat directly under the gaze of the exhorter, the "holy band" of zealous young helpers to pray individually with the religiously smitten. His approach produced an explosion of emotional piety that entrenched a revivalistic "Presbygationalism" in the western regions. Although he was ordained a Presbyterian minister, Finney's "New School" Calvinism led him far from the belief in original sin and the hell fire and damnation of traditional American Protestantism. He embraced the optimistic doctrine of free will and laced his sermons with a call to perfectionism that urged social reform as well as personal salvation. Because Finney's doctrine, like the ones of a number of evangelists including Peter Cartwright, required "work as well as belief," it suggested that the redemption of American society could accompany the moral perfection of the individual. It was no accident, then, that among Finney's disciples were Theodore Dwight Weld and Arthur and Lewis Tappan, abolitionists who combined religious enthusiasm with moral reform.

Most revivalists started from positions they would have regarded as theologically orthodox, but like Finney they were more interested in the effectiveness, the preachability, of what they were saying than in its theological correctness. They quickly found that it was easiest to evoke the desired emotional response by preaching that God was anxious to save sinners, that sinners need only accept God's love. Many Presbyterians and the more conservative Protestants of all denominations in the South resisted this tendency, but the main body of American Protestantism moved gradually and unconsciously toward a Romantic theology. Love was viewed as the essence of the Christian life. God was love, freely offering his love to all who would accept it. Conversion was the emotional experience of acceptance and loving response. In some versions, as with many Methodists and in the theology that Finney himself taught, conversion was viewed as carrying with it a kind of spiritual perfection. The tone of this Romantic Protestantism was clearest perhaps in hymns like "O Love That Will Not Let Me Go" and its juvenile counterpart "Jesus Loves Me."

UTOPIANISM AND HUMANITARIANISM

Wherever the Great Revival burned — and especially in the frequently ravaged "burned-over district" of western New York — it left behind a bed of glowing embers ready to be fanned into varied reform, perfectionist, and utopian movements. Many were millennialist, expecting Christ's early return to establish the Kingdom of God on earth. When the Reverend William Miller calculated from biblical prophecies the time a Second Coming would take place, his followers reacted by disposing of their worldly possessions and expectantly gathering together at the appointed time. But they were disillusioned when the event did not occur, either in the originally predicted spring of 1844, or (after Miller had corrected his calculations) on October 21 of that year.

Various groups that looked forward to an early millennium sought in the meantime to assemble those who had been "perfected" through conversion and to form communities that would be without sin or blemish. Because they emphasized the primacy of love in all relationships and the freedom from sin that comes with salvation, these perfectionist utopians had particular difficulty with conventional notions about the proper relations between the sexes. One group, led by John Humphrey Noyes, established a flourishing community at Oneida, New York; its members rejected both private property for common ownership, and exclusive marriage for a carefully regulated system of "complex marriage" in which the men were husbands to all the women, and the women wives of all the men. A more long-lasting group, Mother Ann Lee's Shakers, solved the problem of exclusive love by practicing celibacy in their many communities. The most durable of all these groups was the Mormons; founder Joseph Smith claimed that he was God's prophet and that in upstate New York he had discovered some buried golden plates containing new divine revelations, which were translated and published as the Book of Mormon. Formed in New York in 1830, the community of Latter-Day Saints met persecution and moved to Ohio and Missouri for a brief time and then settled for a somewhat longer period in Nauvoo, Illinois. In the face of violent opposition to its developing practice of polygamy, the group moved in 1847–1848 to the virtually uninhabited Mexican territory of the Great Salt Lake Valley, where it thrived under the forceful leadership of Brigham Young.

In addition to the religiously oriented utopian movements, the Romantic age produced many secular utopian communities. Perhaps the best known was short-lived Brook Farm (1841–1847), founded at West Roxbury, Massachusetts, by the Unitarian minister George Ripley. A cooperative community of intellectuals, Brook Farm enjoyed the support of many people on the fringes of the Transcendentalist movement and such writers as Nathaniel Hawthorne and Margaret Fuller. A more ambitious socialist community at New Harmony, Indiana, was founded in 1825 by Robert Dale Owen, son of the English textile manufacturer and social reformer Robert Owen. The most extensive movement in secular communitarianism was inspired by Charles Fourier, a French social philosopher who had calculated the optimum size and organization for the ideal socialist community, which he called a "phalanx." Attracting the support of the prominent New York editor Horace Greeley, the Fourierists established some 40 or 50 phalanxes in the United States. In general, the secular utopias did not fare as well as those that had a religious motivation to keep their members loyal to the communitarian ideal. Many of the latter survived late into the nineteenth century, dwindling away only as the ebbing of religious revivalism dried up their source of recruits.

The perfectionist impulse that produced the utopian communities also inspired a broader series of movements aimed at wiping out every individual and social evil that the age could identify. Much of this reform activity was devoted to previously neglected classes of unfortunates. Dorothea Dix led the crusade that persuaded state legislatures to establish institutions for the care of the mentally ill. A related movement induced a number of states to undertake extensive programs of penal reform, emphasizing rehabilitation rather than merely punishment of criminals. For the first time, facilities were developed for educating the deaf, dumb, and blind. Indeed, the great movement for publicly supported common schools for all children got its real start in this perfectionist age, with Horace Mann's ambitious program in Massachusetts leading the way.

The reform movements that had the greatest impact were those most closely associated with the Great Revival. In the early stages of his revivalist campaign in Connecticut, Lyman Beecher devised the technique of organizing through local churches voluntary societies of lay members to promote various moral and evangelical objectives. By the late 1820s, these local societies had developed into a group of regional and national federations with paid agents to organize new local societies, raise funds, and carry out the various objectives of the federations. The American Home Missionary Society, which hired evangelists to carry the Great Revival into the West, was one of the first of the national federations. It was soon joined by other national societies that devoted themselves to such religious objectives as foreign missions, distributing Bibles and religious tracts, promoting Sunday schools, and saving sailors. Leadership and financing for all these societies came from the same group of revivalistic "Presbygational" ministers and philanthropists led by Beecher and Finney.

The developing Romantic theology of the Great Revival soon inspired a reform impulse that went beyond the evangelical objectives of the earliest societies. Finney in particular was preaching that conversion caused a disposition of "disinterested benevolence" in the converted, and his revivals left behind numbers of converts anxious to find some object on which to lavish their disinterested benevolence. The first object to be discovered was the drunkard.

The remarkable consumption of whiskey, hard cider, and rum in the early Republic constituted a serious social problem. The national liquor bill in 1810 ($12 million) exceeded the federal budget; in 1823 the annual per capita consumption of spirits was estimated to be 7.5 gallons, up from the 2.5 gallons consumed by each American three decades earlier. The problem prevailed even among the clergy — one beer was named Ordination Brew — and in 1816 the Methodists forbade their preachers to sell alcohol. Moved by the evangelical spirit of the age and alarmed by the widespread misuse of "demon rum," reform-minded Lyman Beecher inspired the organization of local temperance societies, which aimed at moderation in the consumption of alcohol. When this tactic proved ineffective, Beecher began campaigning for total abstinence, and in 1826 the American Society for the Promotion of Temperance was organized. Sending evangelists through the country to persuade people to sign a pledge of total abstinence, the Society's Temperance Union claimed 5,000 local branches with one million members by 1834.

Turning to politics to secure legal prohibition, temperance forces gained a local option law in Massachusetts in 1838, and the first statewide law prohibiting the manufacture and sale of liquor was passed in Maine in 1851. Soon most of the northern states had legislated against alcohol. In contrast to twentieth-century prohibitionism, the nineteenth-century movement was much weaker in the South, where only the border states of Delaware and Tennessee resorted to legislative prohibition.

Temperance was merely the first of the reform movements inspired by the Great Revival. By the 1830s, the headquarters for the benevolent societies had shifted from Boston to New York City, where Finney had been established as pastor of a great "free" church (charging no pew rents) for the poor and where the two leading financial angels of the general benevolence movement, the merchant brothers Arthur and Lewis Tappan, resided. New societies were continually being organized: to foster the pseudoscience of phrenology, to promote international peace, to encourage healthier diets, to stop the carrying of the mails on Sunday, or to prohibit the wearing of corsets. Into New York every May poured an army of the benevolent-minded from every part of the country to attend a series of annual conventions of all the societies.

WOMEN'S RIGHTS

Animated by the same humanitarian and moral impulses as men, women played significant roles in reform movements. Very often, however, their effectiveness was severely limited by the fears and prejudices of the men with whom they sought common cause. Angelina and Sarah Grimké, for example, left their South Carolina home and went north to aid in the antislavery cause. But their efforts to speak in its behalf were frequently opposed by male abolitionists and howled down by audiences unaccustomed to such "unladylike" endeavors. In 1840, Lucretia Mott, Elizabeth Cady Stanton, and a half-dozen other American women traveled to London to attend the World Anti-Slavery Convention only to be excluded because of their sex. In the 1850s, Susan B. Anthony had much the same experience in the temperance movement, where "ladies" were expected to be seen but not heard. The irony of such discrimination by men and by organizations dedicated to humanitarian causes was not lost on this generation of women. With Angelina Grimké, not a few of them would ask: "What can a *woman* do for the slave when she herself is under the feet of man and shamed into silence."

The sexual prejudices of the male reformers were mirrored and magnified by the larger society they sought to uplift. In the eyes of the law, women were perpetual minors, the wards of male guardians without whom they had no separate legal identity. Although often idealized by men for their tenderness and purity, women could not vote, hold office, sit on juries, or speak in public. They enjoyed few property guarantees, suffered gross education and job discriminations, and had no legal claim to their own incomes. Women found divorce laws stringent and prejudicially administered. They were legally subject to their husbands, even to corporal punishment by them; until 1850, nearly every state permitted wife beating "with a reasonable instrument" (defined by one Massachusetts judge as a "stick no bigger than my thumb"). Men also enjoyed a virtual monopoly on property rights. Except in Mississippi (after 1837) and New York (after 1845), women who owned real estate — generally only single women could — did so only through the authority of a male guardian.

Confronted by such disabilities, women (usually of the upper-middle class) organized for their own relief, often combining women's rights with temperance, abolition, public education, and prison reforms. Except for some highly significant breakthroughs in the fields of literature and education, their successes were few; throughout the period, feminism remained little more than an attitude shared by a few intrepid social pioneers. Sarah Grimké's *The Equality of the Sexes* (1838) and Margaret Fuller's *Women in the Nineteenth Century* (1844) were important early women's manifestoes. Amelia Bloomer's sensible but much ridiculed crusade for dress reform, Lucy Stone's repudiation of marriage laws that gave a husband "injurious and unnatural superiority" over his wife, and Stanton and Mott's Seneca Falls declaration (1848) of women's independence ("We hold these truths to be self-evident: that all men *and women* are created equal") symbolized a heightening feminist consciousness. But the work of these early feminists scarcely touched the lives of the vast majority of women. Sisterhood was not powerful in antebellum America. For all the vigor of their protest, the Susan B. Anthonys and the Angelina Grimkés of that era organized more effectively for causes other than their own. Despite the reform enthusiasms of the age, nineteenth-century concerns were nearly always restricted to the rights of *men*, not women.

ABOLITION

While the women's movement probably owed little directly to evangelical Christianity, religion was clearly a principal engine of abolition. The unfocused impulses of disinterested benevolence fostered by the Great Revival found their great and absorbing object in the institution of human bondage. Before 1830, the organized antislavery movement had been small and ineffectual, drawing its support mainly from those persons, notably Quakers, with strong religious scruples against the institution. A scattering of manumission societies, principally in the upper South, encouraged owners to free their slaves. Since 1821, Benjamin Lundy had published *The Genius of Universal Emancipation*, a newspaper dedicated to "olive-branch" abolitionism: genteel persuasion, gradual manumission, and compensation to slave owners. In addition, the American Colonization Society had been promoting (without much success) the migration of free blacks to Africa; this conservative approach to the problem aroused the suspicion of both the defenders and the critics of slavery.

Only after the British Parliament's widely publicized debates over emancipation came to the attention of the leaders of the American benevolence movement did antislavery become a major force on this side of the Atlantic. In 1830 the Tappan brothers, caught up in the religious fervor of the Great Revival, helped organize an antislavery society in New York. The next year in Boston, young, radical William Lloyd Garrison left Benjamin Lundy's employment to set up his own militant antislavery newspaper, *The Liberator*, which was "harsh as truth," "uncompromising as justice," and untainted by moderation. In the following years, Garrison and the small group of zealous antislavery reformers he inspired in New England furnished an uncompromising ideology of "immediatism" — emancipation without delay, condition, or compensation — for the growing antislavery movement, while the Finney-Tappan benevolence movement committed its substantial support, stretching west from New York, to the cause.

At first, antislavery was only one among many causes espoused by the Tappans and their associates. A turning point came when one of Finney's ablest young converts and apprentice evangelists, Theodore Dwight Weld, shifted his energies from temperance to become wholly devoted to abolitionism. In 1833, Weld enrolled at Lane Seminary in Cincinnati, a school that had just been established under Lyman Beecher's presidency to train Finney's converts for the ministry. Proselytizing among his fellow students, Weld provoked the famous Lane Debate, a revivalistic discussion of slavery that lasted for 18 days and nights and ended with the conversion of virtually the entire student body to the abolitionist cause. Meanwhile the Tappan and the Garrison groups had come together in uneasy alliance to form the American Anti-Slavery Society, which now employed Weld and his fellow Lane converts as agents. During the mid-1830s these and others conducted a whirlwind evangelistic campaign through New England, New York, Pennsylvania, and the Old Northwest, which resulted in the conversion of some whole communities to antislavery and the organization of over 1,000 local antislavery societies with more than 100,000 members.

The abolitionism preached by Weld and his associates emphasized the moral evil of slavery and the religious duty of good people to align themselves against it. In fact, most abolitionists were intensely pious people, driven by religious sentiments that portrayed good works as the result of salvation. At first they naively hoped to persuade slaveholders to abandon the institution by sending into the South tons of pamphlets portraying the sin of holding human beings in bondage. The slaveholders countered, however, with religious arguments of their own, for the proslavery argument, too, found its moral base in biblical texts.

Although the leadership of the antislavery movement remained largely white, blacks were vitally active in its ranks from the beginning. Before 1800, the Free African Society of Philadelphia and such black spokesmen as the astronomer Benjamin Banneker and the church leader Richard Allen had denounced slavery in the harshest terms. By 1830 there were 50 black-organized antislavery societies, and blacks participated in the formation of the American Anti-Slavery Society in 1833. In a movement notable for impassioned oratory, black speakers on the antislavery circuit were among the most compelling. Isabella, an illiterate former slave better known as Sojourner Truth, moved audiences in New England and the West, while the brilliant fugitive slave Frederick Douglass emerged as the foremost abolitionist orator, lecturing to audiences throughout the North and England. Blacks also helped run the Underground Railroad; Harriet Tubman, its most notable "conductor" and herself an escaped slave, was said to have led more than 300 blacks to freedom.

Generally, black abolitionists shared the nonviolent philosophy of the Garrisonians. But black anger could not always be contained. Both David Walker's *Appeal* (1829) and Henry Highland Garnet's address to a Convention of Colored Citizens (1843) urged the slaves to arms. "Strike for your lives and liberties," Garnet commanded. "Rather die freemen than live to be slaves."

Not the least of the black abolitionists' frustrations was the racism they found within antislavery ranks. Moved by both tactical considerations and race paternalism, white abolitionists tried to limit their black counterparts to peripheral roles and sometimes either assigned them to separate-but-equal auxiliaries or excluded them from local organizations. The deeds of the ambivalent white abolitionists, Garrison and Weld included, did not always match their egalitarian rhetoric. Outside the movement, the mood was less simplistic. Despite the rapid spread of antislavery sentiment, abolitionism remained highly unpopular in much of the North, particularly in Indiana and Illinois. Deeply infected with the same race prejudice that bolstered slavery in the South, many Northerners feared that abolitionism threatened established racial practices. Others with no great fondness for slavery were still afraid that antislavery agitation imperiled the Union. Abolitionists had to face hostile mobs, official indifference, and police hostility; one white editor, Elijah P. Lovejoy, was killed in 1837 for his antislavery views.

The abolitionists, however, gained support far beyond their own ranks when they moved into politics in the mid-1830s with a petition campaign asking Congress to abolish slavery and the odious slave trade in the District of Columbia. Many Northerners who shied away from the constitutionally difficult question of abolition in the slave states were glad to support the abolitionist petitions with reference to the national capital over which Congress had unquestioned jurisdiction. Northern opinion was generally indignant when Congress responded to southern pressure in 1836 by adopting a "gag rule" refusing to consider petitions related in any way to slavery. At this point, ex-president John Quincy Adams, who served in the House of Representatives, took up the cause. Originally not an abolitionist, "Old Man Eloquent" was infuriated by this denial of the constitutionally guaranteed right of petition. Supported by a growing body of northern opinion, he carried on a dogged fight against the gag rule until it was eventually repealed in 1844. Though the North was still far from abolitionized, the steady agitation of the question was gradually conditioning increasing thousands of voters to view the slaveholding section of American society with hostility.

THE SOUTH AND SLAVERY

Meanwhile white Southerners were being forced to re-examine their attitudes toward their "peculiar institution." Christianity and the liberal principles of the Declaration of Independence affected Southerners just as much as Northerners. During the latter part of the eighteenth century, many of the South's outstanding leaders had emancipated their slaves, denouncing slavery as incompatible with the ideals of the Revolution. Thomas Jefferson and other liberal Southerners had counted on the gradual operation of economic forces to eliminate slavery in the South as was already being done in the North. As late as the Missouri debate in 1820, southern members of Congress refused to defend slavery in the abstract, arguing instead that the unfortunate institution had been inherited and was difficult to eradicate.

Southern opinion had already begun to shift in a direction that would ultimately lead to civil war. The fundamental cause for change was the market revolution. Until the end of the eighteenth century, the stronghold of slavery had been in the Chesapeake tobacco region of Virginia and Maryland. The economic depression in this region following the Revolution had encouraged the spread of antislavery sentiment and afforded some grounds for Jefferson's hope that the institution might wither away. But farther down the coast the great plantations of South Carolina had continued to flourish; with the perfection of the cotton gin in 1793, high profits stimulated the rapid spread of plantation slavery into the up-country. South Carolina was the only state that permitted a resumption of the barbarous foreign slave trade before its prohibition by Congress in 1808.

The most spectacular expansion of plantation slavery came during the boom years following the War of 1812 when it flooded over the newly opened lands of Alabama, Mississippi, and Louisiana. Taking deep root as a flourishing economic system, the chief source of wealth, and a spur to enterprise, slavery became increasingly impossible for white Southerners to surrender. The cotton boom in the lower South dampened antislavery tendencies in the upper South by creating a heavy demand at high prices for the surplus slaves of the declining tobacco kingdom. Nonslaveholders, too, came to feel that they had a stake in the institution. Only about one-fourth of the white families in the South ever owned slaves, and even among the slaveholding minority only 12 percent owned as many as 20 slaves. But the South was as deeply infected as any other part of the country with the spirit of enterprise that the market revolution generated, and in the South the acquisition of slaves was becoming the primary and almost the exclusive means of raising one's economic and social status.

At the same time, another factor was reinforcing the white South's growing economic attachment to slavery. Thomas Jefferson had assumed that deep antipathies between whites and blacks would make emancipation unthinkable without some plan for removing the emancipated slaves from the United States. This conviction that the two races could not live side by side in freedom received a powerful impetus in the 1790s when the slaves of the nearby French West Indian island of Santo Domingo rose in rebellion, murdering or forcing into exile thousands of their former masters. From this time on, the more the white South became attached to slavery as an economic institution, the more it feared its slaves and, consequently, the more it insisted on slavery as an institution for controlling this dangerous population. Alarms over threatened slave insurrections became more frequent, some with a basis in fact and others arising more from imaginations made excitable by fear and guilt.

A real insurrection finally came in August 1831, when a slave named Nat Turner led an uprising in Southampton County, Virginia. Over 60 whites were killed before the rebels were crushed. A wave of hysteria washed over the whole domain of slavery, and the Virginia legislature was frightened into the Old South's only full and free debate over the peculiar institution. Not a voice was raised to justify slavery in the abstract, and proposals for gradual emancipation were barely defeated.

The entire South sensed that a fateful choice had been made. The fears of slave insurrection had culminated just at the time when slavery was becoming too entrenched as an economic institution to be surrendered and at the very moment when the American antislavery movement was launching a massive propaganda barrage against slavery, appealing to Christian and liberal values that white Southerners shared. Slowly and reluctantly, Southerners faced the fact that, if slavery were to be retained, they could no longer ease their consciences with hopes for its eventual disappearance or tolerate the expression of such hopes in their midst. Southern minds must be nerved for a severe struggle in defense of the institution to which they now saw themselves committed. So southern leaders of the Calhoun school began trying to convince themselves and others that slavery was not merely a "necessary evil" but a "positive good," while southern legislatures abridged freedom of speech and the press, made manumission difficult or impossible, and imposed tighter restrictions on both slaves and free blacks.

Proslavery arguments never succeeded in relieving the majority of white Southerners from varying degrees of moral uneasiness or feelings of guilt. Like all people unsure of their ground but unable to change it, Southerners responded to attacks on slavery with mounting vehemence. Even in the 1830s, when both Southerners and Northerners were still preoccupied with the Jacksonian political issues, the abolitionists' petitions provoked such violent congressional debates that the gag rule had to be imposed. Within another decade, the explosively emotional quarrel over slavery would move to the center of the political stage, there to remain until blood was shed.

CONFLICTING HISTORICAL VIEWPOINTS: NO. 5

How Brutal Was Slavery?

In his monumental studies American Negro Slavery *(1918) and* Life and Labor in the Old South *(1929), Ulrich B. Phillips set forth the classic defense of slavery as a labor system beneficial to both master and slave. A tireless re-*

searcher and a prolific writer, Phillips uncovered a wealth of new material and contributed enormously to our factual knowledge of the "peculiar institution." But the work of this Georgia-born scholar was seriously flawed by racial prejudice. The slave, he believed, was innately inferior and naturally submissive. In his view the plantation was a school in which primitive and uncouth blacks were purged of their African savagery and offered the blessings of western civilization and Christianity.

This sympathetic interpretation of a benign and paternalistic institution dominated American historical writing for almost three decades before World War II. But in the increasingly enlightened climate of racial opinion following the war, historians began reassessing traditional assumptions about the antebellum South's labor system. In American Negro Slave Revolts *(1943), Herbert Aptheker, a Marxist historian and a passionate civil rights advocate, portrayed a rebellious and discontented slave work force that contrasted sharply with the carefree darky of Phillips's idyll. The most sweeping revision, however, was Kenneth Stampp's broad synthesis* The Peculiar Institution *(1956). A distinguished liberal scholar who argued that "Negroes are, after all, only white men with black skins," Stampp viewed slavery as a harshly cruel system degrading to both exploiter and exploited. The typical slave, he concluded, hated both the institution and the master.*

Not all of Phillips's critics agreed with Stampp. In Slavery *(1959), Stanley Elkins, for example, offered a controversial study that blended Stampp's harsh criticism of slavery with Phillips's view of the slave as contented Sambo. Using social science and comparative history techniques, Elkins concluded that the labor system of the Old South was so brutal and dehumanizing that it infantilized its victims. According to this interpretation, the typical slave was thus childlike, docile, and convinced of self-inferiority.*

During the 1970s historians rejected Elkins's conclusions and moved beyond Stampp's. Increasingly the direction has been away from studying slavery as an institutional problem toward analyzing day-to-day life in slave quarters. Masters now attract less scholarly attention than slaves, and though the physically and emotionally coercive side is not discounted, the emphasis has shifted to the vigorous black culture largely independent of white influence. John Blassingame's study of plantation life and labor from the slaves' vantage point, The Slave Community *(1972), for example, describes the evolution of a remarkable, semi-autonomous black community and culture that inhibited white control and gave plantation blacks the means to survive an otherwise brutal and dehumanizing system. Eugene Genovese's* Roll, Jordan, Roll *(1974) also portrays (as its subtitle promises) "the world the slaves made." A leading Marxist historian who views American slavery as an essentially feudal, pre-bourgeois system of class exploitation, Genovese describes the slaves' deft manipulation of the two-edged sword of paternalism, "a doctrine of reciprocal obligations," of patronage and dependence, of mutual rights and mutual duties. He argues that by creating their own religion and maintaining strong family ties and a separate cultural identity, slaves "rendered unto Caesar," but they managed to fix the limits of white authority, to "assert manhood and womanhood in their everyday lives," and to resist the "moral and psychological aggression" of slavery and white supremacy. Although differing in important particulars, Herbert Gutman's* The Black Family in Slavery and Freedom, 1750–1925 *(1976) also focuses on the autonomy, rather than the dependence, of black society. Examining the black family and extended kinship network, Gutman finds close multi-generational ties, settled monogamous unions, and little evidence that African-American institutions were shattered by the slavery experience. A final example is Lawrence Levine's* Black Culture and Black Consciousness *(1977). Imaginatively examining the folk expressions of a creative slave society that was anything but degraded or pathological, Levine concludes that slaves were not wholly powerless to influence the patterns of their own lives — they were not "perfect victims." "For all of its horrors," he writes, "slavery was never so complete a system of psychic assault that it prevented slaves from carving out independent cultural forms." Although not completely ignoring the unjust and often unspeakably cruel dimensions of slavery, these scholars concluded that slaves' lives were often joyful, exuberant, and personally meaningful. Most of all, these writers appreciated the adaptive and creative capabilities of a people who, within an exploitive system, found a measure of cultural and personal autonomy. In recent years, however, some historians have suggested that the slave studies of the 1970s and 1980s overstated the theme of slave autonomy. In* American Slavery *(1993), Peter Kolchin argues that while the focus on slave culture and community has greatly expanded our knowledge of slave life, the emphasis on slave autonomy fails to convey adequately the reality that slavery ultimately oppressed and degraded those held in bondage.*

Another and far more controversial approach to the institution of slavery is in Robert Fogel and Stanley Engerman's Time on the Cross *(1974). Emphasizing the more salutary dimensions of the slave economy, the book attracted much public interest and scholarly criticism. This computer-based analysis contends that slave labor was more efficient and productive than free labor and that slaves lived comparatively well-provisioned, secure, and comfortable lives. "Over the course of his lifetime," the authors argue, "the typical slave field hand received about 90 percent of the income he produced." These conclusions, although less novel than the authors claim, provoked a storm of controversy. Many blacks found them offensive, and many scholars — including most historical quantifiers — faulted the data and research procedures upon which they were based. An example of scholarly criticism of* Time on the Cross *can be found in Herbert Gutman's* Slavery and the Numbers Game *(1975), which finds particular fault with Fogel and Engerman for their neglect of the beliefs and behavior of the slaves themselves.*

FOR FURTHER READING

In the absence of an adequate general account of Romanticism in American thought, much can be learned from the splendid segment of a study left uncompleted by Perry Miller, *The Life of the Mind in America from the Revolution to the Civil War* (1965). An older work by Octavius B. Frothingham is still the fullest account of *Transcendentalism in New England* (1876), but Anne C. Rose offers a good portrayal of *Transcendentalism as a Social Movement* (1981). General accounts of antebellum reform can be found in Alice Felt Tyler's *Freedom's Ferment* (1944) and Ronald G. Walter's *American Reformers, 1815–1860* (1978); Russell Nye's *Society and Culture in America* (1974) examines antebellum cultural and intellectual life. For the Great Revival and its impact on perfectionism and reformism, see Whitney Cross, *The Burned Over District* (1950); William McLoughlin, *Revivals, Awakenings, and Reform* (1978); Timothy Smith, *Revivalism and Social Reform* (1957); and Robert H. Abzug, *Cosmos Crumbling* (1994). David Rothman in *The Discovery of the Asylum* (1971) argues that antebellum reformers were moved less by humanitarianism than by a desire for social control. For other perspectives on antebellum social conditions and the reform impulse, see Ellen Du Bois, *Feminism and Suffrage* (1978); Nancy Cott, *The Bonds of Womanhood* (1977); Nancy Hewitt, *Women's Activism and Social Change* (1984); Stephen J. Stein, *The Shaker Experience in America* (1992); Paul E. Johnson, *A Shopkeeper's Millennium* (1978); W. J. Rorabaugh, *The Alcoholic Republic* (1979); and Ian Tyrrell, *Sobering Up* (1979).

Important studies of the Old South include Bertram Wyatt-Brown, *Southern Honor* (1982); James Oakes, *Slavery and Freedom* (1990); Elizabeth Fox-Genovese, *Within the Plantation Household* (1988); John Hope Franklin, *The Militant South* (1956); J. William Harris, *Plain Folk and Gentry in a Slave Society* (1985); and Mills Thornton, III, *Politics and Power in a Slave Society* (1978). Aspects of the peculiar institution are analyzed in Deborah Gray White, *Ar'n't I a Woman?* (1985); Barbara J. Fields, *Slavery and Freedom on the Middle Ground* (1985); William Scarborough, *The Overseer* (1966); and Charles B. Dew, *Bond of Iron* (1994). Ira Berlin's *Slaves Without Masters* (1974) portrays the life of the free black. Differing views on the origins of abolitionism are offered by Gilbert Barnes in *The Anti-Slavery Impulse* (1933) and by Louis Filler in *The Crusade Against Slavery* (1986). William S. McFeely's *Frederick Douglass* (1991) details the life of an important black abolitionist; Bertram Wyatt-Brown is the author of *Lewis Tappan and the Evangelical War Against Slavery* (1969); Gerda Lerner examines *The Grimké Sisters from South Carolina* (1967); Aileen Kraditor in *Means and Ends in American Abolitionism* (1969) emphasizes variety and conflict within the abolitionist movement; Robert H. Abzug in *Passionate Liberator* (1980) considers the life of radical abolitionist Theodore Dwight Weld; and Richard Sewell's *Ballots for Freedom* (1976) is a history of antislavery politics. The interpretations of a number of scholars on various aspects of abolitionism are presented in a volume of essays collected by Martin Duberman, *The Anti-Slavery Vanguard* (1965).

TABLE 6. PRESIDENTIAL ELECTIONS AND MAJOR EVENTS, 1840–1852

1840 **William Henry Harrison** (Whig) elected over Martin Van Buren (Democrat).

1841 Vice President **John Tyler** becomes President on death of Harrison.
Whig Congress repeals the independent treasury system.
Land Act of 1841: Pre-emption principle allows settlers to buy public lands they occupy at minimum price.
Tyler vetoes successive bills chartering a national bank and is disowned by the Whig party.

1842 Tariff of 1842, a Whig measure, extends substantial protection to American manufactures.
Webster-Ashburton Treaty with Great Britain settles the Maine boundary and other disputed matters.

1844 Tyler's treaty for the annexation of Texas defeated in the Senate.
James K. Polk (Democrat) elected over Henry Clay (Whig).

1845 Texas annexed by joint resolution of Congress.

1846 Democratic Congress reinstitutes the independent treasury system.
Tariff of 1846 substantially reduces rates.
Polk's veto of Rivers and Harbors bill checks policy of internal improvements.
Oregon controversy with Great Britain compromised.
Polk precipitates Mexican War by insisting on extreme Texas boundary claim.
Wilmot Proviso proposed to bar slavery from any territories acquired from Mexico.

1848 Treaty of Guadelupe Hidalgo ends Mexican War, with the United States paying Mexico for a vast cession in the Southwest.
Zachary Taylor (Whig) elected over Lewis Cass (Democrat) and Martin Van Buren (Free Soiler).

1849 Gold Rush to California.

1850 Vice President **Millard Fillmore** becomes president on death of Taylor.
Compromise of 1850: (1) California admitted as free state; (2) Utah and New Mexico territories organized on principle of squatter sovereignty; (3) Texas surrenders claims to area in New Mexico, and United States assumes Texas debt; (4) slave trade abolished in the District of Columbia; (5) a more stringent Fugitive Slave Law enacted.

1852 **Franklin Pierce** (Democrat) elected over Winfield Scott (Whig).

13

★ ★ ★ ★ ★ ★

Manifest Destiny and Sectional Conflict, 1840–1852

THOUGH the Whig and Democratic leaders continued to battle each other in the early 1840s over tariffs, the national bank, and internal improvements, these old issues no longer excited Americans as they had in Jackson's day. The market revolution had completed its psychological conquest of the country, and with hard times receding, an enterprising generation was engrossed in the pursuit of wealth and status.

For countless thousands, the pursuit led west toward the perennial American goal of cheap land and a fresh start. But now, for the first time in the American experience, there seemed a limit to the supply of cheap, fertile land. In the South the tide of settlement rolled up to the boundary of the Mexican province of Texas. Farther north it was nearing the treeless Great Plains, which were thought unfit for cultivation.

Yet neither political nor geographical boundaries were to halt the 200-year advance of the American frontier. Since the 1820s, American settlers had been pouring into Texas, where in 1836 they rebelled against Mexican authority, defeated a Mexican army, and set themselves up as an independent republic looking toward union with the United States. During the same period, wagon trains from the Missouri frontier had been crossing the plains along the northern borders of Texas and pushing on to trade with the ancient Spanish-Mexican settlement of Santa Fe on the upper Rio Grande. Still farther north, fur traders had followed in the tracks of Lewis and Clark, exploring the Rocky Mountains and bringing back tales of new promised lands beyond in the Oregon country and Mexican California. Meanwhile, the enterprising merchants of Boston and Salem and New York were sending their ships around Cape Horn at the southern tip of South America to pick up hides on the California coast and were becoming excited about the possibility of dominating trade with the Orient from the magnificent Pacific harbors at San Diego, San Francisco, and Puget Sound.

While Americans were discovering the far West, romantic assumptions were intensifying their faith in the superiority and glorious destiny of their free institutions. Rapidly the idea grew that it was the "manifest destiny" of these free institutions to spread over all the vast, thinly inhabited, and lightly held territories between the Mississippi Valley and the Pacific Ocean.

The growing enthusiasm for territorial expansion further confused an already tangled political situation, while raising an ominous question. The decade of the 1840s opened with the Whigs and Democrats still battling inconclusively over old issues that no longer stirred the voters, and both parties were for different reasons somewhat demoralized. Under these circumstances the issue of expansion was a godsend to ambitious politicians with various axes to grind. But it was a dangerous issue. The controversy over slavery was making the country edgy. The mounting hostility between North and South was becoming too apparent to be wished out of consciousness. A great crusade to fulfill the manifest territorial destiny of the United States might reunite Americans in enthusiastic patriotism. But it could also incite a disastrous sectional conflict over the territorial spoils.

TIPPECANOE — AND TYLER TOO

Such possibilities were still far from most people's minds as the Whigs took over the national government following their great victory in the presidential election of 1840. President Harrison called a special session of Congress to pass the traditional Whig program — repeal of the independent treasury system, a new national bank, a higher protective tariff, and a scheme for distributing the federal land revenues among the states. Yet the Whigs were the unluckiest of the major political parties. Within a month after his inauguration, "Old Tippecanoe" died, leaving the Whig program at the mercy of the vain, stubborn vice-president, John Tyler of Virginia (see Table 6, p. 165).

Tyler had left the Democratic party when Jackson threatened to coerce the South Carolina Nullifiers in 1832, and he retained much of the old-fashioned Virginian attachment to state rights. He went along with Clay in repealing the independent treasury system, but after indicating a willingness to approve a national fiscal agency, he vetoed two successive bills chartering a new national bank. By other vetoes, Tyler made it clear that Clay could have either a higher protective tariff or distribution but not both. Clay chose increased protection for manufacturers, and the Tariff of 1842 raised duties generally to the levels that had existed before the Compromise Tariff of 1833. Meanwhile, in a futile effort to secure distribution, the Whig Congress included in the Land Act of 1841 the principle of *pre-emption*. Pre-emption enabled any head of a family to settle on 160 acres of the public domain before they were offered for sale at the customary auction and then to bid them in at the minimum price of $1.25 an acre.

Thus the stubborn Virginia president frustrated every part of the Whig program except the higher tariff and caused Clay to accept a pre-emption system for which he had no great enthusiasm. The overwhelming majority of the Whig members of Congress, both northern and southern, turned on Tyler in fury and read him out of the Whig party. Every member of his cabinet resigned, Secretary of State Daniel Webster tarrying only a little longer than the others. Webster's delay was partly to enable him to complete the negotiations with England that led up to the Webster-Ashburton Treaty of 1842, compromising a dispute over the boundary between Maine and Canada. Bereft of party support, Tyler took up the issue of expansion, hoping that it might enable him to run for president in 1844. Secretly, his administration began negotiating with the Texas authorities for a treaty of annexation.

The Texas question had long been regarded as a threat to the delicate sectional balances that held the two parties together as national organizations. From the moment of the Texas Revolution in 1836, antislavery people had been denouncing it as a plot by southern filibusters to extend the area of slavery, and even Jackson, despite his warm friendship for the Texas leader Sam Houston, had delayed recognition of the new republic until after Van Buren was safely elected. Van Buren had similarly avoided the question of annexation during his administration as being too dangerous to the harmony of the Democratic party.

Thus, by pushing the Texas question to the fore, Tyler hoped to embarrass the old party leaders and either to run for president as the candidate of a pro-Texas third party or to displace Van Buren as the Democratic nominee. The potential for sectional conflict over the Texas issue was increased when Tyler brought in Calhoun as his Secretary of State to complete the secret negotiations for an annexation treaty. The treaty was signed and sent to the Senate in April 1844. Along with it, Calhoun sent a copy of a dispatch he had written to the British minister, Richard Pakenham, denouncing British interference in Texas, defending slavery as a positive good, and justifying annexation mainly as a measure in defense of slavery. Calhoun's Pakenham letter, irritating even moderate antislavery people, doomed the treaty to defeat in the Senate and produced violent political turmoil on the eve of the presidential nominating conventions.

THE PRESIDENTIAL ELECTION OF 1844

Clay and Van Buren had both seemed assured of nomination by their respective parties, and both wished to keep the Texas issue out of the campaign. At the end of April, hard on the heels of Calhoun's Pakenham letter, they published simultaneous letters opposing immediate annexation. Shortly thereafter, Clay was nominated by the Whig convention, but Van Buren's Texas letter aroused a storm of opposition against him at the Democratic convention.

Although a majority of the delegates to the Democratic convention had originally been instructed for Van Buren, the late developing Texas excitement had produced, especially in the southern and western states, a decided popular reaction in favor of a pro-Texas candidate. Van Buren's Texas letter was the signal for pro-Texas and anti-Van Buren factions to join forces in a last-ditch fight to block his nomination. Their strategy was to insist on a two-thirds majority for nomination. Many delegates who felt bound by their instructions to vote for Van Buren on the early ballots were nevertheless able to vote for the two-thirds rule that made his nomination impossible.

But if Van Buren could not muster a two-thirds majority, neither could his leading rival, Lewis Cass of Michigan. The deadlock might have destroyed the Democratic party if the convention had not finally hit upon a compromise candidate. James K. Polk had recently suffered two successive defeats in campaigns for governor of Tennessee, but he was almost the only Democrat of any prominence who could command the confidence of all the feuding factions. The hard-money Van Buren wing of the party respected him as a protégé of Jackson and able leader of the Democratic forces in the House of Representatives during the Bank War, while as a slaveholding Southerner and outspoken advocate of immediate annexation, he was acceptable to the expansionist, anti-Van Buren wing.

Having nominated Polk by acclamation, the convention adopted a platform calling for "the reoccupation of Oregon and the reannexation of Texas, at the earliest practicable moment." The Oregon question had recently generated considerable enthusiasm in the Northwest, but even there it had been overshadowed by the Texas question. The Oregon plank seems to have been included primarily to remove the sectional sting from the inescapable Texas issue.

The ensuing election reflected the nearly equal division of popular strength that the matured two-party system had by this time produced. In the closest presidential race to this time, Polk received 49.6 percent of the popular votes to 48.1 percent for Clay. Polk's majority margin in the electoral college was provided by New York, where the diversion of a small number of normally Whig votes to an antislavery third-party candidate swung the balance in favor of the Democrats.

The pro-Texas people interpreted this narrow victory as a mandate for annexation. Just before Polk's inauguration in early 1845, Congress approved, by joint resolution rather than treaty, the admission of Texas as one of the United States.

THE POLK ADMINISTRATION

Polk was one of the hardest working and most effective men ever to occupy the White House. Unimaginative, undramatic, and without much prestige when he entered office, he was nevertheless spectacularly successful in getting what he wanted from a deeply divided Democratic party and Congress and from other countries. And he wanted a great deal.

Polk was first of all an old-fashioned, doctrinaire Jacksonian Democrat. He wanted an independent treasury system reinstituted, and from his first Congress in 1846, he got it. He wanted a drastic downward revision of the tariff, and the same Congress gave him a tariff act incorporating the antipro-tectionist principle of moderate rates designed chiefly for revenue and ex-pressed in uniform percentages — with only moderate discrimination in fa-vor of the most important American manufactures. He wanted an even further reduction in the already circumscribed federal expenditures for in-ternal improvements, and his vetoes of long sanctioned appropriations for river and harbor improvements were sustained. Thus, under Polk, the tra-ditional Democratic policies were finally established, to remain substantially unchanged until the Civil War.

While cleaning up this unfinished Democratic business, Polk was simul-taneously moving aggressively along the new line of expansionism. With the Texas issue settled, he wasted not a moment in turning his attention to the Oregon country. This vast expanse of territory — stretching from the Rock-ies to the Pacific and from the border of Mexican California at 42° on the south to Russian Alaska at 54°40′ on the north — had been jointly occupied by the United States and Great Britain with the proviso that either nation could terminate the joint occupation by giving one year's notice. In the early 1840s, American settlers began finding their way to Oregon in substantial numbers and disputing possession of the land with the well-established Brit-ish posts of the Hudson's Bay Company. This migration had created consid-erable interest in Oregon in the states of the upper Mississippi Valley, north-western Democrats had begun agitating for a more vigorous assertion of American claims to the country, and the Democratic platform had declared that "Our title to the whole of the Territory of Oregon is clear and unquestionable."

Polk's inaugural address echoed the Oregon plank in the Democratic plat-form, but he felt bound to renew once more his predecessors' offer of a compromise boundary along the 49th parallel, an offer the British had re-jected several times. When the British minister rudely rebuffed this pro-posal without even referring it to his government, Polk took a more bellicose line. Calling on Congress to give notice of the termination of joint occu-pancy, he asserted the American claim to the whole of the territory.

For a time war threatened, but both sides were ready for any face-saving solution along the 49th parallel. Polk allowed intimations to reach the British that if they made a proper proposal he would submit it to the Senate for advice. Such a proposal came in June 1846, and the Senate advised its ac-ceptance. The 49° boundary already established east of the Rockies was ex-tended west to the Pacific with a short detour down the Strait of Fuca to leave Britain the whole of Vancouver Island. (See map on page 109.)

THE MEXICAN WAR

Polk's bold Oregon game with the British was rendered more dangerous by his bellicose diplomacy in another quarter. For a time, he seemed to be courting simultaneous wars with Great Britain and with Mexico. The prin-cipal prize in the latter case would be Mexican California with its splendid

Pacific harbors. There can be little doubt that Polk was determined to secure the vast domain between the southwestern borders of the United States and the Pacific and that he deliberately provoked war when the Mexicans refused to sell it.

Having won its independence from Spain in 1821, Mexico was a proud young republic with a political system so unstable that any government compromising the national honor was sure to be driven from office. The Texas Revolution had been a severe blow to Mexican pride. Stubbornly refusing to recognize Texan independence, the Mexicans regarded the annexation of Texas by the United States as an act of aggression and had broken off diplomatic relations.

It was at this point that Polk entered the White House. One of his first acts was to order an American army to the western frontier of Texas to ward off any attack by Mexico while the formalities of annexation were being completed. He was less justified in authorizing the army to advance beyond the traditional Texan boundary at the Nueces River and in announcing his determination to enforce the unfounded Texas claim that its territory extended to the Rio Grande River. Then he sent a minister to Mexico with an offer that the United States would assume the unpaid claims of American citizens against Mexico for property losses during the Mexican Revolution in return for Mexican acceptance of the Rio Grande boundary. In addition, the envoy was to try to purchase New Mexico and California.

Since the Mexicans had not indicated any willingness to reopen regular diplomatic negotiations, it should not have been surprising that they refused to receive Polk's minister. Nevertheless Polk chose to regard this rebuff as a cause for war. He had already ordered the American army to advance to the Rio Grande, and he prepared to ask Congress for a declaration of war. The Mexicans saved him the trouble by precipitating hostilities. A Mexican force encountered an American patrol just east of the Rio Grande, and in the ensuing skirmish 16 Americans were killed or wounded. Polk got the news just in time to modify his war message. Mexico, he told Congress, "has invaded our territory and shed American blood upon the American soil." War was declared on May 13, 1846. Presidential claims of "invasion" and of the shedding of American blood on American soil were properly questioned in Congress — to little avail. Polk wanted war and a continental empire, and his conduct of relations with Mexico illustrated the almost unlimited power of the president in foreign policy and as commander-in-chief.

The Mexican War, whatever its morality, was militarily the most successful of American wars. General Zachary Taylor led the army on the Rio Grande into north central Mexico and at Buena Vista in February 1847, won a brilliant victory over a superior Mexican force commanded by General Santa Anna. Shortly thereafter, another American army under General Winfield Scott landed at Vera Cruz on the Gulf Coast and by September had occupied the enemy capital, Mexico City. Meanwhile Colonel Stephen Kearney had led another American army across the plains from Missouri, seizing Santa Fe on the upper Rio Grande and then moving on west across the mountains and deserts to establish American authority in California.

When General Scott captured Vera Cruz, President Polk sent Nicholas P. Trist, chief of the State Department, to accompany Scott's army and seize upon any opportunity for negotiating a peace that would give the United States the territory it wanted. The fall of Mexico City reduced that country to political chaos, and by the time Trist found a government stable enough to negotiate, he had infuriated President Polk by insubordinate behavior. Defying an order to return home, Trist went ahead and negotiated the Treaty of Guadelupe Hidalgo, signed in February 1848. By this treaty, Mexico recognized the Rio Grande boundary and ceded New Mexico and California, while in return the United States was to assume the claims of its citizens against Mexico and pay Mexico $15 million. Since these were the terms Polk had instructed the repudiated diplomat to secure, he signed Trist's treaty, and the Senate ratified it.

TOWARD THE FIRST SECESSION CRISIS

Despite the brilliance of its military victories and the vastness of its territorial acquisitions, the United States emerged from the Mexican War more deeply divided and distracted than ever. The enthusiastic expansionism of people like President Polk had been partly an effort to find a cause that would unite all Americans in a new burst of patriotic nationalism and furnish a vaccine against the insidiously spreading infection of sectional enmity. But the infection had already taken too firm a hold, and the remedy served to intensify rather than alleviate the disease.

The enthusiasm for expansion was most widespread in the Northwest and the Southwest and among Democrats; in the East and among Whigs, the transparently aggressive character of the Mexican War had made it unpopular with many from the beginning. The Whigs carried on a constant criticism of the administration's war policy, and northern Whigs began to denounce the war as a southern project for expanding the area of slavery. Northern voters were told, too, that a slavery-dominated Democratic party had demonstrated its indifference to the interests of the free states by reducing the tariff, cutting off appropriations for rivers and harbors, and surrendering the American claim to the whole of Oregon. The war helped to crystallize in thousands of northern minds the conviction that the area of slavery and the political power of slavery must not be allowed to expand.

In the summer of 1846, while Congress was debating a bill appropriating money for negotiations with Mexico, a Pennsylvania Democrat named David Wilmot offered an amendment declaring that slavery should be forever barred from any Mexican territories to be acquired. The Wilmot Proviso, though defeated when first introduced, infuriated southern members of Congress and provoked a struggle of such mounting violence that within three years it would bring the country to the brink of secession and civil war.

The end of the Mexican War made it indispensable to enact some legislation for government in the new territories, but no legislation could be passed without settling the status of slavery there. Northerners dominated the House of Representatives and insisted on the Wilmot Proviso while Southerners, relying on a Senate still evenly balanced between slave and free states, asserted their right to migrate with their property, including slaves, into the territory they had helped to win. President Polk urged that the Missouri Compromise line of 36°30' be extended to the Pacific as the boundary between slave and free territory, telling Northerners that slavery could never get a foothold in the arid Southwest no matter what Congress provided. But Polk made the serious blunder of announcing that he would under no circumstances accept a second term. Having expended his patronage in getting his ambitious program through his first Congress, he was less and less able to control Democrats in Congress as his term neared its end, and the extremists, both North and South, defeated his and all other efforts to reach a compromise solution.

It was in this atmosphere that the presidential election of 1848 occurred. The free-soil issue had split both parties deeply along sectional lines. The rift was potentially deeper among the Whigs because antislavery sentiment was stronger in the northern wing of their party, but they successfully obscured their differences by again adopting the strategy of nominating a military hero. This time he was General Zachary Taylor, the hero of Buena Vista, a plain, honest old soldier who owned a plantation and slaves in Louisiana. Democratic differences were more conspicuous because Polk's no-second-term position had prompted a prolonged intraparty struggle over the nomination. At the cost of great bitterness, the Democratic convention finally nominated Senator Lewis Cass of Michigan, hated by the Van Burenites for his role in blocking their chieftain's nomination four years previously.

The major party nominations provoked the formation of a formidable antislavery third party. Deeply suspicious of the slaveholding Taylor, the more fervently antislavery Whigs organized a Free Soil party with the Wilmot Proviso as their platform. They were quickly joined by the "Barnburners," or Van Buren Democrats, who were just as anxious for revenge against Cass and the rival "Hunker" faction of the New York Democratic party as they were to stop the spread of slavery. The new party nominated Van Buren for president and Charles Francis Adams, Whig son of John Quincy Adams, for vice president.

Taylor's personal popularity, his nonpartisan posture, the special appeal that his slaveholding status gave him in the South, and the Barnburner secession from Cass in the North made the outcome a foregone conclusion. "Old Rough and Ready" did not have to say where he stood on the territorial question, while Cass advanced a compromise solution of great future significance but little immediate appeal to the more zealous defenders of the southern and northern positions. This compromise was the doctrine of popular sovereignty by which the settlers in the territories would be left to settle the status of slavery for themselves. Taylor won handily, while the Free Soilers garnered a substantial popular vote and elected nine representatives.

THE COMPROMISE OF 1850

By the time Taylor took office in March 1849, the discovery of gold in California had attracted a horde of unruly immigrants and created a desperate need for legislation providing government in the new territories. Meanwhile, Southerners had been further infuriated by proposals in Congress to abolish slavery and the slave trade in the District of Columbia. Calhoun was passionately exhorting Southerners to abandon the old parties and unite in a new sectional party to defend the South's rights and safety. The more radical Southerners were demanding that the South secede if the Wilmot Proviso were applied in any form to any territory, and a number of southern governors and legislatures took measures looking toward secession in such an eventuality. In this crisis, the new president, to the shock of those Southerners who had supported him because he was a slaveholder, encouraged the Californians to bypass the territorial stage, to draw up a state constitution without congressional authorization, and to apply directly for admission as a free state. Thus Taylor's first Congress met in December 1849, to find a free California waiting on its doorstep and passions running so high that members carried Bowie knives and revolvers and the House of Representatives took three weeks and 63 ballots to elect a Speaker.

The aged Henry Clay now stepped forward to rally the forces of moderation and compromise, presenting a series of proposals as an "omnibus" settlement of all the disputed questions arising from the slavery issue: (1) California was to be admitted as a free state; (2) the remainder of the Mexican cession was to be organized into two territories, Utah on the north and New Mexico on the south, leaving the status of slavery for their inhabitants to settle. The Utah territory was to provide a government for the large body of Mormons who had migrated to the shores of the Great Salt Lake in 1846 after being driven out of their settlements in Missouri and Illinois. The New Mexico territory involved an additional complication because Texas claimed that its territory extended to the upper Rio Grande, embracing Santa Fe and half of the old Spanish-Mexican province of New Mexico. Clay therefore further proposed that: (3) Texas should give up its claims to the New Mexican area in return for which the United States would assume the Texas public debt; (4) the slave trade but not slavery should be abolished in the District of Columbia; and (5) the old federal Fugitive Slave Law of 1790, the enforcement of which had been increasingly defied and impeded in the North, should be strengthened.

Southerners complained that Clay's compromise would cost the South its equal strength in the Senate while making only the single concession to the South of a stronger fugitive slave law. Formidable opposition also came from President Taylor and the bulk of the northern Whigs, who were determined that the advance of slavery should be decisively halted. Even after Taylor died in July 1850, and was succeeded by the procompromise Vice President Millard Fillmore, Clay was unable to gain a majority for his omnibus proposal. Only when the Illinois Democrat, Stephen A. Douglas, took command and broke Clay's omnibus bill into separate proposals did the various compromise measures pass.

The success of the compromise depended on the willingness of the aroused lower South to accept it. In Georgia, Mississippi, and other states, party lines broke down as Whigs and moderate Democrats joined forces to defeat the advocates of secession. The country's factions breathed sighs of relief, and the majority of politicians everywhere committed themselves to the compromise measures as a "final solution" of the slavery controversy.

In the presidential election of 1852, the Democratic nominee, Franklin Pierce of New Hampshire, won because of his allegiance to the compromise. Again the Whigs had turned to a military hero, nominating General Winfield Scott. But Whigs in the South could no longer sustain themselves as copartisans of the increasingly antislavery northern Whigs. With southern Whigs being forced into the Democratic party, the Whig party was already dying as a national entity, and Scott was its last presidential candidate.

FOR FURTHER READING

Frederick Merk has written an important work on *Manifest Destiny and Mission in American History* (1963); Ray A. Billington is the author of the best general account of *The Far Western Frontier, 1830–1860* (1956); and Henry Nash Smith's *Virgin Land* (1950) is a brilliant interpretation of the meaning of the West for the American imagination. The trade between Missouri and Santa Fe is described by a participant in Josiah Gregg's *Commerce of the Prairies* (1844); the fur trade is vividly and soundly reconstructed in James P. Ronda's *Astoria and Empire* (1990). Francis Parkman's account of his experiences along *The Oregon Trail* (1849) is a classic, while John D. Unruh's *The Plains Across* (1979) provides a scholarly examination of overland migration from 1840 to 1860. Marquis James's *The Raven* (1929) is a vivid biography of the Texas leader Sam Houston; Frederick Merk has collected essays on *The Oregon Question* (1967); Norman Graebner explores the *Empire on the Pacific* (1955); and David Alan Johnson is the author of *Founding the Far West* (1992). The political history of the 1840s is best followed through three biographies: Robert Seager, II, *And Tyler Too: A Biography of John & Julia Gardiner Tyler* (1963); the third volume of Charles M. Wiltse, *John C. Calhoun* (3 vols., 1944–1951); and Charles Sellers, *James K. Polk, Continentalist: 1843–1846* (1966). Robert W. Johannsen in *To the Halls of the Montezumas* (1985) describes the war with Mexico, and Elbert B. Smith covers *The Presidencies of Zachary Taylor and Millard Fillmore* (1988). David M. Potter's *The Impending Crisis* (1976) offers a full analysis of the developing sectional controversy of the late 1840s; Joseph G. Rayback's *Free Soil* (1970) examines the election of 1848; Chaplain Morrison's *Democratic Politics and Sectionalism* (1967) probes the Wilmot Proviso; and Holman Hamilton's *Prologue to Conflict: The Crisis and Compromise of 1850* (1964) explains the temporary resolution of the controversy.

TABLE 7. PRESIDENTIAL ELECTIONS AND MAJOR EVENTS, 1852–1861

1852	**Franklin Pierce** (Democrat) elected over Winfield Scott (Whig). Harriet Beecher Stowe publishes *Uncle Tom's Cabin*.
1854	Kansas-Nebraska Act repeals Missouri Compromise and organizes Kansas and Nebraska territories on principle of squatter sovereignty.
1856	**James Buchanan** (Democrat) elected over John C. Frémont (Republican) and Millard Fillmore (American).
1857	*Dred Scott* vs. *Sanford*. Roger B. Taney's Supreme Court declares that Congress cannot bar slavery from the territories. Buchanan fails to force the admission of Kansas to statehood under the proslavery Lecompton Constitution. Hinton Rowan Helper publishes *The Impending Crisis of the South*.
1858	Lincoln-Douglas Debates. In his contest with Abraham Lincoln for Senator from Illinois, Stephen A. Douglas argues, in his "Freeport Doctrine," that slavery cannot survive in a territory without positive supporting legislation.
1859	John Brown's raid on Harper's Ferry.
1860	Radical Southerners break up the Democratic party by withdrawing when the Charleston convention refuses to endorse their demand for a congressional slave code. **Abraham Lincoln** (Republican) elected president over Stephen A. Douglas (Northern Democrat), John C. Breckinridge (Southern Democrat), and John Bell (Constitutional Unionist).
1860–1861	Seven states of the lower South secede and organize the Confederate States of America.

14

★ ★ ★ ★ ★ ★

A House Dividing, 1843–1860

HOPING that the Compromise of 1850 had finally settled the slavery controversy, the American people again turned their energies to the march of enterprise. The 1850s were a decade of unprecedented economic growth and prosperity, the climax of the market revolution and the further development of the industrial revolution. Yet the very process of economic growth and physical expansion provoked a renewal of sectional conflict that could be resolved only by civil war.

CULMINATION OF THE MARKET REVOLUTION

The exuberance of the forces generating the market revolution had also generated boom-and-bust cycles that had periodically inhibited the country's full potential for economic growth. Not until the years between 1843 and 1857 did the developed market economy have a chance to show what it could do in an extended period without a major depression.

The results were spectacular. Between 1844 and 1854, the total value of all commodities produced rose by 69 percent, the highest gain for any decade until the 1880s. Accompanying this rise in gross production was an equivalent gain in the efficiency of production, with output per worker rising by 10 percent in the 1840s and 23 percent in the 1850s, the latter increase again to be unequaled until the 1880s. This rapid economic growth was in part a further acceleration of the market revolution in its various aspects following a slackened pace during the 1837–1843 depression.

Commercial agriculture resumed its growth at a faster rate than ever. By 1846 the formerly protectionist Northwest was exporting so much wheat to foreign markets that it turned toward free trade and provided the votes by which the tariff reductions of that year were passed. By 1850 the Northwest exceeded the Northeast in wheat production, and this was only a prelude of things to come. The advance of the agricultural frontier north into Wisconsin and west across Iowa into eastern Kansas and Nebraska, coupled with the widespread use of Cyrus McCormick's mechanical reaper, pushed northwestern wheat production from some 30 million bushels in 1850 to almost 100 million bushels in 1860. Meat packing and the production of corn and hogs expanded almost as spectacularly.

Similarly in the South, the cotton crop increased by 60 percent in the 1840s and 100 percent in the 1850s. Sugar production in Louisiana rose fourfold between the mid-1830s and 1859. The increasing productivity and profitability of southern agriculture were reflected in the rising price of slaves. In the 1790s, a prime field hand could have been bought for $300; by 1840, the price had risen to $1,000; by 1860, it ran up to $1,500.

The impressive growth of a regionally specialized commercial agriculture was closely related to the perfection of a national system of transportation and communication that provided facilities for swift, cheap, and efficient interregional and international exchanges of goods and services. Turnpikes, canals, and steamboats had been effective enough for the earlier stages of the market revolution, but not until the 1850s was the transportation system brought to full efficiency by the creation of a great railroad network.

Although railroad construction had received a start in the 1830s, only local lines had been completed before the depression of 1837–1843 stalled further progress. As late as 1848, the country had only 6,000 miles of track. Mileage doubled in the next four years and reached 30,000 by 1860. By 1857 the country had invested a billion dollars in railroads, two thirds of that during the preceding seven years.

Particularly important was the completion in the early 1850s of five great trunk lines connecting the Atlantic ports of Boston, New York, Philadelphia, Baltimore, and Charleston with the Ohio and Mississippi valleys by way of Albany and Buffalo, Pittsburgh, Wheeling, and Atlanta and Chattanooga. From these terminals the eastern trunk lines rapidly developed new western railroads to the emerging transportation and commercial centers of Chicago, St. Louis, and Memphis. By 1855 a passenger could travel in two days from one of the Atlantic cities to Chicago or St. Louis for a fare of $20. Radiating out from the trunk lines were feeder lines that brought cheap transportation and commercial production to virtually every part of the country.

The flood of products harvested by an expanded agriculture and brought to the coast by a perfected transportation system helped push American exports from $144 million worth of commodities in 1850 to $334 million worth in 1860. Imports climbed to an even higher level, the trade deficit being bridged by exports of California gold, which rose from $5 million in 1850 to $58 million by the end of the decade. This swelling of foreign commerce brought with it a vigorous revival of the American shipping trade.

Another element in the economic expansion was the upsurge of immigration from abroad, especially from Germany and Ireland after the potato famine created widespread destitution in 1846. Immigrants to the United States had not numbered more than 10,000 a year before 1825, but exceeded 100,000 in the mid-1840s and reached an annual level of around 400,000 in the early 1850s. Between 1844 and 1854 nearly 3 million new Americans arrived from abroad. Many of these people supplied the labor for the factories that were springing up in the East; others did the hard, dirty work in railroad and canal construction. The Germans established strong colonies in such northwestern cities as Cincinnati, St. Louis, and Milwaukee, while still other immigrants swelled the tide of agricultural migration into Wisconsin, Iowa, and beyond.

INDUSTRIAL DEVELOPMENT

The impressive economic gains of the late 1840s and the 1850s were more than a matter of growth along established lines. The rounding out of the vast and lucrative national market set the stage for the industrial revolution in the United States. A new sector of the economy was moving into the dynamic role. Earlier, the profits of the American carrying trade during the Napoleonic Wars had provided the initial impetus that jarred the economy out of its static staple-exporting phase. Then the swelling flood of commercial crops, cotton above all others, had fueled the transportation revolution and the creation of a national market economy. From the 1850s on, industry became the primary stimulant for a sustained and massive expansion of production that would create the most abundant economy that history had yet known.

At mid-century, manufacturing had spread far beyond New England. In fact, capital investments and value of industrial production in the Middle Atlantic states were nearly twice that of New England. Pennsylvania and New York led all states in manufacturing. To be sure, the nation's industrial economy remained immature and, despite rapid antebellum industrial growth in the Ohio Valley and the Chicago area, was concentrated in the East. The trans-Mississippi West, of course, was undeveloped, while the South was overwhelmingly agricultural. Farm products still accounted for the bulk of the nation's exports. Farm employment claimed nearly 60 percent of its labor force, compared to only 12 percent for manufacturing and the remaining percentage in trade and service occupations. And American consumers still depended heavily on foreign-made goods.

Yet the surge in American manufacturing activity, particularly in the 1840s and 1850s, was spectacular. During the 1850s the value of manufactured goods nearly doubled, from $1 billion to just under $2 billion; between 1842 and 1860 the output of pig iron quadrupled. In those decades the value added by American manufacturing — the difference between the value of raw materials used and the value of finished goods — soared higher than in other decades of the nineteenth century.

Cities grew in much the same fashion. In 1820 only 6 percent of all Americans lived in places having 2,500 or more people. By 1860 the percentage had more than tripled, and New York became the first city to contain a million people. The greater part of this urbanization occurred after 1840. Much of it was produced by the increased volume of international and interregional trade that funneled through the cities, creating jobs. But industrial development and new technology were also important to urban growth. The advent of the stationary steam engine as a substitute for waterpower in the 1840s freed manufacturing from riverside locations; this greatly accelerated the tendency of industry to settle in cities and thus contributed to urban growth. In 5 of the 15 largest cities in 1860, more than 10 percent of the population were engaged in manufacturing, while some of the newer and smaller cities like Newark, Lowell, and Lynn were almost wholly industrial. Thus, by any measure, a rapidly transforming economy was approaching what some economists call the takeoff stage. On the eve of the Civil War the United States remained an agricultural nation, but it trailed only England in industrial production and would soon become the world's industrial leader.

Labor conditions, however, were anything but ideal, and not for many decades would industrial workers begin to share in the vast wealth created by the industrial revolution. The steady trend away from domestic manufactures to the factory system — toward the concentration of production in ever larger industrial units — undermined the independence of the old artisan class and created a growing new working class of permanent wage earners. This shift in the status and prospects of working people gave rise in the 1820s and 1830s to a number of labor unions of skilled artisans in such crafts as printing, shoemaking, tailoring, and the building trades. The craft unions organized city federations in New York and Philadelphia; workers' parties entered local politics; and there were strikes for the 10-hour day. In 1834 a National Trades Union was formed. The mass of workers — the unskilled or semiskilled laborers who staffed the new mechanized factories — remained unorganized, however. Then, even the early craft-union movement was swept away by the Panic of 1837. As prosperity returned in the 1840s, the craft unions were reborn. Strikes became numerous and successful enough so that the 10-hour-day was standard by the mid-1850s. Again a National Trades Union was organized, and again a depression in 1857 largely wiped out skilled labor's organizational gains.

CONFLICT AGAIN

With North and South riding the greatest tide of prosperity either section had ever known, it may seem strange that the decade of the 1850s ended in intersectional strife. Indeed direct conflicts of economic interest between the sections over national legislation seemed at the lowest ebb since the Panic of 1819. Southerners were no longer frustrating the Northwest's demands for federal aid to internal improvements; between 1850 and 1860, the federal government granted 18 million acres of the public lands to aid construction of 45 railroads in 10 states. The tariff issue no longer engaged passions as northern industry continued to flourish under the low rates of 1846.

Yet the very lushness of prosperity and growth was fostering imperial visions in the two sections: in the South an expanding cotton-slavery empire, and in the North an expanding free-soil empire. As these competing expansionist impulses headed toward a collision, they were inevitably intensified by the moral dimensions of the slavery question

The South's growing insecurity over the institution of slavery was particularly dangerous. By the 1850s the North was rapidly outstripping the South in population and potential political power; Northerners were demonstrating their deepening disapproval of slavery by blocking enforcement of the stringent new Fugitive Slave Law, one of the few concessions to the South in the Compromise of 1850. These circumstances help explain the mounting stridency with which Southerners proclaimed the merits of slavery, and explain more specifically the South's hysterical reaction to two famous books published during the 1850s. The first, Harriet Beecher Stowe's novel *Uncle Tom's Cabin* (1852), was a sentimental portrayal of slavery's brutal impact on some appealingly drawn slave characters. The second, Hinton Rowan Helper's *Impending Crisis of the South* (1857), was an all too effective argument by a nonslaveholding North Carolinian that slavery was disastrous to the nonslaveholding white majority in the South. Both books were not only denounced, but violently suppressed in the South, while in the North they won wide audiences and helped harden antislavery sentiment.

Paradoxically, the South had more power in the federal government in the 1850s than it had had since Jeffersonian days. The campaign of 1852 demonstrated that the northern and southern wings of the Whig party were too far apart on the slavery question to hold together any longer, leaving the Democrats as the one great national party. Northern Democratic politicians competed against each other for promotion in the party and the federal government by going as far as they could toward satisfying southern demands and thereby winning southern support. Therefore the South came to have the dominant voice in the Democratic presidential administrations of Franklin Pierce and James Buchanan. As long as the Democrats remained a national party and the South's northern Democratic allies could win elections in a good part of the North, the South could in effect control the country and counteract the northern advantage in population and representation. But eventually the South, out of its insecurity, demanded more from its northern Democratic allies than they could grant without losing elections in the North.

What the South was demanding in the 1850s was the right for slavery to expand. This insistence grew out of complicated motives. This southern demand was in part the cotton-slavery imperialism of a prosperous and expansive social and economic system. The demand for slavery was also an effort to bolster the South's slipping proportion of representation in the federal government through the creation of additional slave states. Finally, the South was demanding that Northerners recognize the moral legitimacy of slavery by acknowledging its right to grow and thus relieve the white South from the intolerable burden of justifying and defending an unjustifiable and indefensible social system.

THE TERRITORIAL QUESTION

By the 1850s there was clearly no further room for new slave states within the territorial limits of the United States under the political arrangements that prevailed. The Missouri Compromise of 1820 barred slaves from the remaining unorganized parts of the Louisiana Purchase, the Oregon territory had been organized on free-soil principles, and geography seemed to prohibit slavery's spread over the arid wastes of the New Mexico and Utah territories.

Under these circumstances, expansionist Southerners turned their attention to the Caribbean area, and the Pierce administration attempted to purchase Cuba from Spain. This effort had the advantage of appealing on nonsectional grounds to a nationalistic "Young America" group which wanted to continue the expansionism of the 1840s. But when a trio of southern-oriented diplomats issued the Ostend Manifesto proposing that Cuba be seized if it could not be purchased, there was such an adverse reaction in the North and in Spain that the Cuba project had to be dropped. Despite this setback, many Southerners continued to agitate throughout the 1850s for expansion into the Caribbean area and to support illegal filibustering expeditions that sought to overturn weak Central American governments and pave the way for American annexations.

With the outlook for foreign expansionism dim, a small group of southern politicians began a fateful effort to push slavery into that part of the Louisiana Purchase reserved as free soil. Democratic Senator Stephen A. Douglas of Illinois was anxious to pass a bill providing territorial government for the Kansas and Nebraska country, partly to facilitate the start of a transcontinental railroad that might terminate in his home town of Chicago. Senator David R. Atchison of Missouri, representing a slaveholding constituency across the Missouri River from the area in question, had staked his political life on a promise that his constituents would be able to take their slaves into the new territory. Atchison joined with a group of powerful southern senators to insist that no territorial bill would pass unless it contained a clause repealing the Missouri Compromise prohibition of slavery. Douglas gave in to their demand, a weak President Pierce was persuaded to use all the power of the national administration to secure enough northern Democratic votes to pass the bill, and the Kansas-Nebraska Act of 1854 was the result.

Douglas argued that the act was simply an extension of the democratic "popular sovereignty" principle already applied to the New Mexico and Utah territories by the Compromise of 1850. But indignation blazed up in the

MAP 4: THE KANSAS-NEBRASKA ACT, 1854

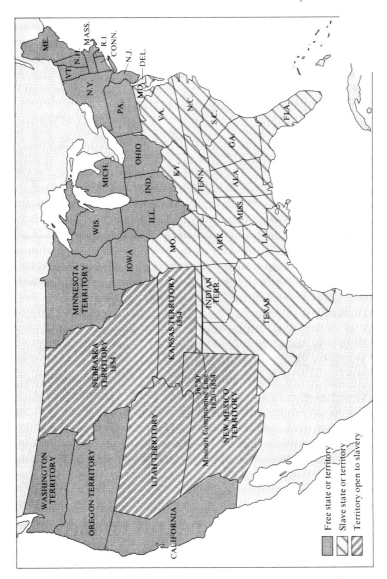

Free state or territory

Slave state or territory

Territory open to slavery

forth at this cynical abrogation of a sacred compromise and at the servile northern Democrats who obeyed an "aggressive slavocracy." While only a small minority of Northerners were disposed to interfere with slavery where it already existed, far more were ready to stop its further spread. With the Kansas-Nebraska Act, cotton-slavery imperialism provocatively challenged free-soil imperialism. The immediate response was the organization of a new sectional party in the North calling itself "Republican" and vowing its opposition to the least extension of the area of slavery.

Meanwhile Kansas, the more southerly of the two new territories, was filled with violence and bloodshed as proslavery and antislavery factions contended for control of the territorial government. New England abolitionists contributed guns and funds for free-soil immigrants, while "border ruffians" from Missouri crossed the river to furnish illegal ballots and armed support to the proslavery faction. When President Pierce again yielded to southern pressure and recognized a proslavery legislature elected largely by illegal voters from Missouri, the enraged free-soilers elected their own legislature and governor. A proslavery force raided the free-soil capital, and in retaliation, a fanatical abolitionist named John Brown invaded an isolated proslavery settlement and butchered five inoffensive residents. In the sporadic violence that followed, more than 200 people were killed.

In retrospect, the demand for repeal of the Missouri Compromise appears to have been a suicidal strategy for southern interests. Southern opinion generally was not strongly in favor of such a demand, and even many of the more radical Southerners admitted that slavery would probably never be established in any of the disputed territories. What the South was really demanding was an acknowledgment of its technical right to take slaves into all territories, an acknowledgment of the legitimacy of slavery. For the sake of this technical right, southern leaders put their northern Democratic allies in an untenable position in their home constituencies and called into existence a formidable antislavery party that would soon destroy their control of the federal government.

BUCHANAN RIDES THE STORM

The new Republican party, drawing heavily from former Whigs and outraged Democrats, grew by leaps and bounds in the North. As the presidential election of 1856 approached, the Democrats were also threatened by another new party, the Americans or Know-Nothings, who appealed to anti-immigrant, anti-Catholic sentiment. To meet this double challenge, the Democratic national convention dropped the discredited Pierce and nominated the cautious, conservative, and prosouthern James Buchanan of Pennsylvania. The new American party nominated ex-President Fillmore and drew a substantial vote, especially from former Whigs in the South, but carried only one state. The major feature of the election was the strong showing of the new Republican party, which carried all but five of the free states for its candidate John C. Frémont. Only by the lavish use of money in Pennsylvania and Indiana and by the support of an almost solid South did the Democrats squeak through with a bare electoral majority.

The attempt to apply the popular sovereignty principle was deepening the chaos in Kansas and Washington. Southerners were insisting that popular sovereignty did not allow the people of a territory to bar slavery until they came to draft a constitution preparatory to admission as a state. Shortly after Buchanan's inauguration in March 1857, a southern majority on the Supreme Court upheld this southern contention in the celebrated case of Dred Scott. Chief Justice Roger B. Taney's opinion denied the slave Scott's contention that he had been made free by residence in the free territory of Iowa; Taney wrote that Congress could not bar slavery from the territories — and it was a logical inference that territorial legislatures could not either.

While northern opinion was reacting to this further evidence of southern aggression, President Buchanan was trying to remove the issue from politics by pushing Kansas into statehood. Failing to get a fair referendum on slavery in Kansas, the president unwisely succumbed to southern pressure and endorsed a proslavery state constitution drafted by a notoriously unrepresentative convention at Lecompton. At this point, Senator Douglas and a number of other northern Democrats, fighting for political survival at home, revolted against the president and blocked the admission of Kansas under the Lecompton Constitution.

At the height of the Kansas crisis in 1857, the further strain of a severe financial crisis hit the country. The Republicans capitalized on the hard times to broaden their appeal. The southern-dominated Democratic Congress had just passed the Tariff of 1857, reducing protection to the lowest level since 1812. It was easy to blame the depression on the new tariff and to win support from hard-hit manufacturers and industrial workers by promises of higher rates. At the same time, the Republicans made themselves more appealing to northwestern farmers by agitating for a homestead act giving free homesteads of 160 acres to settlers on the public lands. A wave of religious revivals following the financial crash further excited the public mind and intensified the Northerners' moral sensitivity on the slavery question.

THE ELECTION OF 1860

Under these unsettling circumstances, the slavery debate began to be dominated by the approaching presidential election of 1860. Stephen A. Douglas of Illinois was the leading aspirant for the Democratic nomination and perhaps the only Democrat who could win enough support in the North to be elected. But Douglas was in an exceedingly difficult dilemma, reflecting the dilemma of his party. In order to be nominated, he had to allay southern suspicions arising from his opposition to the Lecompton Constitution, but it was questionable whether he could allay these suspicions and win the nom-

ination without taking a position so prosouthern that he would lose the subsequent election. And in the meantime, he had to win re-election to the
Senate against the leading Illinois Republican, a shrewd Springfield lawyer
named Abraham Lincoln.

In the famous series of seven debates between Douglas and Lincoln across
Illinois in 1858, Douglas sought to escape his predicament by taking an ambiguous position. On the one hand, he maintained his doctrine of popular
sovereignty, which would technically permit Southerners to take their slaves
into the territories and deny territorial legislatures the right to bar slavery
before statehood. But at the same time he assured the Illinois voters, in what
came to be called the Freeport Doctrine, that slaves could never be successfully held in a territory unless the territorial legislature had passed a
slave code or positive legislation for protecting and policing slave property.
Douglas won the senatorial election in the Illinois legislature by a narrow
margin, but his Freeport Doctrine made him even less acceptable to Southerners as a presidential nominee. Lincoln emerged from the debates as a
major Republican figure in a Midwest increasingly committed to the modernizing ideas of "free soil, free labor, and free men." Affirming his own
moral aversion to human bondage as "an unqualified evil" and his party's
opposition to any extension of slavery, he had held his own against a formidable debater. He had also articulated the hope of many Northerners, including immigrants and disaffected Democrats, that the nation's territories
remain "places for poor people to go to, and better their condition."

The South, however, was committed to slavery. Still a premodern and
pre-industrial society, the southern states demanded a Union that would
maintain slavery, not create freedom. Following the Lincoln-Douglas debates, southern demands reached an extreme of presumption and folly. The
more radical Southerners had already begun to suspect that slavery, as
Douglas claimed in the Freeport Doctrine, could not be sustained in the
territories without a slave code. Now they moved beyond the claim that
neither Congress nor territorial legislatures could bar slavery from the territories and began demanding that the federal government protect and guarantee slavery in the territories through enactment of a congressional slave
code. Most Southerners were not insistent on this radical demand, and certainly very few Southerners thought of actually taking slaves into the territories. But as tension increased and excitement mounted, southern politicians feared to be outdone in defending their constituents' supposed
interests, and the most extreme positions came to the fore. Southern insecurity had generated demands for more and more guarantees and assur-
ances; these apparently aggressive movements of the slaveholding section
had frightened the North into more determined resistance and spawned the
Republican party; and this hardening resistance in the North had intensified
southern insecurity and generated even greater demands.

Southern insecurity reached a peak of near hysteria in October 1859,
when the violent abolitionist John Brown, of Kansas fame, led a raid on the
federal arsenal at Harpers Ferry, Virginia, seizing guns and ammunition with

which he planned to arm a wholesale slave rebellion. Though Brown and his followers were quickly subdued, a paroxysm of terror ran through the South, and terror quickly turned to rage when it was learned that respectable antislavery people in the North had backed the plot.

Against this background, the Democratic national convention assembled at Charleston, South Carolina, in April 1860. Radical Southerners insisted that the convention endorse their demand for a congressional slave code. When the pro-Douglas majority refused, after violent debate, the delegates from eight states of the lower South withdrew, and the convention had to adjourn. Two separate Democratic conventions then met in Baltimore, the northern-dominated one nominating Douglas and the southern-dominated one nominating John C. Breckinridge of Kentucky. Meanwhile, the Republicans, who had no support in the South, had met in Chicago to nominate Abraham Lincoln, and union-minded, old-line Whigs from the border states, calling themselves the Constitutional Union party, had put John Bell of Tennessee into the running as a fourth candidate. In effect, this four-way contest was not one election but two. Free-state voters chose between Lincoln and Douglas; in the slave states, the contest was between Bell and Breckinridge. At this critical moment, the American party system no longer operated in a nationwide context. In the realm of partisan politics, the erosion of unionism was all but complete.

Lincoln had no support *outside* the free states, but in the free states he made an almost clean sweep that was by itself enough for a majority in the electoral college (but only 39 percent of the popular vote). For the rest, Breckinridge carried most of the South handily; Bell won three border slave states; and Douglas, though running second to Lincoln in popular votes, won the electoral votes of only Missouri and half of New Jersey.

SECESSION

For years the small but steadily growing body of radical southern fire-eaters had been looking forward to this day, and they lost no time in making the most of their opportunity. South Carolina had been in a secessionist mood since the days of nullification, impatiently waiting for her stolid sister states to awaken to their danger. At last enough of the southern population was sufficiently aroused by the election of Lincoln, a "Black Republican," and South Carolina could lead the way. Hastily calling a state convention, the Palmetto State formally repealed its ratification of the federal constitution on December 20, 1860. Within six weeks, South Carolina was followed by the six Gulf States: Mississippi, Florida, Georgia, Alabama, Louisiana, and Texas.

As the border states hesitated, the waning Buchanan administration fretted in helpless impotence. The politicians at Washington scurried about seeking a formula for compromise, but the victorious Republicans would not listen to a proposal that countenanced the slightest extension of slavery, while the Southerners demanded at least a token concession on the territorial question. Meanwhile the seceded states sent delegates to Montgomery, Alabama, organized themselves as the Confederate States of America, and chose Jefferson Davis of Mississippi as their president.

CONFLICTING HISTORICAL VIEWPOINTS: NO. 6

What Caused the Civil War?

The Civil War is perhaps the best illustration of the ancient truism that the historian's view of the past is colored by his or her perception of the present. Southerners and Northerners debated the causes across regional lines. State's-rightists, nationalists, and economic determinists offered their own predictable explanations for the catastrophe's origins.

The first scholarly assessment came from the pen of James F. Rhodes, a turn-of-the-century historian with a strong nationalist persuasion. In his History of the United States *(7 vols., 1893–1906), Rhodes argued that the war was fought over the issue of slavery: "Of the American Civil War it may safely be asserted [that] there was a single cause, slavery." Almost universally accepted for two decades, Rhodes's thesis was disputed and ultimately displaced during the 1920s and 1930s. But during the period of civil rights activism following World War II, his interpretation won renewed support. In an authoritative modern reaffirmation of the slavery hypothesis, Allan Nevins concluded that "the main root of the conflict . . . was the problem of slavery with its complementary problem of race-adjustment." Nevins's magisterial* Ordeal of the Union *(4 vols., 1947–1971) also identified "minor roots," including constitutional, political, and economic factors. But the issue of slavery and the future of blacks in American society, he insisted, were fundamentally the causes of the Civil War.*

On the eve of the Great Depression, Charles and Mary Beard argued that economic conflict, not slavery, caused the war. In The Rise of American Civilization *(2 vols., 1927), the Beards viewed the conflict as one between rival forms of capitalism. According to this reform-minded husband-and-wife team, the Civil War was a "Second American Revolution" in which northern industrialists sought successfully to dominate southern agriculturists. Although Charles Beard would later abandon this interpretation, it has remained popular among radical scholars. Both William Appleman Williams's* The Contours of American History *(1961) and Barrington Moore's* Social Origins of Dictatorship and Democracy *(1966) offer variations on the Beardian theme.*

Other historians interpreted the war as an inevitable clash of regional rivals. Arthur C. Cole, for example, argued in his The Irrepressible Conflict *(1934) that the North and the South were two distinct civilizations, two separate societies drawn ineluctably into conflict by the very nature of their differences. But other scholars denied there were irreconcilable ideological, institutional, or economic differences between the sections. Indeed,*

James G. Randall (The Civil War and Reconstruction, 1937), Avery Craven (The Repressible Conflict, 1939), and Kenneth Stampp (And the War Came, 1950) viewed the Civil War as an avoidable and needless conflict. Writing in the eras of World War II and the Cold War, these anti-war historians blamed blundering politicians and moral fanatics for a holocaust that should never have happened.

In one form or another, each of these major interpretations has sup-porters among the present generation of historians. For example, in The Impending Crisis *(1976), the latest and perhaps the best synthesis of this much analyzed period, David Potter returns to the theme of Rhodes and Nevins. Although not arguing the issue of inevitability, Potter agrees that the institution of slavery lay at the heart of the problem. Exploring the paradoxical relationship between an ascendant American nationalism and a growing and disruptive sectionalism, he finds no basic nor irresolvable ideological, economic, or cultural differences dividing North from South. The conflict, then, was one over values — values centering on the issue of slavery. Likewise, Kenneth Stampp has recently updated his repressible conflict interpretation in* America in 1857 *(1990). Closely examining the events of that crucial year, Stampp places much of the blame for civil war on the shoulders of President Buchanan and his "tragic miscalculations," especially his decision to support the pro-slavery minority in Kansas, which divided the Democratic party and paved the way for Republican electoral success in 1860.*

Perhaps the conflict that divided the Union more than a century ago will inevitably continue to divide the scholarly community. As Thomas J. Pressly remarked in his analysis of how Americans Interpret Their Civil War *(1954), "The further the Civil War receded into the past, the greater the strength of the emotions with which these divergent viewpoints were upheld."*

FOR FURTHER READING

For economic development in the 1840s and 1850s, the references listed at the end of Chapter 9 will continue to be useful. Marcus Lee Hansen's *The Atlantic Migration, 1607–1860* (1940) and Kerby A. Miller's *Emigrants and Exiles* (1985) are good accounts of the upsurge of immigration during these years. John Commons and others have written the standard *History of Labor in the United States* (4 vols., 1918–1935); Bruce Levine weaves together the themes of German immigration, labor conflict, and the com-ing of the Civil War in *The Spirit of 1848* (1992); and Robert May exam-ines *The Southern Dream of a Caribbean Empire* (1973). The drift toward Civil War is traced by Avery Craven, *The Growth of Southern National-ism, 1848–1861* (1953); by William J. Cooper, *The South and the Politics of Slavery* (1978); and by Michael Holt, *The Political Crisis of the 1850s* (1978). In *Origins of Southern Radicalism* (1988), Lacy K. Ford describes the secession movement in South Carolina; Michael P. Johnson does the same for Georgia in *Toward a Patriarchal Republic* (1977). Thomas Alexander has analyzed congressional voting in the 1850s as an index to *Sectional Stress and Party Strength* (1967), and Eric Foner's *Free Soil, Free Labor, Free Men* (1970) is a major study of early Republican ideology. The more illuminating biographies include David Donald, *Charles Sumner and the Coming of the Civil War* (1960); Robert Johannsen, *Stephen A. Douglas* (1973); Glyndon Van Deusen, *William Henry Seward* (1967); and Drew Gilpin Faust, *James Henry Hammond and the Old South* (1982). *The Dred Scott Case* (1978) is an account by Don Fehrenbacher, while *The Slave States in the Presidential Election of 1860* (1945) have been analyzed by Ollingen Crenshaw. Modern readers will gain much insight from those two famous books of the 1850s, Harriet Beecher Stowe's *Uncle Tom's Cabin* (1852) and Hinton Rowan Helper's *The Impending Crisis of the South: How to Meet It* (1857).

15

★ ★ ★ ★ ★ ★

The Civil War, 1861–1865

WHEN Abraham Lincoln arose to deliver his inaugural address on March 4, 1861, few people had any very clear idea of how the secession problem should be handled. Some voices in the North counseled letting the "erring sisters depart in peace." The abolitionist minority called for a holy war to free the slaves. Majority opinion in the North was increasingly convinced that the Union must somehow be preserved, but there was no clear mandate for military coercion of the seceded states. The war that finally came, like most wars, came not because anyone deliberately willed it, but out of a chain of circumstances whose result reflected only imperfectly the conscious collective will of North or South. Insofar as a guiding will affected the outcome, it was the will of Abraham Lincoln.

LINCOLN AND THE SECESSION CRISIS

The new president was known to the country only as a tall, homely, and apparently uncultivated lawyer-politician from the prairies of Illinois. He had won brief notice years earlier when his opposition to the Mexican War caused Illinois voters to repudiate him after a single term in Congress. Not until his debates with Douglas in the senatorial campaign of 1858 had he attracted national attention. Elected president by a minority of the voters, he had given little public indication of his policy in the months between the election and the inauguration. Actually he had blocked all efforts at compromise by privately opposing any arrangement that left the slightest room for the expansion of slavery. But this position could be put down to political expediency — compromise on the territorial question would have left the infant Republican party little reason for existence — and gave no clue as to what he would do when he assumed office.

Certainly Lincoln was not prepared to lead a crusade to free the slaves. He had insisted that slavery was wrong and that its expansion should be

TABLE 8. PRESIDENTIAL ELECTIONS AND MAJOR POLITICAL EVENTS, 1860–1865

1860	**Abraham Lincoln** (Republican) elected over Stephen A. Douglas (Northern Democrat), John C. Breckinridge (Southern Democrat), and John Bell (Constitutional Unionist).
1860–1861	Seven states of the lower South secede and organize the Confederate States of America.
1861	Confederates bombard Fort Sumter, beginning the Civil War. Virginia, North Carolina, Tennessee, and Arkansas secede and join the Confederacy. Morrill Tariff. Substantial upward revision of duties, beginning a long period of high protection. *Trent* affair. Union naval officer seized two Confederate diplomats from a British vessel.
1862	Homestead Act provides free farms of 160 acres to actual settlers. Morrill Land Grand Act grants land to the states for agricultural and mechanical colleges. Pacific Railroad Act. Federal subsidies for a railroad from Omaha to California. Slavery abolished in the territories and the District of Columbia. Second Confiscation Act. Freeing escaped or captured slaves of Confederates.
1863	Lincoln's Emancipation Proclamation. Declaring free all slaves in Confederate areas. National Bank Act, with a supplementary act of 1864, establishes a system of banks issuing a uniform paper currency based on holdings of federal bonds. Turning point of the war in July, when Union forces capture Vicksburg on the Mississippi and stop Lee's invasion at Gettysburg. Lincoln announces his "10 percent plan" for the easy restoration of the seceded states to the Union.
1864	Lincoln vetoes the Wade-Davis bill, containing a harsher congressional plan for restoration of the seceded states to the Union. **Abraham Lincoln** (Republican) re-elected over George B. McClellan (Democrat).
1865	Lee surrenders to Grant at Appomattox Courthouse. Lincoln assassinated. The Thirteenth Amendment abolishes slavery throughout the United States.

stopped so that the country might look forward to its eventual peaceful extinction. But he had repeatedly denied any disposition, "directly or indirectly," to interfere with slavery where it already existed. Nor were his social values notably advanced. In his debates with Douglas the lanky Republican denied that he was "in favor of bringing about in any way the social and political equality of the white and black races." A "physical difference" would prevent the two races from ever living together on equal terms, he had said, and, therefore, "I, as much as any other man, am in favor of having the superior position assigned to the white race." He wanted slavery excluded from the territories so that "white men may find a home — may find some spot where they can . . . settle upon new soil and better their condition in life . . . as an outlet for *free white people everywhere.*"

The inaugural address revealed both a leader of unsuspected stature and a position around which northern opinion could rally. With an eloquence that no president since Jefferson had attained, Lincoln pleaded for preservation of the Union. "The mystic chords of memory," he said, "stretching from every battlefield and every patriot grave to every living heart and hearthstone all over this broad land, will yet swell the chorus of the Union, when again touched, as surely they will be, by the better angels of our nature." In trying to touch these chords, he reassured the South in the most positive terms that he would countenance no act against slavery in the states where it already existed.

But the address also had a vein of iron. The Union, said Lincoln, was perpetual, any violent acts against the authority of the United States were "insurrectionary or revolutionary," and these statements were to be taken "as the declared purpose of the Union that it *will* constitutionally defend and maintain itself." Though the federal government would not initiate hostilities, the president told the South, it would "hold, occupy, and possess" the federal forts and other property in the seceded states and collect the import duties there.

In retrospect, Lincoln clearly committed himself to a course that led directly to one of the bloodiest wars in history. But war was not his purpose. Eight of the 15 slave states were still in the Union. By refusing to recognize secession while at the same time declining to proceed forcibly against the secessionists, Lincoln was seeking to reinforce the manifest Unionist sentiment in the upper South. He wanted to keep the upper South from seceding, hoping that latent Unionism would eventually overcome secessionism in the seven seceded states of the lower South.

There were weaknesses in this union-saving strategy. One was that Lincoln exaggerated the strength of Unionist sentiment in the lower South. Another was the likelihood that the effort to hold the federal forts in the seceded states would lead to armed conflict. Armed conflict was the more likely because the more fiery secessionists were ready to provoke a crisis that would force the upper South to choose sides.

The issue of peace or war reached a crisis at Charleston, South Carolina. Practically all the federal forts and other property in the lower South had been taken over by the seceding states before Lincoln's inauguration. Of the few posts remaining in federal hands, the unfinished and lightly garrisoned Fort Sumter, located in the entrance to Charleston's harbor, had become the symbolic focus of the whole controversy over federal property. Sumter had sufficient supplies to hold out only six weeks, and a decision about its future could not be postponed. Lincoln finally informed the Confederate authorities that he was sending a naval expedition to reprovision Sumter. They in turn ordered their general at Charleston to demand the fort's immediate evacuation and, in case of refusal, to bombard it. The demand was made and refused, and on April 12, 1861, the Confederate shore batteries opened fire.

Lincoln responded by calling on the states for 75,000 troops. Rather than make war on their fellow Southerners, four states of the upper South — Virginia, North Carolina, Tennessee, and Arkansas — reluctantly followed the lower South out of the Union. The four slave states of Delaware, Maryland, Kentucky, and Missouri remained with the Union, though the last two had strong secessionist movements and furnished many soldiers to the Confederacy. The tables were turned on the secessionists when the strongly Unionist western section of Virginia seceded from Virginia and laid the basis for the new state of West Virginia under the aegis of the Union. Meanwhile the Confederacy acted to consolidate the adhesion of the upper southern states by moving its capital from Montgomery to Richmond, Virginia.

THE WAR BEGINS

A spirit of martial ardor swept over both sections in the spring of 1861. Northerners expected a short and easy war, while Southerners seemed oblivious to the overwhelming superiority in human and material resources against which they would have to contend. The 5.5 million free people of the 11 Confederate states faced a population of 22 million in the 23 Union states. The North had a four-to-one advantage in free males of fighting age and would muster twice as many soldiers. Even if one southern soldier was worth two Yankees — as Southerners loudly proclaimed — how were southern armies to be supplied and transported? The North had 80 percent of the country's factories and most of the coal and iron. Approximately 22,000 miles of railroad traversed the North compared to 9,000 in the South, and the North's rail network included a series of vital trunk lines between its eastern and western areas, whereas the sprawling southern regions lacked such efficient rail connections.

Not least of all, the North had Abraham Lincoln. Lincoln was never a very popular president, yet he was a consummate politician, an eloquent and inspired statesman, the symbol of an enduring Union, and an astute war leader whose military judgments were often better than those of his generals. The Confederacy, on the other hand, was less effectively led. For all his humanity, courage, and dignity, Jefferson Davis possessed neither the political nor the military gifts of his Yankee counterpart.

At the war's outset, however, the Union's advantages were not obvious. The South made a remarkable military showing, and some seasoned international observers thought it would prevail. In part, the South's initial successes were due to the strategic advantage of fighting a defensive war. The North was compelled to attack and not only to invade but to occupy the South. Southern commanders had the logistical advantage of shorter supply lines. Moreover, Jefferson Davis had at his command several outstanding generals: Albert Sidney Johnston, Joseph E. Johnston, Thomas J. ("Stonewall") Jackson, and pre-eminently Robert E. Lee. After much soul-searching, these officers had left the United States Army and had taken up arms for a new nation against the country they had once sworn to defend. Secession stripped the Union of many of its more talented officers, and Lincoln was several years in finding a truly able commander.

The Appalachian highlands, thrusting deep into the South, divided the war theater into two zones. Throughout the conflict, the greatest public attention was focused on the East, where the rival armies menaced each other's capitals, which were only 100 miles apart. The Confederate armies, magnificently led by Joseph E. Johnston and then by Robert E. Lee, repeatedly repelled Union invasions aimed at Richmond. In the first major battle of the war in July 1861, Union General Irvin McDowell's army of 30,000 was turned back by a smaller Confederate force at Bull Run in northern Virginia. Lincoln's next commander, 34-year-old General George B. McClellan, was a brilliant military administrator but not an able field commander. The cocky "Little Mack" ferried an enormous, well-trained invasion force down Chesapeake Bay and up the York River to the eastern outskirts of Richmond. But his troops were driven back by Lee and Stonewall Jackson in the series of hard fought battles that constituted the Peninsula Campaign of May–June 1862. Later that summer (August 29–30), Lee trounced another Union army led by John Pope in the second battle at Bull Run. Lee followed up this victory with an audacious advance across the Potomac River into Maryland; McClellan's army caught up with Lee's at Antietam Creek, some 50 miles northwest of Washington, in September 1862. In one of the war's crucial battles, the much larger Union army (70,000 Northerners to the 40,000 Confederates) inflicted so much damage that Lee had to withdraw to Virginia. In a single day of fighting, each side sustained some 12,000 casualties. Typically, the cautious McClellan failed to press his advantage and lost the opportunity to defeat Lee decisively.

Back on his home ground, Lee was again invincible. He defeated the blundering General Ambrose E. Burnside, McClellan's replacement, at Fredericksburg, Virginia, in December. In May 1863, Lee and Stonewall Jackson's forces repelled a Union army of more than double their numbers, led by Major General Joseph E. ("Fighting Joe") Hooker, Burnside's replacement, at Chancellorsville, Virginia. In the latter encounter, Jackson was killed accidentally by his own troops. Seeking to capitalize on the victory at Chancellorsville, Lee risked everything in a June invasion of the North, hoping to cut the east-west trunk railroads in Maryland and Pennsylvania, to imperil Washington, and to persuade the Union to make peace before the North's superiority in arms and materiel became irresistible. On July 1, 1863, Lee's 70,000 men and the 90,000 Union soldiers of George G. ("Old

Snapping Turtle") Meade, Hooker's replacement, assembled on opposing ridges outside the southern Pennsylvania town of Gettysburg. For three days during the greatest battle of the war, wave after wave of gray-clad Confederates swept against the entrenched Union position. On the hot, dry afternoon of July 3, Lee committed the costliest blunder of his career. In a last desperate charge against the center of the Union line, he sent General George Pickett with three divisions (15,000 troops) across the valley and up the Union-held Cemetery Ridge. The Confederates were cut down by withering Union fire. Casualties on both sides were staggering: the Confederates sustained more than 28,000 killed, wounded, or missing; the Union losses were slightly fewer. Repulsed at fearful cost, the South's last hope of victory gone, Lee had no recourse but retreat to Virginia.

While Lee's gamble was failing in the East, the Confederacy's military doom was being more plainly spelled out in the West. At long last Lincoln found a winning general, Ulysses S. Grant — an obscure, former junior officer in the Mexican war who had come out of retirement to join the Union cause. Using the Mississippi, Tennessee, and Cumberland rivers, which offered natural invasion routes for Union gunboats and armies, Grant drove steadily, from Cairo, Illinois, into the South. Forts Henry and Donelson, guarding the Tennessee and Cumberland rivers, fell to him in February 1862. Pressing southward on the Tennessee River, Grant inflicted a severe blow to the main Confederate army in the west during the bloody two-day battle at Shiloh (April 6–7). Both sides suffered severe losses; the outnumbered Confederates lost one-quarter of their forces, 11,000 troops compared to the 13,000 Union casualties. Also, Confederate General Albert Sidney Johnston, like many others in this era of primitive medical care, died of a minor wound. The southern troops retreated to Mississippi. Meanwhile, Union gunboats steamed up the Mississippi River from the Gulf of Mexico to take New Orleans, and others came down the Mississippi from the north to destroy a Confederate fleet at Memphis, Tennessee. The last stronghold on the river, Vicksburg, Mississippi, fell to Grant in July 1863, following a six-week siege, which exhausted Confederate forces and reduced the civilian population to eating rats and mules. With the surrender of General John C. Pemberton and 30,000 troops at Vicksburg, Grant had cut the Confederacy in two.

THE CONFEDERACY AT WAR

The burden of directing the Confederate war effort fell almost wholly on the shoulders of Jefferson Davis. Lacking able subordinates in his cabinet and in the Confederate Congress, Davis perhaps took on too much of the burden of detailed administration and sometimes made poor decisions concerning military strategy and commanding officers. But only an able and conscientious executive could have kept the Confederacy operating and its armies fighting, given the staggering difficulties that he faced.

At the beginning of the war, Davis had high hopes of aid from Europe. France's Napoleon III was openly sympathetic as were the ruling upper classes in Great Britain, and both of these countries went so far as to recognize the Confederacy's belligerent status. But Davis was counting on the economic power of the South's cotton to produce more substantial aid — full diplomatic recognition, financial assistance, and perhaps even military intervention. The South might have built up large credits for the purchase of supplies in Europe by shipping its cotton abroad. Instead, the Confederate authorities placed an embargo on cotton exports, expecting that this would force British cotton mills to close and thus bring pressure on the British government to intervene more openly on behalf of the Confederacy. Unfortunately for the Southerners, the British mills had a year's surplus of raw cotton on hand, some alternative sources of supply were available, and although some of the cotton mills eventually shut down, their unemployed workers remained sympathetic to the more democratic North and exerted their influence against any aid to the South.

The South's best chance to drive a wedge between Great Britain and the North came in November 1861 when a United States naval vessel stopped the British ship *Trent* on the high seas and took off the Confederate diplomats James M. Mason and John Slidell. But the United States promptly released Mason and Slidell, and Lincoln's skillful minister in London, Charles Francis Adams, was increasingly successful in preventing the British from aiding the Confederacy either directly or indirectly. And France refused to act without British support.

Meanwhile Lincoln had ordered the Union navy to blockade southern ports; by the time the Confederacy decided to ship cotton to Europe in exchange for supplies, this was no longer possible. Cut off from all outside goods (except a trickle brought in by swift blockade runners), the Confederacy was increasingly hard put to supply its armies with munitions or its people with the ordinary necessities of life.

As the struggle wore on and as the Confederacy's prospects expired under mounting Union industrial and military strength, the South's early optimism was replaced by growing discouragement, apathy, and disaffection. Secessionist sentiment was anything but universal in the Upper South and mountain regions. In the hill counties, the Confederate conscription law, which exempted overseers and owners of 20 or more slaves, was especially resented. Having no direct interest in slavery, some poor Southerners came to view the struggle as "a rich man's war and a poor man's fight." The disparity in materiel was also a factor. Union soldiers were adequately provisioned; sometimes encumbered federal soldiers jettisoned their unwanted articles. Often Confederate troops, on the other hand, lacked food and clothing and depended on captured Union supplies for arms. Draft evasion in the South increased following the Union victories of July 1863, and desertion became so widespread that by the end of 1863 one-third of the Confederate army was absent without leave — clearly, the morale of poorly paid Confederate soldiers was at low ebb. Desperate for manpower, the Confederacy in 1864 reached out to "the cradle and the grave," drafting men from 17 to 50 years of age; by war's end, it had resolved to draft slaves.

The South's enthusiasm for the war was probably less than wholehearted from the beginning. Its tradition of localism bred dissention. Fractious governors in some states and even Vice President Alexander Stephens resisted the inevitable centralizing policies necessary to the conduct of the war and defied the Richmond government. Raging inflation, transportation shortages, and a federal blockade brought extreme civilian privation and unrest; in 1863 bread riots broke out in several cities, including Richmond where President Davis helped restore order. The Confederacy's most serious problem, however, lay in the growing indifference of many wealthy and powerful Southerners. Never unreservedly committed to a separate southern nation, substantial portions of the planter class resented the "usurpations" of the Richmond government, particularly policies that hurt their financial interests. A growing disenchantment with the Confederate cause was thus a major factor in the South's military collapse.

LINCOLN AND THE WAR

Like Davis, Lincoln also faced troubles, for wartime dissent was not confined to the South. In the border states (slave states that remained in the Union), anti-Union sentiment was widespread, and in the non-slave North, support for the war was not universal. As civil strife dragged on unsuccessfully for the North, "Copperheads" — allegedly disloyal Democrats who were as dangerous as poisonous snakes — stepped up their demands for a negotiated settlement. Led by such spokesmen as Clement L. Vallandigham, former congressman from Ohio, and supported by Old Northwestern newspapers, these "Peace Democrats" found their greatest strength in Illinois, Indiana, and Ohio. Unlike the "War Democrats," who despite their differences with a Republican administration followed Stephen A. Douglas in supporting the war effort, the Peace Democrats opposed Lincoln's government at every turn. A diverse group, they included some southern sympathizers, but most were loyal Unionists who for varied reasons decried "King Abraham's" leadership and thought the war to be ill-advised, unnecessary, and even unconstitutional.

Much opposition centered on conscription, a novel wartime expedient that ran counter to the nation's tradition of voluntary military service. The draft law of 1863 exempted not only the unfit, but also those wealthy enough to hire a substitute or to pay $300. Since conscription fell disproportionately on the urban poor and immigrants, the law was widely resented. Riots occurred in a number of cities. The bloodiest riot took place in New York City, where for three days predominantly Irish working-class gangs vented their anger on blacks until federal troops arrived to end the looting and lynching. Not the least of Lincoln's problems was this unwillingness of whites to risk life and limb in what they viewed as a black cause.

Problems were also created by those strongly opposed to slavery. Lincoln was hounded by a group of "radical" Republicans who wanted to make the war an antislavery crusade and who advocated a punitive policy toward the South. Under the leadership of people like Senator Charles Sumner of Massachusetts and Representative Thaddeus Stevens of Pennsylvania, the Radicals gained great power in Congress. They set up a joint congressional Committee on the Conduct of the War, which constantly criticized and interfered with the president's conduct of military operations.

The split between radical Republicans and moderate or administration Republicans did not affect cooperation on common interests, and a series of major laws was passed by the wartime Congresses. The Morrill Tariff Act of 1861 marked a turn toward higher protective duties, and subsequent legislation of 1862 and 1864 pushed duties to unprecedented levels, inaugurating an era of extravagant protectionism that would last into the twentieth century. The long fight for free land culminated in the Homestead Act of 1862, granting 160 acres to any family that wished to settle on the public domain. The Morrill Land Grant Act of 1862 donated public lands to the states for support of agricultural and mechanical colleges. In the same year Congress finally authorized the long projected transcontinental railroad, granting 30 million acres and millions in federal bonds to the Union Pacific and Central Pacific railroad companies to build a line from Omaha to the Sacramento River. By an act of 1863, Congress established a national banking system, with member banks issuing a stable currency of uniform national bank notes on the basis of their holdings of federal bonds. In passing these important measures to serve the interests of northern farmers and business enterprise, the Congress was simply legislating the Republican platform since Southerners were no longer there to oppose it.

No measures aroused the controversy in the Republican party that the subject of slavery created. Anxious to mollify the loyal slave states of Delaware, Maryland, Kentucky, and Missouri, Lincoln stoutly resisted doing anything to suggest that abolition of slavery was a northern war aim. In the fall of 1861, he removed the Radicals' favorite general, John C. Frémont, from command in Missouri for declaring that the slaves of rebels were free. Meanwhile he sought unsuccessfully to interest Congress and the loyal slave states in a plan of gradual, compensated emancipation with the federal government footing the bill. His constitutional amendment would have granted states up to 37 years to abolish slavery.

The Radicals were determined to force the issue, and in 1862 pushed through Congress legislation abolishing slavery in the territories and in the District of Columbia. More important was the Second Confiscation Act of 1862, declaring forfeit the property of all persons supporting the rebellion and proclaiming escaped or captured slaves to be "forever free." By this time, Lincoln was becoming aware that an emancipation policy would be of value in helping to win the war, especially by gaining friends for the Union in Europe. Finally, on January 1, 1863, he issued his Emancipation Proclamation. This famous proclamation was not the universal measure it has often been said to be. It freed only those slaves living in rebel areas — those who were at the moment beyond the reach of Union law — and justified even this largely rhetorical gesture on the grounds of "military necessity." Only as the Union armies advanced did the freedom proclaimed by Lincoln's document become an actuality for the slaves. Not until 1865 did the Thirteenth Amendment, forbidding slavery throughout the country, become a part of the Constitution.

The Emancipation Proclamation did not allay the Radicals' suspicion of Lincoln, but they failed to block his renomination for president in 1864. In this wartime election, the Lincoln Republicans ran as the Union party, appealing to War Democrats by nominating for vice president Andrew Johnson, the Tennessee Senator who had remained loyal to the Union. The regular Democratic nomination went to General McClellan, many of whose supporters were calling for peace negotiations. The long string of Union defeats in the East has so strengthened antiwar sentiment that Lincoln might have been defeated but for some timely military successes in the West on the eve of the election.

Despite his political difficulties, the war so changed the structure of American government and society that Lincoln wielded presidential power that his predecessors could never have dreamed of. Commanding vast land and naval forces, initially without benefit of competent professional military leadership, he intruded more often into day-to-day military operations than he wanted. A civil libertarian, he nevertheless stretched executive authority in the name of national security by ordering the arrest of disloyal and disruptive citizens. Under his direction, the government tampered with private mail, closed several dissident newspapers, suspended in "extreme" cases the writ of habeas corpus (traditional safeguard against arbitrary arrest), and incarcerated without trial thousands of men for draft evasion or suspected disloyalty.

The government's role, moreover, was greatly expanded. To ensure efficient transportation and communication, the government subsidized a transcontinental railroad, built additional track, and assumed the direction of telegraph and rail lines. To finance a war that required daily expenditures of up to $2 million, Congress taxed and borrowed heavily; at war's end, the national debt was $2.6 billion. Congress created a Bureau of Internal Revenue and imposed the first income tax. It doubled the protective tariff, reformed the banking and monetary system, and fostered scientific agriculture. During the war the federal bureaucracy necessarily burgeoned, and afterward, federal expenditures never again fell to prewar levels.

TOWARD APPOMATTOX

The fall of Vicksburg to Grant and Lee's failure at Gettysburg, both in July 1863, doomed the Confederacy. And Lincoln had finally found a successful general. Before leaving the West, Grant consolidated Union control of Tennessee with a victory at Chattanooga. In the spring of 1864, Grant was made general-in-chief of all the Union armies. Now his grand strategy was a two-pronged final offensive against the South, with General William T. Sherman leading one great Union army south from Chattanooga into Georgia and with Grant himself leading another army from Washington toward Richmond.

The twin offensives were launched simultaneously in May 1864. The two Union armies of around 100,000 each pressed back Confederate armies of around 60,000. In the West, Sherman steadily pushed the Confederates south and by September won the important rail center of Atlanta. He made an audacious decision to abandon his line of supply and wage a war of destruction between Atlanta and the sea. Devastating the countryside as he went, he was in Savannah by December, and the Confederacy was further segmented. Turning north, Sherman reached Columbia, South Carolina, in February 1865 and by March was in east-central North Carolina.

By demoralizing the Confederate areas south of Virginia, Sherman greatly facilitated Grant's advance on Richmond. In the Spotsylvania Wilderness and at Spotsylvania Courthouse in May 1864, Lee inflicted heavy casualties on the invading Union troops as he had so often done in the past. But this Union general did not withdraw to lick his wounds as had all his predecessors. By flanking movements, he kept pressing south toward Richmond. At Cold Harbor, Lee again inflicted frightful losses on the Union army, but still Grant pushed inexorably south, passing just east of Richmond and crossing the James River. Lee managed to shield Richmond as Grant moved around it to the south and southwest toward Petersburg. By June, the two armies were entrenched facing each other in a long line bending from Richmond southward around the southern side of Petersburg.

Grant would not let go, and as the siege went on through the summer and fall and winter, his superiority in numbers began to tell. Remorselessly he kept extending his line to the west, and Lee's line became steadily thinner and more vulnerable. By April, Lee could extend his line no more and had to pull out of his entrenchments, abandoning Richmond and Petersburg. But by this time Grant had cut off all the roads leading south over which Lee might effect a junction with the only remaining Confederate army of any strength. On April 9, 1865, at Appomattox Courthouse, Lee bowed to the inevitable and surrendered. One month later the fleeing Jefferson Davis was captured in disguise in Georgia and imprisoned at Fortress Monroe. The Confederacy was dead — and so were some 260,000 Confederate and 360,000 Union soldiers. In blood, if not in dollars, it was the costliest war in American history.

LINCOLN AND THE SOUTH

The treatment of the vanquished South was a point of contention between Lincoln and the Radicals. Lincoln wished to bring the rebellious states back into full membership in the Union as rapidly and painlessly as possible. By the time Union forces occupied Arkansas in December 1863, the president was ready with his "10 percent plan" of reconstruction. Under this plan he proposed to extend amnesty and restore confiscated property to all Confederates who would take a simple loyalty oath, excluding only high civil and military officers of the Confederacy or its states. As soon as 10 percent of a state's 1860 electorate had taken the oath, the state could write a new constitution and rejoin the Union.

The Radicals, however, feared with considerable reason that if the southern states were reconstructed on this basis, the old ruling class would return

MAP 5:   THE CIVIL WAR

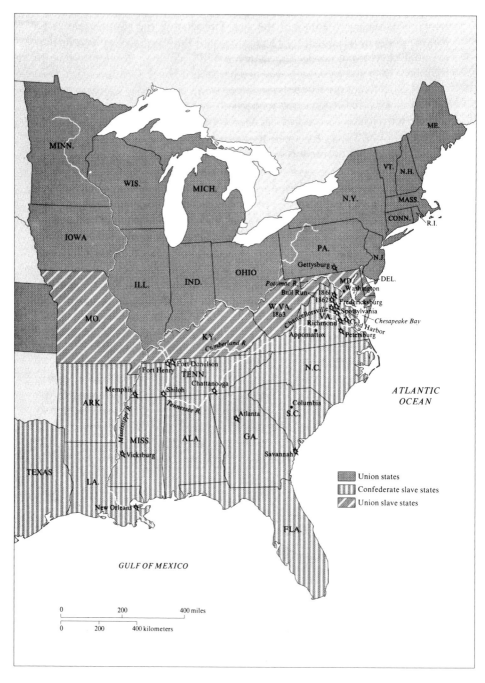

to power and the freed blacks would be little better off than they had been under slavery. Anxious for a thorough reconstruction of southern society, they insisted that black men be given the ballot and that the old rebel leadership be effectively excluded from political life. As a counter to Lincoln's plan they secured the passage in 1864 of the Wade-Davis bill. This measure required a majority, rather than 10 percent, of the 1860 voters to take a loyalty oath before reconstruction could begin and further insisted on disfranchisement of ex-Confederate leaders.

Lincoln allowed the Wade-Davis bill to die by pocket veto, but the Radicals had one tactical advantage. A state would not be fully restored to the Union until its representatives were seated in Congress, and the Radical-controlled Congress had full power over the admission of members. The Radicals used this power to deny admission to the first southern representatives who appeared under Lincoln's 10 percent plan. In March 1865, as the war drew to a close, the Radicals gave a further indication of their objectives by creating the Freedmen's Bureau to assist the ex-slaves in adjusting to freedom and to protect their rights.

The sharpening struggle between Lincoln and the Radicals was suddenly cut short on Good Friday, April 14, 1865, five days after Lee's surrender at Appomattox. As Lincoln sat in a box at Ford's Theater in Washington, John Wilkes Booth, an actor and Confederate sympathizer, fired a fatal bullet into the president's head, crying *"Sic semper tyrannis! The South is avenged!"*

A grieving nation suddenly discovered a tragic hero. To Lincoln's strength, humility, eloquence, and magnanimity was added the quality of martyrdom. He had presided over the bloodiest war in the American experience, preserving the Union as the land of liberty and last best hope of humanity. Hesitantly and grudgingly, but in the end unmistakably, he had also made the war a struggle to enlarge the sphere of American liberty. Yet the Emancipation Proclamation and the Thirteenth Amendment were only a beginning. It was Lincoln's Radical critics who saw most clearly that the task of completing emancipation still lay ahead, and even his great talents could hardly have been equal to this Herculean task. Perhaps it was a timely martyrdom that translated Abraham Lincoln — a man groping toward an ideal only dimly perceptible in his society and age — into the Great Emancipator. For a century and more to come, Lincoln, the symbol, would remind his fellow Americans that the egalitarian dream was still unfulfilled.

FOR FURTHER READING

The best one-volume history of the Civil War is James M. McPherson's *Battle Cry of Freedom* (1988), but Allan Nevins's classic *Ordeal of the Union* (4 vols., 1947–1971) is still important. Divergent interpretations of the North's reaction to secession are presented by David M. Potter in *Lincoln and His Party in the Secession Crisis* (1942) and by Kenneth M. Stampp in *And the War Came* (1950). The northern conduct of the war can be followed through the biographies of Lincoln. One-volume studies include *With*

Malice Toward None (1977) by Stephen B. Oates, *The Presidency of Abraham Lincoln* (1994) by Philip S. Paludan, and *Lincoln* (1995) by David Herbert Donald. For greater detail, see the chronologically successive volumes by James G. Randall (completed by Richard N. Current) on *Lincoln the President* (4 vols., 1945–1955). LaWanda Cox analyzes *Lincoln and Black Freedom* (1981). Special aspects of the North during the war are treated in George Fredrickson's *The Inner Civil War* (1965), Phillip S. Paludan's *A People's Contest* (1988), and Iver Bernstein's *The New York City Draft Riots* (1990). The blacks' role in the struggle is analyzed in Joseph T. Glatthaar's *Forged in Battle* (1990), Dudley Cornish's *The Sable Arm* (1956), and Benjamin Quarles's *The Negro in the Civil War* (1953). Emancipation and its legacy are explored in Eric Foner's *Nothing But Freedom* (1983) and Clarence L. Mohr's *On the Threshold of Freedom* (1986). Emory Thomas surveys *The Confederate Nation* (1979), while both Richard E. Beringer, et al., in *Why the South Lost the Civil War* (1986), and Paul D. Escott, in *After Secession* (1978), explore the weaknesses of Confederate nationalism. The Confederacy's *King Cotton Diplomacy* (1966) is the subject of Frank L. Owsley, while D. P. Crook's *The North, the South, and the Powers* (1974) examines the maneuverings of both sides. The military history of the war from the viewpoint of the northern armies may be followed in the vivid volumes by Bruce Catton: *Mr. Lincoln's Army* (1951), *Glory Road* (1952), and *A Stillness at Appomattox* (1954). A more detailed and professional evaluation of the northern military effort through 1863, with greater attention to the western campaigns, is Kenneth P. Williams's *Lincoln Finds a General: A Military Study of the Civil War* (5 vols., 1949–1959). Herman Hattaway and Archer Jones offer a general military survey in *How the North Won* (1983). The fighting as viewed from the southern side is best followed in the distinguished study by Douglas Southall Freeman, *R. E. Lee: A Biography* (4 vols., 1934–1935). Thomas L. Connelly, in *The Marble Man* (1977), critically examines the life and legend of Robert E. Lee. Alfred M. Josephy, Jr., reports on *The Civil War in the American West* (1991). John F. Marszalek details the life of *Sherman* (1993), and Charles Royster looks at the Civil War careers of both Sherman and Stonewall Jackson in *The Destructive War* (1991). Bell Wiley has described *The Plain People of the Confederacy* (1943) and the common soldiers of the South in *The Life of Johnny Reb* (1943); Reid Mitchell explores the everyday lives of northern soldiers in *The Vacant Chair* (1993); Catherine Clinton and Nina Silber have collected essays on women and the war in *Divided Houses* (1992); and George C. Rable's *Civil Wars* (1989) looks at white women in the South during the war. Of the multitude of personal accounts of contemporaries, three very different ones may be singled out as having special interest: the *Personal Memoirs* (2 vols., 1885–1886) of General Grant; *A Diary from Dixie* (1905) by Mary Boykin Chestnut; and *The Diary of Edmund Ruffin* (3 vols., 1972–1989), edited by William K. Scarborough.

The Civil War and Reconstruction

President Lincoln issued the Proclamation of Emancipation in 1863 before the end of hostilities. This lithograph of the proclamation made in 1865 by J. Mayer & Co. shows "before and after" scenes of a slavery sale and free blacks. *(Library of Congress)*

Lincoln, as Commander-in-Chief, is shown with General George B. McClellan and a group of officers at the headquarters of the Army of the Potomac. Photograph by Matthew Brady. *(Library of Congress)*

Union troops — the
96th Pennsylvania
Infantry — at Camp
Northumberland
near Washington.
Photograph by
Matthew Brady.
(*Library of
Congress*)

With the aggressive leadership of Generals Grant and Sherman, Union victories wrought destruction on southern cities and countryside. The ruins of Richmond, Virginia, on the James River, were photographed by Matthew Brady. (*Library of Congress*)

Confederate troops often lacked uniforms and other supplies, as this photograph of an army camp reveals. The Union army was generally better equipped. (*Library of Congress*)

Often unsuccessful in its early encounters with Confederate forces, the Union Army sustained many deaths and casualties. In June 1862, Matthew Brady photographed the wounded at a Union field hospital at Savage Station, Virginia. (*Library of Congress*)

Blacks fought on both sides of the conflict. This black gun crew participated in the battle of Nashville. (*Chicago Historical Society*)

FROM THE PLANTATION TO THE SENATE.

During Reconstruction, blacks were elected to the U.S. Congress. This poster shows, from left to right: Senator Hiram R. Revels, Representative Benjamin S. Turner, the Reverend Richard Allen, Frederick Douglass, Representatives Josiah T. Walls and Joseph H. Rainy, and the writer William Wells Brown. (*Library of Congress*)

Black sharecroppers in the South often found conditions after Reconstruction little better than slavery. Victims of white discrimination and the crop lien system, they lived in poverty and too often in virtual peonage. *(Brown Brothers)*

16

★ ★ ★ ★ ★ ★

Reconstructing the Union, 1865–1890

IN THE GENERATION after the Civil War, economic expansion absorbed most of the nation's energies. The people's attention, however, centered at first on the Reconstruction of the Union and the new order in the defeated South. They faced difficult questions involving the rights of the freed slaves.

THE PROBLEM

The problems of Reconstruction were numerous. The most obvious and easiest problem was the physical rebuilding of shelled cities and ruined railroads. Harder to reconstruct was the defeated section's economic life. The South's industry was at a standstill; much of its farming land was lying idle. Its labor system was destroyed, investment capital was lacking, the savings of many people were wiped out by the collapse of Confederate currency and bonds. Beneath every other problem lay that of a new relationship between the South's two races. All that was clear about the country's 4,500,000 blacks was that none of them remained a slave. Some 286,000 were Union soldiers; a few were settled on confiscated plantations in the sea islands off the Carolinas; and many were simply wandering, drifting from Union army camps to southern cities with great hopes and no means of support. Nearly everybody assumed that they were to continue to work on the land. A few radicals had suggested that they would become landowners, and the sea islands experiment raised some hopes. White Southerners assumed that blacks would work as laborers for white landowners.

By 1865 three southern states were already reconstructed under the easy terms offered by President Lincoln, which demanded only that 10 percent of the citizens take an oath of future loyalty and recognize that slavery was ended. Once this was done, elections were held for both state governments and federal Congress. But Congress refused to admit these delegates.

To settle this difficulty, Americans turned to the Constitution. What was the status of a sovereign state that had seceded and been forced to return to the Union? Was it still a state or was it, as Thaddeus Stevens insisted, merely a conquered province? Who would decide: Congress or the president? The president was commander-in-chief of the armed forces and had the power to pardon. But Congress had the right to admit new states, to make rules for territories, and to judge the qualifications of its own members. Long before Lincoln's death, the executive and congressional branches of government had been at loggerheads over these issues. In this unprecedented situation, the Constitution offered few unambiguous answers to these questions.

More important in the long run than the constitutional question was the state of mind of three main groups: the ex-slaves, the defeated white Southerners, and the victorious Northerners. Though able black leaders soon appeared, most of the ex-slaves were not only illiterate but inexperienced, both in participating in politics and in dealing with such economic institutions as wages and rent. Many pathetic stories are told about the strange hopes and fears of these displaced people. Yet the basic desires of the freed blacks were clear. What they wanted was real freedom, and the signs of that freedom were the right to move around the country, access to education, and ownership of land.

Right after the war, according to northern travelers in the South, shock rather than bitterness was the most common state of mind among southern whites. With their institutions destroyed, what was to become of them? Most pressing of all, without slavery, how was the cotton going to be picked and planted? At first, many looked northward for their answers.

Northern whites comprised the third and largest group, which was by no means a united body. Nearly half were Democrats. Only a few Democrats had been willing to accept the breakup of the Union, but many had sharply criticized the conduct of the war and had opposed emancipation. The sole purpose of the fighting, the party's leaders had insisted, should have been the restoration of "the Union as it was." In the 1864 elections, the Democrats had lost some ground, yet they still mustered a formidable 45 percent of the votes. Not even the Republicans were sure of what they wanted. The group called "Radicals" agreed that Lincoln had been too weak, too lenient on the South, but they agreed on little else. Republicans were also divided on such matters as the tariff and finance, and few had thought through the future status of the blacks.

Two paradoxes made constructive action inordinately difficult. First, slavery had been abolished and the ex-slaves armed by a nation that believed overwhelmingly in the inherent inferiority of the black race. Even among the abolitionists, only a few had accepted blacks as intellectual and political equals.

Second, during Reconstruction the government had to undertake a program of drastic, even revolutionary measures. Yet nearly all nineteenth-century Americans had been taught that government action should be sharply limited. This had been said by Jefferson, Jackson, and Lincoln. Schools and colleges taught as gospel truth the maxims of *laissez-faire* political economy, that is, minimum governmental interference in the economy.

The choice faced by the North, in its simplest terms, was the choice offered to every victor: occupation or conciliation. Most Northerners preferred the latter, but they wanted conciliation on northern terms: the South must recognize its errors and govern itself — according to northern ideas.

Yet to whom in the South could government be confided? To the ex-rebels who were, many Northerners believed, still rebels at heart? To the ex-slaves whom most Northerners regarded as members of an inferior race? Even if they were given the vote, the freedmen, inexperienced in politics and a minority in all but two states, could hardly govern alone. They would have to have the support either of a substantial number of southern whites or of sufficient occupying forces. With or without black suffrage, the same choice existed: conciliation or occupation.

PRESIDENTIAL RECONSTRUCTION

The first alternative, conciliation, was attempted under the authority of Presidents Lincoln and Johnson and is often referred to as Presidential Reconstruction. It is hard to tell how Lincoln's "10 percent plan" might have worked if it had been continued. This plan had already been sharply challenged by Congress, and Lincoln himself had said that it was only one of many possible approaches. The Wade-Davis bill, the most extreme congressional substitute, had been left unsigned by Lincoln.

Like Lincoln, President Andrew Johnson embodied the log-cabin tradition of humble origins. He was a tailor by trade and learned to read only as an adult. A resident of eastern Tennessee where slaves were few, and a former Jacksonian Democrat, he had been an outspoken opponent of secession and a lifelong enemy of the southern planter class. Yet he was not committed to either rights of blacks or the Republican party. Though honest and able, Johnson lacked Lincoln's gifts of patience and political realism. Soon the very Republicans who had hailed his remarks about the infamy of treason and the punishment of traitors found him to be too soft on the former Confederates and too eager to forget and forgive.

Like his predecessor, Johnson offered amnesty to those who would sign an oath of allegiance. Exceptions included important Confederate officials and Confederates who owned more than $20,000 worth of property, seemingly the leaders of the Old South. Those who took the oath were to vote for constitutional conventions for each state, which were, in turn, to repeal the ordinances of secession, to abolish slavery, and to repudiate Confederate war debts. The state thus reconstructed could then elect a new government and send representatives to Washington. By the end of 1865, all the states had actually passed through either the Lincoln or the Johnson version of this process, and in conservative and southern eyes, Reconstruction was over. Southern government was functioning, and the people, black and white, were returning to work.

Much in the new order was deeply disturbing to northern opinion. Some reconstituted states elected prominent Confederates to state and federal office. Most enacted special "Black Codes" to regulate the conduct of freed blacks. To former slaveholders, such rules seemed natural and necessary; to freed blacks and many Northerners, the rules looked much like the slave codes of the antebellum period. In some states, blacks were not allowed to assemble, to intermarry with whites, to possess alcohol or firearms, or to pursue a skilled trade. In others, the labor of petty offenders could be sold at auction; in some, black children could be apprenticed to white men without the consent of indigent parents. Most codes provided for strictly enforced compulsory labor contracts, and for the binding out (forced apprenticing) of unemployed blacks declared vagrant. In South Carolina, the code spelled out the intent of such contracts: blacks were to engage only in agricultural labor or in domestic service. In Mississippi, blacks could work, but not own, agricultural land. Even some white Southerners found these measures to be unduly provocative of Yankee sensibilities.

In 1865–1866, northern opinion was further affronted by outbreaks of racial violence in the South. Responsibility for race riots was of course disputed, but the victims nearly always turned out to be blacks or pro-black whites. To Radical Republicans, it seemed that life was not safe in the South for those who supported a change in southern society, and this change the Radicals were determined to bring about. To some this was a moral duty; to others, a political necessity.

In the spring of 1866, Congress extended the life of the Freedmen's Bureau, a wartime organization designed to supervise and aid the ex-slaves, and passed a Civil Rights Act prohibiting many kinds of discriminatory legislation. Congress also refused to admit the representatives of the new southern state governments, among them former Confederate officials: the vice president, six cabinet officers, four generals, and numerous other high-ranking civilian and military leaders of the secessionist government.

Johnson could not expect to carry forward his policy without regard for such formidable congressional opposition. Yet the imprudent Johnson, like other presidents in other battles with Congress, seemed to grow steadily less flexible and more defiant. He blamed southern race riots on the Radicals, minimized southern denial of black rights, and pardoned thousands of southern leaders. In the spring of 1866, he vetoed both the Freedmen's Bureau bill and the Civil Rights Act, arguing that such measures were unconstitutional and that blacks were not ready for full citizenship. When the Fourteenth Amendment was proposed to guarantee blacks equality before the law, he condemned it on similar grounds.

By this time, Johnson had gained the support of Democrats and solidified the Republican party against him. In the fall, he toured the country and violently denounced his opponents as traitors, particularly Thaddeus Stevens and Charles Sumner. In the November congressional election, Johnson was repudiated at the polls. The Republicans won two-thirds of both Houses, and the Radical leadership moved into key positions of power. The pendulum of power had swung to the congressional side; a new phase of Reconstruction was at hand.

CONGRESSIONAL RECONSTRUCTION

During congressional, or Radical Reconstruction, the alternative to conciliation, military occupation, was finally given a trial. The purpose behind this move was still reform; the South was to be occupied only until her society could be altered and a new electorate formed. This meant attempting something like social revolution, and it was clear that in this revolution blacks must play a major part.

The Freedmen's Bureau and Civil Rights bills, both repassed over the president's veto, established that the former slaves were to be protected by the federal government during a transitional stage. They were not, however, to be given land; in this property-loving age only a few suggested such an extreme measure, and local experiments in this direction (including one in Mississippi on land owned by Jefferson Davis) were abandoned. Ultimately, the failure to attempt some form of land redistribution and provide some measure of economic security for former slaves assured their continued dependence on their former masters.

Federal protection for blacks already implied a change in the relationship between the federal government and the states, and this change was spelled out in the Fourteenth Amendment submitted to Congress in June 1866. The first section of this amendment provided that no state should infringe any citizen's "privileges or immunities," nor "deprive any person of life, liberty or property, without due process of law," nor deny to any person "the equal protection of the laws." Thus individuals were guaranteed by the *Union* against oppression by the *states*. (The Bill of Rights already protected individual liberties from the federal government.)

The second section of the amendment edged toward black suffrage. It provided that if a state denied the vote of any of its male citizens, its representation should be reduced accordingly. The third and fourth sections barred leading Confederates from Congress or federal office and forbade states to repudiate the federal or recognize the rebel debt. Obviously this all-important amendment could not be ratified by three-fourths of the states without some southern support. As President Johnson urged southern states not to ratify, Congress moved on to still more drastic reconstruction action.

The First Reconstruction Act, passed in March 1867, divided the South into five military districts, wiping out the existing state governments. Under military supervision, each state was to elect a constitutional convention. Delegates to these conventions would be chosen by vote of the whole male population, including the freed blacks and excluding leading Confederates.

Each constitution was to be ratified by a majority of the state's new electorate and approved by Congress. When the new state had ratified the Fourteenth Amendment, its representatives might be admitted to Congress. This act was clarified and tightened by further legislation, and in 1870 Radical Reconstruction was completed by the ratification of the Fifteenth Amendment, once and for all forbidding suffrage discrimination on the basis of "race, color, or previous condition of servitude."

All these actions were taken against the firm opposition of the president and in the face of the nearly certain disapproval of the Supreme Court. To safeguard Radical Reconstruction, Congress made the most drastic attempt in American history to establish the dominance of a single branch of government. To disarm the court, Congress simply withdrew certain kinds of cases from Supreme Court jurisdiction, and the court prudently refrained from challenging this action. Johnson, however, could be rendered powerless only by impeachment and conviction for "treason, bribery, or other high crimes or misdemeanors." Failing after much effort to find serious evidence of "crimes," Congress saw its best chance for impeachment in the Tenure of Office Act passed in 1867. This act, of dubious constitutionality, forbade the removal of cabinet officers without congressional sanction. Johnson challenged it by trying to remove Secretary of War Edwin Stanton, an appointee of Lincoln. In the spring of 1868, the House of Representatives impeached the president in a long, confused, and shaky set of charges. Anger ran so high that his accusers failed by only one vote to secure the two-thirds of the Senate votes necessary for conviction.

RADICAL RECONSTRUCTION IN ACTION

How did the Radical program actually work in the South? To this crucial question, historians have developed two opposite answers. A generation ago, most accounts said that Radical Reconstruction had been a dreadful mistake. According to this traditional view, southern state governments, dominated by ignorant blacks, self-seeking carpetbaggers, and despicable southern "scalawags" (that is, collaborationists) had imposed a reign of terror, extravagance, and corruption. Finally the South, supported by a revival of moderate opinion in the North, had risen in revolt and thrown off the yoke. The very name given to those who overthrew Reconstruction, *redeemers*, speaks to the conclusions of this perspective.

More recently this version has been challenged by an opposite one. According to this second, neo-Radical view, Radical Reconstruction was a long overdue attempt to bring justice and progress to the South. It was sustained in the South not only by federal forces but by determined black support. Its defeat was brought about by brutal terrorism and northern betrayal.

The truth about this abortive social revolution is various and complex. It is clear that some Radical governments were indeed both extravagant and blatantly corrupt. Yet the redeemer governments that followed were not notable for political or fiscal probity, and both extravagance and corruption were common in both the North and South. Moreover, the Radical governments scored some accomplishments, bringing to the South broader suffrage for whites as well as blacks, relief for the poor, and the beginnings of free, popular education. Taxes did go up (though not to northern levels), but tax monies were put to valid social uses.

Could Radical Reconstruction have effected a permanent change in southern institutions and customs? Successful Reconstruction would have demanded either prolonged northern occupation, repeated federal intervention, or some degree of cooperation between southern whites and blacks. For the first two alternatives, Northerners proved to have no enduring appetite. The third — white-black cooperation — seemed initially more promising. Many southern whites did make an effort to accept the new situation, though many did not. Contrary to legend, some scalawags were well intentioned, just as many carpetbaggers were honest and many black leaders were well informed and moderate. But any permanent alliance among these elements faced great difficulties. The cooperating southern whites were willing to accept black voting only under white leadership; the blacks demanded political equality. Predictably, the necessary coalition failed.

Conservative whites quickly regained power. With this shift in power, violence against blacks and their political allies continued to escalate; at first determined to suppress the Ku Klux Klan and other secret terrorist organizations, Congress grew weary of the attempt. In one state after another, with differing degrees of fraudulent and forcible action, conservative southern whites achieved victory at the polls. In 1877 when President Hayes withdrew the last federal troops, the cycle was complete: the South was "redeemed" and restored to native white rule. At first, the new "lily-white" governments, mostly led by the prewar planter class, allowed blacks some token participation in politics. Then in the 1890s, governments claiming to represent poor whites came to power. Denouncing the alleged political "fusion" of aristocrats and blacks, these governments effectively nullifed the Fifteenth Amendment (universal manhood suffrage) and drove southern blacks out of politics. These acts were accomplished partly by violence and intimidation and partly by the discriminatory application of such legal sophistries as the grandfather clause, the literacy test, and the poll tax. Faced with the most flagrant violations of federal law, the federal government and northern public opinion looked the other way. White Northerners, including some former abolitionists, came to value national harmony more than equal rights.

SOCIAL RECONSTRUCTION

Since blacks never received the "40 acres and a mule" for which they had longed in 1865, they had to work for white landowners. As money to pay them was lacking, the only possible solution was some form of tenantry. The result was the sharecrop and the crop-lien systems. Throughout the South, sharecroppers, both white and black, received their seed, tools, and staple necessities from landlords to whom they turned over a third or a half of their produce. Most, and often all, of the remaining produce went to pay long-standing debts accumulated by the tenants at country stores or plantation commissaries with high monopoly prices and exorbitant rates of interest. The system was not slavery, and it got the crops planted and harvested. Yet the black farmer — forever in debt and unable to move, without education or political privileges, subject to white courts and terrorism — could hardly be called free. Indeed, recent research suggests that the shadow of slavery still darkened southern race relations as *peonage* (the use of laborers bound in servitude because of debt) was fairly widespread. To make matters worse, planter-class paternalism was supplanted by an increasingly virulent race hatred among whites who feared their inability to control their former slaves.

In the 1880s, the white-ruled South put on a spectacular drive for industry. Heavy inducements were offered to attract capital, and much was accomplished in developing steel, lumbering, tobacco, and, especially, textile industries. However, by the turn of the century, the region had barely held its own; the South's percentage of the nation's industry was about that of 1860. Even this, in a rapidly expanding economy, was a considerable achievement. But the price was heavy. In southern mill towns, disease and child labor were endemic. Most industry profits were flowing out of the section. Until World War II, the South remained both poor and overwhelmingly agrarian.

Perhaps the saddest chapter in all American history is the general acceptance in the North of the failure of so much effort. Thirty years after the war, most people took for granted a southern system that included not only disfranchisement, economic dependence, and rigid social segregation of blacks, but also recurrent violence. In 1892 and 1893, for example, more than 150 blacks were lynched each year; they were often sadistically tortured, and virtually always the crimes went unpunished. If Reconstruction was a tragedy, it was because it heightened interregional tensions without either lessening racial hatred or securing a place in the national mainstream for the former slaves.

How could the people who had defied the Fugitive Slave Act, fought the war, and voted for Radical Reconstruction accept this situation? First, it was easy to emphasize the seamy side of Radical Reconstruction, the greed and corruption with which the process was sometimes executed. Next, most white Northerners shared the white southern assessment of black worth. White supremacist assumptions were reinforced by turn-of-the-century American imperialism. If the "little brown" Filipino was a lesser breed of man in need of the firm, guiding hand of a superior white American nation, should not the Afro-American be left to the direction of his southern white betters? Moreover, the conventional wisdom of the age argued that stateways could not change folkways, that government was powerless to change customs or alter social mores. Thus a failure of northern resolve partly explains the failure of Reconstruction. The courts, Congress, the White House, and a popular majority all came, in time, to accept the view that white Southerners knew best how to handle the race problem. It also seems likely that failure was built into the system itself. Federalism, whatever its

TABLE 9. EVENTS OF RECONSTRUCTION, 1863–1877

Date	General tendency	National events	State events
1863	**Presidential Reconstruction**	Lincoln Plan announced.	Governments set up in Louisiana, Arkansas.
1864		Wade-Davis Plan pocket-vetoed by Lincoln.	
1865		Lee surrenders. Lincoln shot. Johnson Plan announced.	Governments partly functioning in Virginia, Tennessee.
1866		Freedman's Bureau bill and Civil Rights bill vetoed. Fourteenth Amendment submitted to states. Congressional elections: Radical gains.	All remaining states reorganized under Johnson Plan. Tennessee readmitted.
1867	**Height of Radical Reconstruction**	Reconstruction Acts. Tenure of Office Act.	Military Rule in effect.
1868		Impeachment of Johnson. Fourteenth Amendment in effect. Grant elected.	North Carolina, South Carolina, Florida, Alabama, Louisiana, Arkansas readmitted under Radical governments.
1869	**Conflict**	Fifteenth Amendment in effect.	Conservative government restored in Tennessee.
1870		First Enforcement Act. Congressional elections: Republican majorities reduced.	Virginia readmitted under moderate government. Moderate government restored in North Carolina. Mississippi, Texas, Georgia readmitted under radical government.
1871		Second and third Enforcement Acts.	Conservative government restored in Georgia.
1872		Grant re-elected.	
1873			
1874	**Restoration of White Rule**	Congressional elections: Democrats gain control of House.	Conservative government restored in Arkansas, Alabama, Texas.
1875		Civil Rights Act (declared invalid 1883).	
1876		Hayes-Tilden disputed election.	Conservative government restored in Mississippi. Federal troops removed from Louisiana, South Carolina.
1877			Conservative government restored in Florida, South Carolina, Louisiana.

other advantages, proved to be an imperfect instrument for the protection of black rights. As the experience of the post–World War II civil rights struggles suggests, the Fourteenth and Fifteenth Amendments were often unenforceable in the face of adamant white opposition. The traditions of federalism, which required wide-ranging deference to local, state, and regional customs, seemed to deny effective enforcement of a colorblind Constitution. In the last analysis, the left wing of the Republican party, for all its apparent radicalism, accepted prevailing constitutional conservatism. The Radicals created a formal structure of racial equality — and in the process no doubt promised much more than most northern whites would willingly see the nation deliver — but they did not challenge a federal system that permitted intransigent southern whites to sabotage congressional intent. Still "old republican" in their fear of the centralized national power necessary to reconstruct the South, the Radicals returned to the old federal balance of national and state power, a position sustained by the Supreme Court in a series of cases beginning in the 1870s.

In the Slaughterhouse Cases (1873) the court found that the Fourteenth Amendment conferred no new privileges or immunities that would protect blacks from state power. In the Civil Rights Cases (1883), it decided that the Fourteenth Amendment did not prevent *individuals*, as opposed to states, from practicing discrimination. In *Plessy* vs. *Ferguson* (1896), the court held that "separate but equal" accommodations for blacks in trains (and by implication in restaurants, schools, hotels, and the like) did not violate their rights. Few inquired very carefully into whether accommodations were indeed equal.

If blacks found the promises of Reconstruction largely empty, the period had a brighter side for whites. A great Civil War had been settled on remarkably magnanimous terms, without the postwar blood-letting, executions, confiscations, and mass incarcerations that have characterized internecine struggles in other times and places. As the two sides inched toward reconciliation, it was all too easy to forget that Afro-America was paying most of the bill for the intersectional accord.

The upshot, then, of the greatest struggle in American history seemed to be a tragic failure. Yet the story had not ended. Blacks had gained a few rights and a great many hopes. And in neither the North nor the South was the national conscience really at ease.

CONFLICTING HISTORICAL VIEWPOINTS: NO. 7

Was Reconstruction a Tragic Era?

Until the 1930s, historians generally agreed that Reconstruction was a period characterized by sordid motives and human depravity. It was the "Age of Hate," "The Blackout of Honest Government," "The Dreadful Decade," and "The Tragic Era." In 1939, however, Francis Butler Simkins, a distinguished southern scholar, urged his fellow historians to adopt "a more critical, creative, and tolerant attitude" toward the period. In a notable essay

(Journal of Southern History, 1939), *Simkins suggested that the traditional interpretation of Reconstruction was rooted in "the conviction that the Negro belongs to an innately inferior race."*

Until Simkins's time, most white students of Reconstruction did in fact approach their work with decidedly racist views. In the first serious history of the era, James Ford Rhodes's enormously influential History of the United States from the Compromise of 1850 *(7 vols., 1839–1906), blacks were described as "the most inferior race." Similarly, in John W. Burgess's* Reconstruction and the Constitution *(1902), blacks were characterized as inherently inferior beings incapable of "subjecting passion to reason." Although Rhodes and Burgess were sharply critical of the motives and actions of congressional radicals, the traditional interpretation of Reconstruction is best identified with the work of William A. Dunning. A Columbia University scholar and the author of* Reconstruction, Political and Economic *(1907), Dunning and his many students uncovered a wealth of factual information about the period. But their work was seriously marred by their pro-southern and anti-black biases. They portrayed the postbellum scene in darkly tragic hues of unrelieved brutality, scandal, corruption, and licentiousness. According to the Dunningities, Reconstruction was not only unnecessary but harshly cruel to the prostrate South and ruthlessly exploitive of the ignorant ex-slaves.*

Black scholars — most notably W. E. B. Du Bois, author of Black Reconstruction *(1935) — vigorously disputed Dunning School conclusions. But in an age of virtually unchallenged white supremacy, few Caucasians thought to question simplistic characterizations of vindictive radicals, venal carpetbaggers, reprobate scalawags, and barbarous blacks. A shift in the climate of racial opinion, however, ushered in a new era of Reconstruction historiography. Reflecting a growing national sensitivity to civil rights, historians since the 1930s have turned Dunning's conclusions inside out. First in a series of monographs and biographies, then later in such sweeping syntheses as John Hope Franklin's* Reconstruction After the Civil War *(1961), Kenneth Stampp's* The Era of Reconstruction *(1965), and Eric Foner's* Reconstruction *(1988), revisionists discarded racial stereotypes and viewed the postbellum period in a generally favorable light. According to Franklin and Stampp, traditional studies grossly exaggerated not only the extent of corruption, fraud, and black rule, but even the length of radical control. Both Franklin and Stampp emphasized that Reconstruction was a tragic era only in that it failed to ensure blacks economic, political, and social equality. Foner's recent survey pays particular attention to the role played by blacks in shaping Reconstruction; he also stresses that although many issues raised during the era were not resolved for decades or remain unresolved today, the bold experiments launched during Reconstruction ultimately represented a revolutionary beginning to America's unfinished effort to integrate the former slaves fully into American life.*

FOR FURTHER READING

Leon Litwack's *Been in the Storm So Long* (1980) lyrically describes the transition from slavery to freedom. Dan Carter's *When the War Was Over* (1985) and Michael Perman's *Reunion Without Compromise* (1973) analyze presidential Reconstruction. Eric L. McKitrick in *Andrew Johnson and Reconstruction* (1965) offers a view of Lincoln's successor. Janet Herman's *Pursuit of a Dream* (1981) and Willie Lee Rose's *Rehearsal for Reconstruction* (1964) examine land redistribution experiments that failed. William Gillette traces the *Retreat from Reconstruction* (1979); Allen Trelease explores the *White Terror* (1979) of the Reconstruction Ku Klux Klan; and Michael Perman explains *The Road to Redemption* (1984). Among numerous state studies, the best are Thomas Holt's *Black Over White* (1977), Joel Williamson's *After Slavery* (1965), and V. L. Wharton's *The Negro in Mississippi, 1865–1890* (1947). James L. Roark's *Masters Without Slaves* (1977) examines planter life and thought during war and Reconstruction, and Lawrence N. Powell in *New Masters* (1980) studies Northerners who became southern planters during or after the war. C. Vann Woodward's justly celebrated trilogy (*Reunion and Reaction* [1951], *Origins of the New South* [1951], and *The Strange Career of Jim Crow* [1955]); Paul Gaston's *New South Creed* (1970); and Ed Ayers's *The Promise of the New South* (1992) are valuable for understanding the South during the post-Reconstruction period. Stephan DeCanio in *Agriculture in the Postbellum South* (1974) and Robert Ransom and Richard Sutch in *One Kind of Freedom* (1977) offer strikingly different conclusions about the nature of the southern economy. Neil McMillen explores the *Dark Journey* (1989) of black Mississippians during the Jim Crow era.

INDEX

Abolitionist movement, 157–159: impact of, on politics, 159; impact of, religion on, 157–158; racism in, 159; role of blacks in, 158–159; Underground Railroad, 159
Act of Toleration (1649), 8, 13
Acts of Trade and Navigation (1660–1672), 22–25
Adams, Abigail, 62, 92
Adams, Charles Francis, 173, 197
Adams, Henry, 107
Adams, John: and independence struggle, 59, 60, 65–66, 76, 81; and presidency, 92–94, 98; as vice president, 85
Adams, John Quincy: and abolitionist movement, 159; and presidency, 131–132, 151; as secretary of state, 106–107, 120
Adams, Samuel, 47–48, 51, 59, 76
Africa, slaves from, 30–31
Age of Jackson (Schlesinger), 147
Agrarianism: post-Revolution evolution of, 68–69; and ratification of Constitution, 79–81
Agriculture, *see* Economic development; *specific crops*
Alcohol, *see* Temperance societies
Algonquin Indians, 26
Alien and Sedition Acts (1798), 93, 98
Allen, Ethan, 72
American party, and presidential election of 1856, 184–185
American Revolution, *see* Revolution, American; Revolutionary War
Andrews, Charles McLean, 52
Andros, Edmund, 15
Anglo-American rapprochement, 105–107
Anthony, Susan B., 156, 157
Anti-Federalists: and Bill of Rights, 86; characteristics of, 79–80; struggle of, with Federalists, 81–82
Appomattox, 201
Aptheker, Herbert, 162
Ark, 7
Arnold, Benedict, 55, 63
Articles of Confederation (1781), 62–63
Assembly-line production, *see* Labor systems
Atchison, David R., 182
Attucks, Crispus, 48
Aztecs, 2–3

Bacon, Nathaniel, 33
Bailyn, Bernard, 53
Balboa, Vasco Núñez de, see Núñez de Balboa, Vasco
Baltimore, Lord, *see* Calvert, Cecilius
Bancroft, George, 52
Banks, national: establishment of, 87–89, 97, 199; resentment of in 1820s, 129–

130; Second Bank of the United States, 120–122, 140–142, 167
Banks, state: establishment of, 119; overexpansion of, 120; reform of in 1830s, 144
Baptist Church, 152
Barnburners, 173
Bassett, John Spencer, 146–147
Battle of Bunker Hill, 55
Beard, Charles A., 81, 188
Beard, Mary, 188
Becker, Carl, 52
Beecher, Lyman, 152, 155
Bell, John, 187
Benevolent societies, *see* Reform movements
Benson, Lee, 82, 147
Berkeley, Sir William, 33
Biddle, Nicholas, 121, 141–142
Bill of Rights, 85–86. *See also* Constitution of the United States
Black Codes, 208
Black Hawk War, 140
Blacks: civil rights of in reconstruction era, 208; conditions for after Civil War, 206–207; and Constitution, 82; culture of, 31, 162–163, 215; employment opportunities for, 211–212; enslavement of, 7; and Revolutionary War, 56–57; role of in abolitionist movement, 158–159; social segregation of, 212; violence against, 211, 212; *see also* Civil rights; Slavery; Voting rights
Blassingame, John, 162
Bloomer, Amelia, 157
Bonus Bill (1817), 121–122
Boorstin, Daniel J., 53
Booth, John Wilkes, 203
Boston Massacre (1770), 48
Boston Tea Party (1773), 49
Braddock, General Edward, 27
Bradford, William, 9
Bradstreet, Anne Dudley, 36
Breckinridge, John C., 187
British East India Company, 48
Brook Farm, 154
Brown, John, 184, 186–187
Brown, Robert E., 53, 81–82
Brown University (Baptists' College of Rhode Island), 39
Buchanan, James: and presidency, 181, 184–185; and secession, 187
Burgess, John W., 215
Burgoyne, General John, 63
Burnside, General Ambrose E., 195
Burr, Aaron, 94

Cabinet, establishment of, 86
Cabot, John, 3

Wool, 114
Worcester vs. *Georgia* (1832), 139

XYZ Affair, 92–93

Yale College, 37
York, Duke of, *see* James II (king of England)
Young, Brigham, 154
Young, Thomas, 48